THE GIRL NOBODY WANTS

THE GIRL NOBODY WANTS

A shocking true story
of child abuse in Ireland

LILY O'BRIEN

This book is based on true events but the names and locations of
characters and events have been changed.

Matador
Troubador Publishing Ltd
9 Priory Business Park
Wistow Road
Kibworth Beauchamp
Leicester LE8 0RX, UK
Tel: 0116 279 2299
Email: books@troubador.co.uk
Web: www.troubador.co.uk/matador

ISBN 978-1780880-334

A CIP catalogue record for this book is available from the British Library

Typeset in Aldine by Troubador Publishing Ltd
Printed and bound in the UK by TJ International, Padstow, Cornwall

Matador is an imprint of Troubador Publishing Ltd

*I dedicate this book to all the children who went through the
institutions in Ireland and to those who took their own lives later in
life as a way to escape from the torment that never left them alone,
and to my baby brother who was one of them.
I will never forget you.*

*I would also like to thank my partner for writing this book for me,
and for never once judging me for what others have done to me.*

THANK YOU.

CONTENTS

CHAPTER 1

My Life with Bad People

It's my 40th birthday today and I'm trying to smile, but as I look in the mirror all I can see is an empty shell, someone waiting to die, and I have a feeling of butterflies in my belly that won't go away and it's making me feel sick. I want to sit down, but as I turn around and head for a chair, I get a nasty taste in my mouth and I have to run to the toilet before I vomit over the kitchen floor. I push the door open and I kneel down next to the toilet, but nothing happens and I wait for the feeling in my stomach to go away.

After a while I feel better, so I lift my head up off the toilet and I try to get up, but as I push my hands against the toilet bowl my stomach lightens and I have to grab hold of the toilet as I vomit into it. My head begins to spin, but my stomach's empty, I haven't eaten a thing in the last 24 hours, so all that comes out of my mouth is green water and I know I need to get up before I vomit again and make a mess of myself. But, it's the same thing for me every day and I've been feeling this way for the last thirty-six years, and I have no idea how I've managed to last this long without cracking up or killing myself.

I get up and walk back into the kitchen and I stand in front of the mirror again. I straighten my clothes and look at myself again and I begin to brush my hair. My hair is long and blonde and I'm very slim, so my hair seems to suit me this way. But I'm only this slim because I keep being sick, and I need to be careful not to brush my hair too hard or I will end up pulling some of it out with the brush, then I will just get fed up with myself for being careless.

I'm still feeling a bit sick, so I sit by the kitchen window, but I don't know what to do with myself, so I think about my partner Tony and then I think about what I've been telling him for the last six weeks and how stupid he must think I am. You see, I've been telling him that I will be dead before my 40th birthday; and each time I told him, all he ever did was to say 'ok' and that's been driving me nuts. God knows, I could never tell anyone else how I'm feeling or what I'm thinking, as they would just think I'm nuts or stupid; but I can tell Tony anything, but all he ever does is say 'ok' and that makes me feel like I want to smash his face in.

And you could never tell that anything was wrong with me by just looking at me, as I dress clean and I keep myself tidy, and I have a smile on my face that hides my emotions and over the years I've become an expert at hiding behind it. My smile also hides my weaknesses from everybody, but I don't know how much longer I can keep the charade up and keep what's left of my life under control. God, I need help. It's only 10 am Monday morning and already I'm picking up the phone to call Tony who's at work. I need him to bring some painkillers home as soon as possible, as I can't cope with the pain in my head and the tingling in my belly any longer. But it's the same for me every day and he knows the drill because he's been doing the same thing for the last twenty-two years.

I call him and he listens while I explain to him what I want, and he only has a chance to say 'ok' before I put the phone down on him. Then I walk into the living room and curl up on my bed waiting for him to come back, while the pain in my head takes control of my mind and I can do nothing to stop it. The pain's awful and it makes me feel like I want to kill everyone; but within half an hour, Tony walks in and throws a packet of painkillers down onto the bed next to me. I quickly move my hand towards the packet and, as Tony turns and heads towards the toilet, I frantically grab the packet, jump off the bed and take four tablets out of the packet while I head into the kitchen for a drink of water.

One by one, I begin to swallow the tablets and then I hear Tony as he walks back along the hall and follows me into the kitchen; he looks over at me and he begins to shake his head from side to side, but then he stops; he knows what I've just done, but he says nothing. He just turns, gives me a kiss on the back of my head and says, 'See you later, I'm off back to work.' And as I drink a glass of water, I turn around and look him in the face, and I say nothing at all, not even thanks for the tablets. He looks at me again and then he walks off down the hall and towards the front door and I head back to my bed; but once I hear the sound of the front door closing and I know that he's gone, I jump off the bed and head back into the kitchen and then I take another four painkillers.

I know he will be back around lunch time and it's only a couple of hours away, so I get back into bed and I close my eyes while I wait for the tablets to work, but my flat's a lonely place when I'm all alone and my mind won't rest and I'm cold. My flat's small and my bed is in the living room, so my two kids can have a bedroom each, and the kitchen door has fallen off its hinges, so I have a bed sheet hanging in its place; but the light and the noise from the street outside the kitchen window is filtering through and it's bothering me.

I feel like I'm going mad, I just can't rest and I want to scream with anger, so I get back up, I search through my handbag, looking for more tablets, and I find a strip of sleeping pills that my doctor prescribed for me. I push the pills out of the strip and swallow half a dozen of them, while the rest fall out of my hand and onto the kitchen table, scattering amongst old fag packets and junk mail that's been sitting on the table for weeks. I know the pills aren't very strong and they will do little to help me, so I take a couple of nerve pills that my doctor prescribed for me. I know the nerve pills will do a better job than the painkillers and sleeping pills will ever do, and they will stop the tingling in my belly and calm the pain in my head for a couple of hours. I know it sounds like a lot of tablets, but I've been taking tablets for most of my teenage and adult life, and now it takes more and more of them to get a reaction from my body and to put some kind of normality back into my head that will last for a few hours.

So anyway, I head back to my bed, lie down and shut my eyes, but still nothing, I just can't rest, so I get back up and I make a cup of coffee and smoke a fag out of the kitchen window. But the people outside in the street can look up and see me looking out of the window, so I quickly finish my fag, take a few more nerve tablets and go back to my bed and lie down again. I know it will be lunchtime shortly and Tony will be back from work soon, so I close my eyes and pull a blanket over my head to block out the light and sound from the street outside and I try to sleep. It's difficult and I only manage to drift in and out of a dazed state of light sleep brought on by the medication, until suddenly I'm woken by the noise of the front door opening.

He's back already; it must be lunchtime and I'm feeling normal at the moment, so I get out of bed and walk into the kitchen and I put the kettle on to make myself coffee. Then Tony walks in behind me and we both sit down and we talk about the weather, the news and our kids just to make some kind of conversation; but we seem to have little in common at the moment, so it's hard work and we both know it. Plus, as the medication starts to take effect and it begins to relax my brain, I begin to feel like I don't give a shit about anything he says to me and we both continue as if everything is fine.

He only has an hour for lunch, and because I have been waiting all morning just for his company and someone to talk to, the hour goes fast and already he has to go back to work. But as he leans over to give me a kiss good bye, I just keep my face blank and I show him no emotions at all; then after he kisses me, I wipe his kiss off my lips with the back of my hand, in an act of I don't know what.

4

It's not that I hate him, it's just that I hate him for having to go back to work and for leaving me all alone again. I know he has to go back to work and within a few seconds he's gone and I can hear him locking the front door from the outside as he leaves.

It's so that I will be safe and so that no one gets into the flat and kills me; ok, I don't really think anyone is after me or that anyone's going to kill me right now, and I asked Tony to lock the front door for me every time he leaves the flat as you never know who's outside. It's just that I feel so much safer when the front door to the flat is locked, and it doesn't matter what time of the day it is, the door has to be locked.

After he leaves, I walk back into the kitchen and I look over at the clock, it's almost two-thirty in the afternoon and I have to go soon and get the kids from school; so I get changed and head for the front door, but as I get to the door I stop. I put my ear against the door and listen; it's quiet outside, so I unlock the front door and walk outside. It's still quiet and no one's around, so I turn around lock the front door and run down the stairs and out of the building and towards my car. Still running, I press the car door release button on the remote so that I can open the car door and jump inside within a couple of seconds; then, once inside the car, I press the remote button again, locking the car doors shut so that no one can get to me inside.

I relax and take a deep breath, then I put the key into the ignition and I begin to turn the key, but the steering lock is on and I struggle with the steering wheel for a moment and then the key turns and the engine starts and I drive off towards the school. It only takes about fifteen minutes to get to the school by car, but within the first couple of minutes I'm already wound-up and I start calling the other drivers cunt's and bastards. 'God, I need a fag to calm myself down before I kill someone', so I wind the car window down and light one up and it works.

I feel much better now and eventually I get to the school; the kids are waiting for me by the side of the road and they tell me that they have been waiting for ages. I'm late, but don't ask me why; I'm late because I just don't know. It must have been the fag or the other drivers going too slow or something like that. Anyway, the kids get into the car and we head back towards the flat and we just about make it back without me cracking up or shouting abusively at the other drivers.

Apart from the one old bitch who kept me waiting a couple of seconds longer than I needed to at the lights while she chatted on her mobile phone, but the kids told me to stop shouting at her, so I did, but I had to have a fag instead to calm myself down. I just can't help it. I just get so wound-up and angry with everyone for the smallest of things and I tend to let off steam that way because the other drivers can't normally hear me when I'm in the car, and I can scream and shout as loud as I want at them without any consequences.

Once home, I make the kids dinner and then I look at the clock, I know Tony should be home from work by now and he's already told me that he's got no money so he won't be getting me anything for my birthday, but it doesn't matter as long as he gets back soon. Because I don't like being on my own all day, as it makes me feel fed up and angry having no one to talk to, but he's late, it's 6.15 pm and he's only just coming through the front door. God, I want to take a dig at him, he should have been home almost an hour ago; but I can see that he's got me some presents and a cake for my birthday, so it makes me feel better and I just can't find any reason to take a dig at him. Plus I'm glad that he's back from work and I have some adult company now.

I walk back into the kitchen and sit by the window, then I light up a fag and talk to Tony while he does the washing up, and once he's finished he makes us both a cup of coffee while I open my presents. He looks over at me and I look back and smile and then I say thanks. It's a couple of bottles of perfume, it's nice but I already have over thirty different bottles of perfume, so now I'm starting to think that he's trying to say something about me in a nice way, like I stink or something.

But I leave it at that for now and I start to cut the cake up into large pieces, but he's hidden all of the kitchen knives from me apart from a small blunt one that we use for everything, and I struggle cutting into the cake and it ends up looking a mess. I ask him if I can have a sharper knife, but he says, 'No, sorry' and I shout at him, 'Why not?', but all he does is smile at me as he continues to drink his coffee. Then a feeling comes over me that makes me feel like I want to kill him, but instead I turn away and put some of the cake onto plates and I take it to the kids, who are in their bedrooms playing.

But they are playing computer games and they have forgotten all about my birthday; I hand them the cake and they say thanks and continue playing. 'It's only my birthday and it doesn't matter anyway.' But before I walk away, I stand by the bedroom door and I take a long look at them both playing and it makes me smile, and I am happy knowing that they are good boys and that I have managed to keep them safe and away from my family for so long. And I think that if it wasn't for them, I would probably be dead already, as without them I have nothing to live for. Plus Tony keeps telling me that they need me and that it would be a selfish thing for me to kill myself and leave them without a mother, and even though it's hard for me to say that he is right, I have to agree with him.

I head back into the kitchen and sit by the window again and have another fag, while Tony makes himself dinner, poached egg and beans on toast, quick and easy. Good, it saves me doing anything for him as it's not my job anyway. The evening drags and I get bored as everyone has something to do apart from me and I begin to feel like everyone is ignoring me, so I take a verbal dig at Tony, but he doesn't get the message and he keeps ignoring me. He's writing something on the computer that he won't tell me about and he doesn't look up. So this time I shout at him and I start an argument on purpose, and now he's talking to me and I feel better with myself, knowing that I have his attention, and I begin to smile.

So I quickly turn around and I walk away ignoring him, and I walk into the kitchen and light up another fag as he gets up and walks in behind me; then he asks me what the problem is, and I tell him to leave me alone and to go fuck off to bed. He says nothing, then he walks out of the kitchen and he gets ready for bed, and I can hear him as he shouts to the kids that he loves them and then he walks back in to me, 'Good night', he says. 'I'm going to bed now.' Then he walks away while I finish my fag by the kitchen window.

I know I won't be able to sleep very well, so before I leave the kitchen I take a few sleeping pills to help me get through the night, then I walk into the living room and towards the bed. The room's dark and I can't see what I'm doing, so I turn the light on and make a big fuss about nothing before I get into bed, and I leave the light on just to wind Tony up. While telling him that if he wants the light off, he will have to get up and turn it off himself, or he can sleep with the light on all night if he wants as it won't bother me. Then I smile to myself as I turn away from him and tuck myself in really tight with the quilt, leaving him very little to cover himself with, but he says nothing and he does his best to get comfortable.

God, I feel like I want to kill him, but he hasn't done anything wrong, so instead of hitting him I get up and head to the toilet. I sit there for a while, resting my chin on the palm of my hand, and I think to myself that Tuesday will be the same as Monday and the rest of the week will be the same as every other week and I hate it, and I hate my life. Then I head back to bed and lie down for the night, knowing that I will have a horrible sleep ahead of me.

But while I lie there, I remember that tomorrow's going to be different, as I have an appointment to see a mental health adviser at 10 am. It was made for me by my GP and he told me that if I don't go to the appointment, he will stop all the medication that I've been on for the last twenty plus years and then strike me off his books for wasting his time. So I need to get up early, have a bath and wash my hair before I go and see the mental health adviser.

But what am I going to tell him and how will I begin, or will he even believe what I tell him? I have so much in my head and it's all a mess; it's like all of my memories are bad ones and they all have a pain connected to them that won't leave me alone. I can't rest, I look up at the ceiling and then I turn my head and look over at Tony. He's still awake, but he's facing the wall, and he's having trouble sleeping too, but not because he has problems troubling him, but because I like to talk to him and I keep him awake. Then, when I do finally fall asleep, I still keep talking and that's bad for both of us.

So before I nod off, I ask him what he thinks about the appointment I have in the morning and if I should go to it. He turns around and smiles, then he looks straight into my eyes and he says, 'Yes, please go', and good night and God bless. Ok, I get the message and I roll back over to my side of the bed and I stare at the ceiling again, while I think of things to tell the person in the morning. I know it's got to be from the beginning, when it all started as that's the only way I'm going to be able to tell him everything about myself and feel that it might help me in some way, so I close my eyes and I look deep into the darkness that I've created for myself. I know I won't see anything like people or places because I've been doing the same thing for years, but if I keep my eyes closed tight for a while, I start to see little flashes of bright white light bursting through the darkness as it passes before my eyes. It only lasts for a split second at a time, but it helps me to drift away from reality and then off to sleep.

But once I'm asleep, my dreams disturb me and after a couple of hours I'm awake again, and I feel cold and confused and I have to get up before my head explodes from the madness crashing around in my head. So I get up and I look at Tony, he's still sleeping, so I walk into the kitchen and I look out of the window; it's still dark outside, great. I sit on a chair by the window and I have a fag and think to myself that I wish my life was all over. I wish I were dead, I mean how can I keep going on day after day when I feel the way I do?

I must have been a very bad person in a past life for me to be tormented like this now. It's a fucking shit hole of a world that we live in and I hate it and what am I waiting for. All my life, people have used me as if I was nothing, and very few people have ever helped me or shown kindness towards me unless they wanted something from me. The only person who has been honest with me is Tony, even my own family have treated me like shit and they have never shown me any kindness or love. I feel so sad.

I can even remember as far back as when I was four years old, when I lived in London with my mum, step dad and some of my brothers and sisters. You would think that it all sounds nice and fine, but even back then, when I was only four years old, one of my older brothers, Paul, was messing around with me and abusing me for his own pleasure and satisfaction. It all started when mum wanted someone to baby-sit for her; my brother Paul would come around to the house and tell mum that he would do the babysitting for her, while she and my step dad, Jim, went out to the pub for a drink. At first, they paid Paul to do the babysitting; but after a couple of weeks, they stopped paying Paul and they kept the money so they could buy even more drinks down at the pub for themselves.

But that didn't stop my brother Paul from coming around to baby-sit for them, and while they were out, he would come into my bedroom and sit and talk to me until they got back. Then after a few weeks of them going out to the pub and leaving Paul alone with me, he began to act more like a child around me and he began to play games with me and he would pull at my nightdress while he tickled me all over my body. And while he was alone with me, he would tell me that I was a very pretty little girl and that my nightdress was beautiful.

Then one night, while mum and my step dad had gone out to

the pub for a drink, Paul got up, locked the front door and turned off all the lights in the house and then he came into my bedroom. It was late, but I was still awake and I could see him standing just inside the doorway of my room; and as he entered the room, he told me to be very quiet. Then he walked over towards me and picked me up out of my bed and he took me out of my bedroom and into the living room. I looked up at his face and I smiled at him while he laid me down onto the living room floor.

At first, I thought it was a game, 'fun', and that he wanted to play games with me in the living room; but as I spoke to him, he told me to be quiet and to stay still, then as he moved back away from me he began to lift up my nightdress. And as he did so, I put my hands out to stop him and to push my nightdress back down, but he got angry with me and he pushed my hands out of the away and he started pulling at my knickers, trying to take them off me. I asked him what he was doing, but he said, 'Be quiet, shush' and then he pulled my knickers down and off me and with both hands he lifted my legs up and wide open, moving me into odd positions like a rag doll.

Then he put my legs back down onto the floor and spread them wide apart, hurting me, and I began to cry. I told him to stop and I tried to get up, but he told me to shut up and he pushed me back down onto the floor and I stayed there while he undid his trousers and took them off. I looked up at him and I tried to get up again, but before I could move away from him, he got on top of me, positioning his body against mine, and he used his whole body to trap me into a position that stopped me from moving away from him. And all of a sudden, he put his dick up against my body and he pushed himself between my legs.

I was frightened and I shouted at him to stop and I thumped him as hard as I could into his belly, and I shouted at him to stop hurting me and to get off me. I wanted to get up, but I couldn't move; he was squashing me with his body and he was pushing his whole body between my legs. My belly was beginning to hurt me and he was squashing me so much that I could hardly breathe; again, I shouted at him to stop. 'Please stop, my belly hurts', I said, but he kept on pushing and squashing me, while all the time telling me to shut up.

And he only stopped when I began to bleed from between my legs and his clothes got wet from the blood. The blood dripped from between my legs and onto the floor and then the blood smudged over his clothes, so he stood up and he used my knickers to wipe the blood from his clothes. My belly was still hurting me, but at least I could breathe again and, as he moved away from me, I began to cry; he looked down at me and then he stood me up and he put my knickers back on me.

God, when I think of it, it makes me feel so sick. The dirty bastard, how could he do that to me and think that it was ok and as if it was nothing at all? I mean I was only four years old and he was fifteen, and when he had finished with me and he was carrying me back to my bedroom, he tripped on the hallway carpet, but he was able to stop himself from falling over and he said sorry to me for tripping and almost dropping me onto the floor. I was in a lot of pain and it was as if my belly was on fire and my legs hurt from him bending me into odd positions and from him trying to have sex with me. I was still crying when he put me back into my bed, but he didn't care, he just turned around, walked away and closed my bedroom door as he left the room. God, what he had done to me was so sick.

And when I got up the next morning and I tried to tell mum what had happened to me the night before, she never said a word, not a thing, nothing about the blood on my clothes or on the carpet. She just took my bloodstained knickers off me and hand-washed them in the kitchen sink with washing-up liquid and then she handed them back to me and that was it. 'All done.'

I blame my mum for what went on. She could have stopped a lot of the abuse by kicking my step dad Jim out of the house in the first place and by sticking up for us kids, but she never did and, as far as she was concerned, her man came first before her kids. Yet Jim treated her like shit and he would push her around all of the time and have sex with her in front of us whenever he felt like it, and she seemed to like it as she always had a smile on her face.

And when they both got drunk, it was even worse. He would brutally hit and rape her and she would never try to stop him, and he would have sex with her whenever and wherever he felt like it; so to the older kids in the family, sex was nothing at all and abusing each other was the normal thing to do. Just like the adults had done to each other.

The only thing is that it wasn't just my brother Paul who was mentally and physically abusing me back then, it was almost all of the adults around me that were abusing me in some way or another. There were just three of us little kids living with mum back then and we had nobody to protect us, not even our own mother, so all the adults around us had plenty of time and opportunities to abuse us and they did. There was just my big sister Daisy who was only five years old and my little brother Simon who was two and myself, all looking after each other, and we had no one else to help us.

The rest of the kids, the bigger ones, mostly boys, lived in squats and used to walk around the streets all day doing nothing. They would only come around to mum's for food or money; otherwise, you wouldn't see them unless they had caused trouble and needed somewhere to hide from the police. It's terrible to think that mum had eleven kids in total, all doing whatever they wanted, and no one ever did a thing to help us. We never went to school and even at the age of four I was allowed to walk around the streets every day with only Simon, my baby brother, and Daisy, my sister, for company and protection.

We would play outside in the streets for the whole day with nothing to eat or drink, and we were always dressed in the flimsiest of clothes and we never had shoes on our feet, only socks. We would run around outside the flats of the council estate that we lived on and we would look through the rubbish bags left outside the bin rooms for something to play with or eat. We never knew what it was that we were playing with or eating from the bags; we just grabbed the things that we found interesting and then we ran off with them, as anything was better than having nothing at all. If it was wet, sticky or colourful, then it was good; and if we could suck, chew or play with it, even better.

God, I feel sick now thinking about it, but it was the same thing every day and the normal thing for us to do because our mum hardly ever did a thing for us. So whenever we went out, we went looking for something to eat first and then we would go and play around the rubbish shoots of the big council blocks, slamming the fire doors on each floor of the building and trying to make as much noise as we possibly could. The sound from the doors slamming was so loud that it would echo throughout the building and shake the panes of glass in the doors and windows of the hallways, and then people would come out of their flats and shout at us while they chased us out of the building. God, it was so good back then and it was about the only fun we ever had together, but we didn't know any better and it wasn't our fault as no one was looking after us or teaching us the difference between right and wrong.

Then one day, when Daisy, Simon and I went into one of the buildings to play games, a tall black man was standing by one of the rubbish shoot rooms that we used to play in and he looked angry. We looked over at him and we could see that he had one of his hands down the front of his trousers and he was moving his hand around inside his underpants and he was doing something to himself, and in his other hand he was waving a packet of biscuits at us. He looked like he was waiting for someone, so we stopped playing and we turned around to go back outside, but as we walked away he shouted for us to stop and he told us that he had food in the shoot room and the food was all for us.

He said that he wanted us to go into the shoot room with him to get the food, so we walked towards him and as we got to the shoot room door he smiled and we walked in, and then we all stood still and looked up at him, waiting for the food. But there was no food, nothing but rubbish, and then the man leaned over our heads and he pushed the door closed behind us and held the door shut with one arm. He then looked down at us and he began to say something to us, but my sister Daisy grabbed Simon and me, and she shouted, 'Quick, run.' So I screamed as loud as I could and I began pulling at the door and as the man let the door go I pulled the door open and we all ran out of the shoot room as fast as we could, and Daisy and I screamed at each other to run. We knew what he wanted; it was the same thing that my older brother Paul had done to me many times before, back at mum's flat when she was out, and it wasn't nice.

Still holding each other's hands, the three of us ran out of the building and we ran straight out into the road, all falling over and all getting cuts on our knees and faces at the same time. We got up off the road and we headed back to mum's. Our clothes were dirty and I was shaking when we got back to the flat, but nobody gave a damn. Mum and Jim never once asked us what we had been doing all day or if we were ok, so we just walked straight past them and into our bedroom and we all sat on the bed.

Our bed was big and all three of us had to share it, but we loved it, as it was big enough for all of us to sleep on together. Simon, Daisy and I were exhausted, so we cuddled up together and you couldn't tell whose arms or legs were whose; we felt very safe and happy on the bed together and we stayed in a big pile on the bed until we got our breath back. And once relaxed, we began to laugh and giggle to each other because we had got away from the bad black man and then we fell asleep on the bed, dirty but happy.

The next day would be the same as all the others, with mum's first words of the morning to us indicating that she wanted us to get out of the flat, and then she would leave us on our own for the whole day, to fend for ourselves as usual. It didn't matter to her if it was winter or summer, raining or baking hot, it just didn't matter to her at all, so long as we all got out of her way for the whole day. But we never went back to the shoot room again. Sometimes while out playing, we would bump into our older brothers and sisters, as they walked along the streets of the council estate we lived on, and we would try to tag along with them, but they would tell us to fuck off and to go pester someone else. And our brief encounter with them would end with them calling us little shit heads and stuff like that, until we left them alone. You never forget something like that and I think it will stay with me for the rest of my life, because when someone hurts you, you never forget it.

Some days, people in the streets would stop us and ask us if we ever went to school or if we had a mummy or a daddy, and then they would give us money and sweets, but we never knew anything about school so we just ran off laughing at them. To us, it was all just fun and games, and running from people whom we didn't know was what we did best and we would run as fast as we could to get away from them.

Then one day, while walking home, an old woman stopped us. 'Hello, children', she said. 'Can you help me? I have locked myself out of my flat and I cannot get back in, but perhaps one of you children could put your little arms through the letterbox and open the door for me from the inside.' I looked at Daisy and she looked back at me, I couldn't wait to do it and I shouted, 'I will do it', and quickly, without another word, I put my arm through the letterbox and pulled on the handle inside and the door swung inwards, with me still hanging on to it with my arm sticking through the letterbox. 'Thank you', she said, then she told us to wait while she went inside to get something, so we waited by the open door and I tried to have a look inside her flat; but before I had a chance to see inside, the old woman came out of the flat and handed us a packet of chocolate buttons each. 'Thank you', she said, and then she went back inside and closed the door.

We felt so happy to have chocolate buttons and I can still remember the feeling I had to this day. From that day on, each time we walked past the old woman's flat, she would be standing at her door waiting for us to come along. It was as if she knew we were coming and she would say the same thing to us about locking herself out, and each time I would put my arm through the letterbox and open the door for her and she would then give us some sweets to say thank you.

Now when I think back to it, I know that she had planned it that way and it was her way of helping us without us knowing what she was doing. We couldn't always run away from the bad things around us and sometimes we just had to take whatever came our way, like having a bath. It might sound simple enough and it can even be a fun time for kids, but taking your clothes off in our house was like throwing meat to the lions.

I could never take a bath on my own or with my sister Daisy or brother Simon, as Jim's rule was that we all had to have a bath one at a time. And I always wanted mum to bathe me, but Jim wouldn't allow it and he always insisted that he bathed me on my own and always with the bathroom door shut. And mum would never try to stop him or come into the bathroom, because she knew precisely what he was doing and she would just let him bathe me just to keep him happy.

Most evenings, it would start with Jim coming home from the pub drunk; he would grab me by the arm and tell me to get into the bathroom and to wait for him. Then he would follow me into the bathroom, strip me naked and make me stand in front of him while he filled the bathtub up with cold water. I would be standing there naked and shivering from the cold of the room, but I would not move an inch for fear of him hitting me, and once the bath was full of cold water he would pick me up. But he would always grab me from between my legs with one hand while he held me steady around my neck with the other hand. Then he would push and poke his fingers in-between my legs, fondling me at the same time as he tightened his grip around my neck and I felt like he could have strangled me within a second; I would stay as stiff as a board and I would never move an inch just in case he hurt me.

Then he would slowly lower me into the bath, making sure that he had plenty of time to touch me between my legs with his fingers as he did so. I didn't like what he was doing and he always hurt me with his fingers, but I said nothing and once I was in the bath he would let me go. He would then get down on his knees next to the bath and once he was in position next to me, he would undo his trousers and put one of his hands down between his legs and then he would position his other hand on top of my head.

And when he was ready, he would grab me by my hair and then he would push and pull my head up and down, in and out of the water whilst he played with himself while next to the bath. And somehow I knew he was wanking himself off at the same time as he forced my head under the water, and it was as if both his hands were moving at the same time and speed, getting faster and faster all of the time until he would finish. And during the whole time, he had a look on his face that would have wiped the grin off almost any adult's face, apart from my mum's. She knew exactly what he was up to and I think that if playing around with me kept him happy, then she was happy too. No matter what the emotional cost was to me, it just did not matter to her and she would never try to stop him from abusing me.

Then after a while, things began to get worse for Daisy, Simon and me, as mum became pregnant again, but this time she was pregnant from him, Jim; and as her belly began to grow, I could tell that Jim hated her for being pregnant. Because he started to kick and push her around even more than he usually did, and she even told me that he was trying to get rid of the baby out of her belly by hurting her, because he didn't want the baby, as it wasn't his. For the next few weeks, Jim made everyone's life hell, and during that time mum's belly grew even bigger and Jim told mum that if she wanted to keep the baby, then she would have to get rid of us little kids because his baby came first. He said that he didn't have the money to keep all of us, so we had to go; and having us around was now causing them both problems. No matter what we did, we couldn't do anything right; and even when we were good kids and never caused any trouble, Jim would still find some way of treating us nasty and upsetting us.

Like when he would come into our bedroom in the middle of the night and wake us all up just so that he could put a spoonful of mustard into our mouths. Mum would be standing behind him, looking over his shoulder at us with her arms crossed, and she would be smiling as if it was a good thing that he was doing to us. Sometimes we would try to keep our mouths shut, but he was too strong and he would force our mouths open and make us swallow the mustard without us making a fuss. Because if we did complain and make a big fuss, he would just make it worse for us, and he would beat and hit us into swallowing the mustard. Then he would add an extra spoonful for the trouble we had caused him, so most nights we would just swallow the mustard the first time so that he would go away and leave us alone and allow us to go back to sleep.

The same thing would happen to us almost every night until one night, after drinking too much alcohol, Jim kicked mum so hard that she started to bleed from between her legs and she had to be rushed into hospital, so that the doctors could take the baby out of her belly before she lost it. However, when she got to the hospital everything was ok, she was fine and she gave birth naturally to a baby boy. Once mum returned home with the new baby, she didn't have much time for us kids anymore, so she arranged for one of our older sisters, Tracy, to occasionally come around to the house and take us kids out for the day. Tracy would pick us up early and then she would let us play around in the streets all day, near the flat that she was living in with her boyfriend, Fred.

Tracy was only seventeen and Fred, her boyfriend, was twenty-three, and they had come over to London from Ireland about a year earlier, just after she and Fred met. At first, I thought that Fred was a nice man, as he would never say or do anything wrong while my sister Tracy was around, and some days, while Tracy was looking after us, they would take us out to the park for the day and Fred would play games with us. He would push us on the swings and he would run around playing chase with us, acting just as a child would. Then, after leaving the park, he would buy us sweets and give us rides on his back while we walked back to the flat and we would always have a lot of fun playing with him, as he acted just like us, and we were getting more attention from him than we ever got back at mum's.

Then one day, Tracy told me that she was going to leave Fred to baby-sit me on his own while she took Daisy and Simon off to the park with her. I thought it was a bit strange and unfair that I was not going with them, so I asked Tracy if I could go, but she said no and she said that I had to stay with Fred until she came back. Then she smiled at Fred and me as she left, leaving me all alone in the flat with Fred.

It felt like hours sitting and waiting for them all to come back and, for most of the time, Fred left me all alone in the living room just sitting and waiting, but then Fred must have got bored because he came and sat down next to me and he began playing games with me. Then, after a while, he put me on his back and he gave me a ride around the living room, bouncing me up and down and shaking me from side to side until I fell off onto the floor and then he tickled me until I begged him to stop. But after a while, he said that we had to stop as it was getting late and he made a bed up in the living room for me to sleep on. He said that it was late and he told me to go over to the bed, to lie down on it and to stay there, so I did; and as I lay down, I gave him a kiss goodnight on the side of his face and he went off into his bedroom and closed the door behind him. I looked around and then I curled up into a ball on my little bed and wished for Simon and Daisy to come back.

But after a couple of minutes, Fred's bedroom door opened and he came back out of the bedroom. I looked over at him and I could see that he wasn't wearing any clothes. He walked straight over towards me and then he looked down at me and, within a second, he bent over and picked me up out of the little bed that he had made for me on the living room floor. Then he carried me in his arms towards his bedroom, I wriggled around and I tried to get up out of his arms, but he held me tight around my legs and my back until he got into the bedroom with me.

Then he laid me down on his bed and climbed over me; I looked up at him and I watched him as he moved around the bed, and then he lay down on the bed next to me and he positioned himself as close to me as he possibly could. I knew something was wrong and I started to shake with fright and I told Fred that I wanted to get up, but as I turned and moved away from him, he grabbed me and pushed me back onto the bed and then he smiled at me.

Then he put one of his hands down between his legs and he began to touch himself while he continued looking over at me. I asked him what he was doing and he told me that it was good for him and that it felt nice, and then he said that his dick was a lollypop and that I should put it in my mouth and suck it for him because it was nice for both of us. I said no, I said that it was not a lollypop and I told him that I wanted to go back into the other room. But as I tried to get up and off the bed, he grabbed me again and pulled me closer to him and he forced my head over his dick and he told me to open my mouth and to suck it for him. I said no and I tried to wriggle away from him, but he held me tight around my head and, with all his strength, he pushed my face next to his dick and he kept pushing me closer until his dick touched my mouth. I struggled and twisted my head to one side to get away from him, but he grabbed me even tighter around my head and then he pushed my head down hard and his dick went into my mouth.

I didn't want to do it and I tried to move my head away from him, but he grabbed me even tighter around my head and neck with both hands, while he told me to suck his dick for him. I said no, but he was holding my head so tight that I could feel the pressure in my head build up as he squashed my skull with both hands and, as I tried to move my head away from him, he just kept moving my head up and down, faster and faster. I had no control over what he was doing to me, I coughed and choked a lot, but it didn't seem to bother him and he just carried on, moving my head up and down on his dick for a few more seconds until he had finished with me.

Then he pushed me over to the other side of the bed and he told me that it was enough and then he handed me a proper lollypop that he grabbed from a glass bowl that was sitting on a cupboard next to the bed. And it looked like he had it all set up in advance and had planed the whole thing, then he told me not to tell anyone about our little secret and that if I was a good little girl for him, he would buy me lots of sweets and toys to play with. I began to cry and I felt sick, but he didn't care and he just put his clothes back on, and then he told me to go back into the living room and to get back into my bed and to be a good girl for him and to be quiet.

I did what he said, but I was upset by what he had just done to me, I was shaking, my belly felt sick and I had a bad pain in my head that wouldn't go away and I wanted to go home. Then Tracy came back with Daisy and Simon and, as she walked into the living room, she walked over towards me and looked down at me and she patted me on the head. She then smiled as she put Simon and Daisy in the bed next to me and then she walked over to the bedroom that Fred was in; and as she walked into the bedroom, she smiled and closed the door behind her. I soon fell asleep, cuddling into Simon, and when I woke up the next morning, Daisy looked over at me and we said nothing. I couldn't wait to go back home to mum's house.

CHAPTER 2

Off to See Daddy in Ireland

After about six months of us going around to Tracy's flat and Fred constantly molesting me, mum told me that I couldn't go there anymore because Tracy was pregnant and she was going to have a baby. Mum said that Tracy had no more time for me and she could not look after me anymore. God, I was so happy, I couldn't believe it; I was finally getting away from Fred. However, it wasn't long before mum decided that she too could not look after me, so she said that she had decided to send all three of us little kids back to our real dad, who lived in Ireland.

We never knew our real dad because mum took us away from him when we were just babies; when she ran off with Jim, left Ireland and came to live in England. Even though mum said that we would be going to our dad in Ireland, we didn't know when we would be going, as she never told us anything, and then one day it just happened. There had been many times before when mum would get us dressed in our best clothes and have us ready for something special, but then she would change her mind about what she was doing and instead she would send us out to play and we never knew what she had been up to. Now when I think back to it, she must have wanted to leave our step dad Jim and run back to our real dad in Ireland many times, but she never did. And until now, we had never heard anything about our real dad, apart from Jim calling him a bastard and a cunt to mum when they were having an argument.

Now the time had come for us to leave and one day, while Jim was at work, mum packed all our clothes into a single small suitcase, and then she waited for one of our older brothers, Kevin, to arrive at the house. Then Daisy, Simon, Kevin and I all went off with mum to the underground station. Mum said that we were all going to Paddington train station and I will never forget the journey because I had never been on the underground before and I had never seen anything like Paddington station, with so many people in such a big place making so much noise all at the same time. It was a world that I had never seen before and it all looked wonderful.

With whistles blowing and people shouting, we all walked along the platforms looking at the trains, but mum couldn't read the signs, so she asked some people if they knew anything about the train that we had to get on to go to Ireland and they said yes, and they explained to her what she had to do. She said thanks and then she began to run along the platform with all of us children running along behind her. It was like an adventure and I loved it. However, as she turned and ran down another platform next to the train that we had to get on, it was just too difficult for me to keep up with her anymore and I fell. I got up and I began to walk behind her, but suddenly mum stopped running, then she turned around and began to grab and lift us one by one onto the train.

I walked towards her and it was my turn. I looked down at the gap between the platform and the train and the gap was so big that I could have easily fallen under the train and onto the tracks; but before I could say anything to her, she grabbed me and, in one huge swoop of her arms, she swung me onto the train. Then she stepped onto the train and shouted, 'Is this going to Ireland?'; but before anyone could shout back, the train began to move and it began to leave the station. She quickly turned around, opened the carriage door and jumped off the train; and as she did, the carriage door swung open and crashed against the side of the carriage and it made a huge smashing sound. But before we could do anything, mum turned around, ran up to the carriage door and slammed it shut, leaving us looking at her through the window.

Then she just stood and smiled, and as the train pulled away from the platform she began to wave goodbye at us. I screamed and shouted at her, 'Mum, stop', but the train kept pulling away and then she was gone. I could not believe what she had just done, I sat down and put my head down onto my lap and I began to cry, then Kevin told me that mum had planed it that way all along and that she never intended to come with us back to Ireland. 'I'm taking you', he said. 'I will be taking all of us all the way to Ireland and all on my own. Now shut up and sit down', he said. But I started to scream at him that we didn't want to go to Ireland without mum and that we wanted to stay in London with her. But he just looked at us and said nothing; he was only sixteen years old and he was taking three little kids hundreds of miles to Ireland, so what could he do with us apart from look and wonder what was going to happen to us all when we finally got to our dad's house in Ireland?

After a while, Kevin told us that it was going to take hours to get to the docks and ferry by train and he said that he had nothing for us to eat or drink with him and that he had no money to spend on food or water while on the train. We looked at each other, not quite understanding what he meant, and then we all looked out of the train windows and watched as the world went by, and I began to cry again; but Kevin just ignored me as if I were not even there. It was a long and difficult journey for us and some of the people on the train began to get fed up with us crying, playing and messing around, but they couldn't do anything about it, apart from complain to Kevin about us, but he couldn't do anything either and we didn't understand what was going on anyway. So, by the time we arrived at the last station, we had worn ourselves out from playing and crying, and we didn't make a fuss about anything Kevin told us to do. Even when Kevin told us to carry all our own stuff, and even when he said that we had to walk over a mile to the docks to catch the ferry, we still said nothing, we just quietly followed him.

As we got nearer to the docks, I could see the ferry in the distance and it looked magical as it towered high above the docks. It was bathed in sunlight and the sea mist and spray was splitting the light reflecting from its side into the colours of the rainbow. I loved the look of the ferry and, as we walked along the dock road and onto a small path, I looked up at the ferry in amazement and I kept looking up at it because it was so big and wonderful, and I had never seen anything like it before. Everything in the docks smelt of fish and the ferry had huge slimy green ropes hanging from its sides.

And as we walked along the path, I tried to grab hold of one of the ropes to swing on it. But as I looked up at the rope, I wandered slightly off the path and tripped over a big metal ring sticking out of the ground that the ferry ropes were tied to and I almost fell into the sea. But Kevin just managed to grab me by my hair and he pulled me back to safety before it was too late. My heart jumped and it missed a beat from the fright I just had, and Kevin and I just looked at each other with shock and, within a second, it was all over and we went on our way as if nothing had happened. But I could hear the sea smashing against the dock wall and the ferry and the sound grabbed my attention and I wanted to look down between the gap, but once again Kevin pulled me away from the edge and I kept walking.

Eventually, we got to the ferries-boarding ramp and many people were pushing and shoving to get on board, so we stepped to one side, and we waited until everyone had calmed down, then we tried to get on board and, an hour later, we eventually did. Once on board, we headed straight to the top deck of the ferry and, as we got to the top, we ran out onto the open deck and we looked over the side and down at the sea. We never quite knew what was going on, but it was so exciting that we soon forgot all about why we were there. What's more, we even forgot all about what was going to happen to us all when we got to Ireland.

It was freezing out on the deck, and after a couple of hours, we decided to go inside. Once back inside, we walked around for a while and, eventually, we found a place to sit down. It was much warmer inside and we soon settled down; but after a while, we noticed that some of the people around us had begun to look at us and one of the ferry staff came over to us and he asked us about our parents, as he wanted to know about who was looking after us. But Kevin just sat down, picked up a newspaper and pretended to read it. And even though we knew that he couldn't read, he did it anyway, just so that he did not have to look or talk to the ferry staff. Daisy knew what he was doing, so she walked over and stood next to him, she then stood up straight and began to tell everyone sitting around us that he could not read and that he was just pretending; but it didn't seem to bother Kevin or the people. So he just kept pretending and he kept it up for hours and hours, only sometimes putting the newspaper down so that he could pop an extra strong mint into his mouth and he even gave us one each just to keep us all happy and to shut us all up until we got to the docks in Ireland.

However, the ferry crossing was slow and it was going to take hours to get to Ireland, so all we could do was to try to sleep most of the time away. Daisy, Simon and I huddled up together on the floor and as I laid my head against the carpet, I could feel the vibrations of the engines penetrating up through the floor. So I pressed my ear hard against the carpet and I could hear the humming of the engines, as they pushed the ferry through the sea, and the vibrations made my ears tingle and the feeling was so nice that it made me feel sleepy and I was able to sleep through most of the journey.

When the ferry finally got to the docks, Kevin woke us all up and he told us to look out of the window, but it was dark and all I could see was bright lights and hundreds of people moving around the docks. We gathered up our belongings and, as we began to walk along the ferry, Kevin told us all to stay together and not to wander off or bad people would take us away and then we would be gone forever. I didn't want to be taken away by bad people, so I held Daisy's hand tight; but suddenly the ferry gave out a loud noise and I had to let her hand go to cover my ears. 'That's the horn', said Kevin, 'and we have to get off the ferry now before it goes back to England.'

We didn't waste any time, we grabbed all our things and we ran down the stairs and on to the exit ramp; and as we ran along the ramp, I looked over the side. I could see cars coming out of the ferry and it all looked very exciting, I couldn't wait to get off, so I grabbed Simon by the hand and we followed Kevin off the ferry. Once we were out of the docks, Kevin walked along the road and we followed him, but then he stopped next to a line of taxicabs and we stood and watched as he pulled a bundle of money out of his pocket. 'Hey', I said. 'I thought you had no money.' 'Mum gave it to me, she told me to get us some food for our trip with it, but instead I'm going to use the money to pay a taxicab to take us all the way home to our dad's house.' He said that it was about a five-hour drive by car and that mum had told him to get the coach to dad's house, but he told us that he didn't want to go by coach as he wanted to arrive in style and that's why he was getting a cab. By now, we had been travelling for almost a whole day, and it was beginning to get dark and we all felt sick from eating mints all day and nothing else. I told Kevin that we all needed food and water, but he said that we didn't have the time to stop for food and then he paid one of the cab drivers and we all got in the back of a cab.

It took what felt like forever to get to our dad's village and, on the way, we had to stop about six times just to go to the toilet. But eventually, the man stopped the cab and turned the engine off, and for a moment there was nothing but silence. I lifted my head to see what was going on and then he told us that we had to get out of the cab and walk the rest of the way to our dad's house. Because the rest of the road was far too bad for his cab to go down and he would get stuck in the mud if he tried to drive down it. So we got out of the cab and Kevin paid the man a couple of extra pounds as a tip and we began walking along the road; but after a couple of seconds, the road disappeared and we had to walk the rest of the way down a wet and muddy lane, in the pitch black of night.

We kept walking, stepping through deep puddles that came up to the ends of our clothes and stepping on cobblestones that stuck up through the mud and were making us trip and slip, every now and then, as we slid over them. We kept walking in an almost uncontrollable manner until we came to the end of the lane and we had to stop in front of an old wooden gate. Exhausted, I put my things down in the mud and then I looked up; only to see a huge dark horse standing in front of me, and the horse was looking down at me as if I were standing in its way and it was waiting for me to move out of its way. But as I turned to get out of the horse's way, a hand appeared from behind the horse and pulled on the chain that was around its neck; and with a rattle and a clanking of the chains, the horse slowly moved to one side, leaving a tall and ageing man standing in its place. I took a step back, but as I moved back, I tripped and fell onto my bum and I ended up sitting in a puddle of mud that splattered over everyone.

The man looked down at me and then Kevin turned to us all and said, 'That's our dad.' And I could tell from the look on dad's face that he knew we were coming, and as I looked up at him, I could just see a twinkle of joy creeping through his hard, cold face that gave me a feeling of being welcome and an instant sense of security. I smiled and picked myself up, and then we all stood still in front of him and we said nothing while we tried to work out what was going to happen next. But before we could say or do anything, our dad opened the wooden gate and told us all to move along and to get inside the house.

So, dragging our little belongings behind us, we walked and splashed our way up past the horse and up towards the front door of the house. Not knowing what was going to happen to us once we got inside the house, Simon and I struggled our way to the top of the one stone step that led up into the house. But just as I stepped inside the doorway, I dropped my things and I had to leave them sitting at the top of the step as the others pushed me into the house.

Once inside, we were swiftly moved into the living room, with our dad moving quickly past us and into the centre of the room, then he placed himself on an old wooden chair where he just sat and looked at us. And with a little smile creeping over his face, he could not control his emotions any longer and he said, 'Come over here to me, my children.' We all looked at each other and we slowly moved closer to him, but before we got a chance to do or say anything, he leapt up off the chair and put his arms around all four of us at the same time; telling us that he loved us, and that he had missed all of us so much and that he was so very sorry for not contacting us. Then he said that he thought our mum was coming back with us. Kevin then told him that she didn't want us anymore and that she did not want to come back to Ireland ever again.

Dad said nothing and he began to cry with happiness and he held us all so tightly together that I could hardly breathe. I looked over dad's shoulder and I could see four other people standing in the room behind him. He then got up, turned around and said, 'These people are just some of your family, your brothers and your sisters', as he pointed at three of the people in the room. Then he grabbed them by their arms and pulled them over to us. 'And this is your aunty', he said, as he grabbed the other person by her arm and pulled her over to touch and cuddle us.

'Come on', she said. 'I will make you some dinner and give you all a drink before I put you to bed.' I had no idea who she was, so I ran back to Kevin and grabbed him by his legs and wouldn't let go. I looked up at Kevin and told him that I wanted to go home, back to mummy in London, but dad told me to let go of Kevin and to go with our aunty. Then he told Kevin to go and get his coat on, as he was taking him down to the pub for a drink and to meet the boys.

Then they both went off to the pub, leaving us with our aunty, who fed us dry cornflakes with no milk, and then she made us all go upstairs where she put us all into one very large bed. I was still wearing the clothes that I had travelled in and so was Simon and Daisy, but she said that it didn't matter and that she would be back later to see if we were ok. I wanted to laugh at her, but I was so exhausted that I never made a fuss; I just lay down on the bed and I shut my eyes and the others did the same. I tried to forget everything that was going on around me and it must have worked, as it wasn't long before I went into my own little world for the rest of the night. I know it sounds strange, but the second my head hit the pillow I felt safe and happy, and I think Daisy and Simon felt the same.

Our aunty never came back that night and when I woke up the next morning, the bed we had all slept in was soaking wet. One of us must have wet the bed during the night, but because we were all so exhausted from the travelling, we had not woken up to go to the toilet and we never knew which one of us had wet the bed. So now, we had to face all the strange people again and we thought they were going to kill us for wetting the bed, so we all got off the bed and we pulled at the sheets, pulling them off the bed, and then we pushed and kicked them under the bed before someone walked in and discovered them.

When we had finished with the bed sheets, it was still very quiet in the house so we opened the bedroom door and we ran down the stairs as fast as we could and, on the way, we made enough noise to wake even the devil. We still had all our clothes and shoes on from the night before, so we thought we could head straight for the front door and escape before anyone realised what we were doing. But as we got to the front door, we couldn't open it as the handle was too stiff to turn, and there was a big bolt sticking out of the top of the door that was pushed into a piece of wood that was keeping the door closed and locked tight.

We stood back from the door and we looked for another way out, but as we stood for a moment, an arm came over the tops of our heads and grabbed the bolt on the door. Then the person slowly moved the bolt to one side and opened it, and then they moved their arm down to the door handle and unlocked the door. I didn't want to look behind me, but I just had to, so I slowly turned around to see who it was and it was our dad and he just looked down at us and smiled as he pulled the front door open, letting us all run out into the daylight and what to us felt like freedom. It didn't matter to us that our clothes were still wet or that we hadn't had any breakfast, all we wanted to do was escape outside and see if everything we remembered from the night before was real and that we had not dreamed it all up, and it was.

The horse was still standing by the wooden gate, but the gate was locked and it was keeping the horse from getting out of the yard. And I could see that the horse was looking over at the tall grass in the field next to the house and I knew the horse wanted to get to the grass, but I was too frightened to go over to the horse on my own because it was so big. Then I looked over the gate and the mud and puddles were just the same as I remembered them from the night before, but then I noticed a boy standing over by a wall in the corner of the garden. He was much older than we were and, as I looked at him, he shouted over at us all that he was our brother and that we had to do exactly what he told us to do or he would hit us.

Then our dad came out of the house and he told the boy to shut the fuck up and to go get some food from someone, anyone, and he said that it didn't matter who the food came from as long as he got something for us. So the boy, our brother, jumped over the wall and ran off down the lane, throwing stones and shouting back at us that he wasn't going to get us any fucking food and to go get it ourselves. We didn't know what to do, so we just walked over to the horse and we pretended that nothing had happened.

Then our dad followed us over to the horse, telling us that the horse's name was Rose and that she was a good horse and she would look after us kids whenever he wasn't around. It all sounded a bit strange to us, but it didn't really matter because we had no idea what he was talking about, so we just patted the horse on the legs and then we smiled up at her. Then dad told us that he loved us and that he was going to be out for the whole day, so someone else would be coming to the house later to see if we were ok. Then he opened the gate and walked off down the lane, leaving us standing alone in the garden, looking at each other and not knowing what to do next. We waited for dad to walk out of sight, then we turned around and went back into the house; we walked into the living room and, not knowing what to do we sat down on the sofa next to each other.

We had only been sitting down for a few seconds when suddenly I heard a strange noise coming from within the room, but I couldn't tell where it was coming from, and then we all heard it. And it was coming from a large old trunk over in the corner of the living room. 'That's strange', I said. Then suddenly the lid of the trunk moved and an old scruffy looking dog pushed the lid open and jumped out. The dog stopped for a moment and then looked at us; but before we could touch it, the dog ran out of the room and out of the front door, with all of us running behind it. Then the dog jumped over the old wooden gate and ran down the lane after our dad, barking and making a big fuss as it ran off and disappeared around the corner and out of sight.

We looked at each other and then we turned around and went back into the house, wondering what to do next; but this time, we closed the front door behind us just in case something else popped up out of the trunk, but nothing did. I had no idea where our other brother had gone after dad shouted at him to get us some food, but we all needed clean clothes and something to eat, so we looked around and we found the case that we had brought with us from London and we opened it. It was full of our old clothes that we used to run around in back at mum's, so we all changed into some dry clothes; and just as we had finished, Kevin came down the stairs and told us all to shut up and to be quiet. He said that he had a bad pain in his head and he felt sick because dad had taken him out to the pub last night and got him drunk. Then he turned around and ran into the kitchen to be sick, but he didn't make it to the sink and he was sick all over the kitchen floor, so he slammed the kitchen door shut and shouted at us to hurry up and to get out of the house.

We quickly put on our shoes and headed towards the front door; but as I reached for the door handle, the door opened and in walked our aunty. She had some eggs, bread and milk with her. 'Go and sit down at the kitchen table', she said and, as we all walked into the kitchen and sat at the table, she began to make us all breakfast; while Kevin hung onto the kitchen sink and continued to be sick.

At first, the smell of the food was so nice and we all stuck our noses up into the air with excitement and anticipation, and I kept turning around in my chair to have a look at what she was doing. 'Yippee, good', I said, but then Kevin began to choke on his own vomit and our aunty had to stop and help him at the sink; but she left the food on the stove and it all burnt, and when she had finished with Kevin she gave the burnt food to us.

And it resembled something that looked like a steaming pile of shit on a plate and she said that it was the best that she could do and that she would give us a drink of milk to make it all taste better. We were so hungry that it didn't matter what it looked like, we just giggled to each other and ate the food as quickly as possible. Drinking the milk at the same time, so the taste of the burnt food wouldn't stay in our mouths for very long, and she was right, it worked. She then said that our dad was a very busy man and we should all be good kids for him when he was around; but for now, we should just go outside and play for the rest of the day until he gets back. So we all got up and we did what she said, but we didn't know what to do or where to go, so we just stood around at the front of the house, looking at each other.

However, it wasn't long before a small group of children

walked up to the front of the house and they said that they were our brothers and sisters; and by the end of our conversation, we were a grand total of seven kids, four girls and three boys. And for the rest of the day, we all sat around and exchanged stories, with them telling us about our dad and Ireland and us telling them about mum and London.

They told us that they all lived in the house with dad and that he would just come and go whenever he felt like it, and sometimes they would not see or hear from him for a week or two at a time. We didn't really understand what they meant, but we could tell that everyone done just about, whatever they wanted to every day and that was the way of life in our dad's house.

We shrugged our shoulders and then we just got on with copying what everyone else did. We knew mum didn't want us anymore and we hoped that everyone in Ireland would like us and that we would fit in, so we did whatever we could to keep out of trouble. And for the next few days, our older brothers and sisters looked after us by showing us around the village and teaching us basic things, like how to steal whatever we needed from farms, shops and other people who lived in the village.

CHAPTER 3

All On Our Own

With dad coming and going whenever he felt like it, it soon became very clear that if we were going to survive we would have to look after ourselves. Occasionally, he would turn up and, when he did, he would leave us some food, but it was never enough and after a few hours, it would be all gone. And when dad was home, he was nearly always drunk and he would just sleep until he was sober enough to go back to the pub again; and while he was drunk, he never once thought about us for one second.

I remember one day he came home with a dead rabbit, it must have been road kill or something as it was almost flat and it looked a mess. He walked into the kitchen with it and he chucked the rabbit onto the table, and with one swift swing of his arm he picked up a large kitchen knife and chopped the rabbit's head off and then its feet, and then he pulled at its fur and skin with his hands until it all came off the rabbit's body. We all stood around and looked at him as he put the rabbit and its feet into a pot of water and then he began to make dinner for us all; but as the pot began to warm up, the rabbit began to stink and the kitchen quickly filled with a nasty smell.

When the rabbit was finally cooked, dad put the whole pot onto the kitchen table and he sat down and ate most of the rabbit himself, while we all stood around him and watched. And when he had finished and his belly was full, he pushed the pot into the middle of the table and left all of us to fight over the scraps, but he had only left a few bones and what looked like the skin for us kids to suck and chew on. And he began to laugh at us as he left the kitchen, and as he walked away he said that we were all little beggars and he told us to fuck off out of his sight.

I grabbed the pot and I ran out of the house with it, but I had forgotten all about the step outside the front door and, as I ran outside, I fell. The pot flew out of my hands and then it hit the ground and rolled over, tipping what was left of the rabbit onto the ground; and within a second, the dog ran over and savaged the remains of the rabbit. I was so unhappy and hungry, I got up and walked back into the house and towards dad, but he just looked straight through me like it didn't matter that I was starving. Then he walked off back to the pub, with the dog following behind him, both with stomachs full from the rabbit they had just eaten, and I stood hungry and sad in the middle of the garden, watching them as they walked away happy and content with themselves.

At the end of each day, I would try to have a wash, but dad never had a boiler in the house, he only had a wood-burning stove to heat the water and it was never lit, so the water was always cold. We never had soap to wash with and I never once saw a towel in the house, so I always smelt bad, my skin was always dirty and my clothes were never washed. I was only five years old, and after playing outside all day, I would be filthy, but no one cared; and at the end of each day, I would climb into my bed covered in dirt and I would have to make the best of a bad situation.

But with four of us girls all sleeping in one bed, it meant that almost every night one of us would wet the bed and we would all have to lie on the wet sheets until morning. Then, when we all got up, we would leave the bed covers pulled back so the sheets could dry out on their own during the day, then in the evening we would climb back into a dry bed again. However, most evenings when I got back into bed, the smell from the sheets was so bad that I would gag and choke for the first few minutes until I got used to the smell again, and I would get dizzy from the fumes off the sheets, but eventually I would fall asleep. I slept in the bed for months until the smell got so bad that I couldn't sleep or even stay in the bedroom without coughing or choking, so I decided to change the sheets myself; but we never had any, so I went out and I stole some from other people's washing lines.

Over the next few months, our situation went from bad to worse and I never heard a thing about mum, our aunty hardly ever came around to see if we were ok and we soon realised that we had to look after ourselves if we were going to survive, as no one else was going to do anything for us. We knew that our dad loved us, but that was about as far as he would commit himself to us; he would never look after us and he used any money he had to drink himself stupid, down at the pub every day. I found it very difficult adjusting to my new life in Ireland and it just became harder and harder for me every day and because we had very little food to eat, if any at all, I began to lose weight fast. My older brothers and sisters could see the state that I was in, so they began to take me out with them each day and they explained to me that I could get potatoes, carrots and other root vegetables from the fields if I used my hands to dig for them.

And while we were in one of the fields and they showed me how to dig into the earth, I had a go and I managed to dig up some carrots, but we couldn't cook them so they told me to eat them raw. I shock the carrots and rubbed the dirt from them with my hands and then I put a carrot into my mouth and I dug my teeth into it, but I couldn't chew it. The carrot was so hard that my teeth became stuck and everyone laughed at me, and I had to pull on the carrot to get it out of my mouth and I thought my teeth were going to come out with it. I was hungry and felt like crying, so one of my bigger brothers took the carrot from me and he put the carrot into his mouth and he began to chew the carrot for me and then he spat the bits out into one of his hands and he gave the bits to me to eat.

He said that my teeth were baby teeth and I was too small and weak to chew the food, and everyone thought it was funny, including me. The farmers knew what we were doing in the fields, but they never stopped us and the only time we got shouted at or chased by them was when we ran past the small farmers' shops in the village and we took an apple or a turnip to eat from outside the front of the shops. We would grab at anything and then run off into the fields with it and hide until we had finished eating what we had stolen.

Most mornings before I left the house, my brother Ted would grab Daisy, Simon and me, because we were the smallest and the easiest of the kids to pick on, and he would make us all stand in line in front of him while he gave us our orders for the day. One of my jobs was to pick up all the fag butts and all the round pebbles that I could find along the roads around the village. The fag butts were for him and my older brothers to make their own fags with and the pebbles were for him to use in his slingshot. He told me that the pebbles had to be perfectly round to do the most damage and if I didn't get it right, he would shoot me with the pebbles that would not work well for him, so I had to get it right or I would be in trouble.

I had to do this for him every morning; even when it was cold and raining, he still sent me out and I had to walk along the road looking down on the surface for pebbles and fags. But after a while, my back would ache from bending over and I would feel sad for most of the time, but I had no choice, as it was my job. Then, when I had finished, I would hand Ted the pebbles and he would go out and use them around the village, doing as much damage as he possibly could, by breaking windows and anything else that caught his eye.

Most days, I would just walk around for a while and then I would go back to the house to see what was going on or to see if dad had come home, and I would hide in the garden until Ted went off, and only then would I feel happy knowing that Ted was not around to bother me. And most of the time, Ted would be out for hours, just walking around, breaking things; but then sometimes he would get on the horse Rose and ride her bareback through the village, as fast as he possibly could, and he would only be holding on to the chain around her neck to steady himself. He would ride along, smashing as many windows as he possibly could with his slingshot and not stopping until he got back to our house.

Then, a couple of hours later, people would turn up at the house looking for our dad, to complain about Ted riding the horse through the village like a madman, and about him smashing all the windows and street lights as he had done so. But dad was never at home and we would tell the people that if they really wanted to find our dad, then they should go down to the pub and ask for him there, but they never did. Next to come along knocking on the door and looking for Ted would be the police, but Ted would just give them even more things to complain about, as he laughed and shouted at them, calling them all kinds of names and telling them to fuck off as he hung out of the upstairs windows. However, they would never go into the house to get him as he always threatened to climb out of the window and onto the roof if they put a foot through the front door.

Almost every time we went out, we would cause some kind of trouble for ourselves; it wasn't because we were bad children, but because there was so many of us that something just had to happen. I remember one morning a woman came to the house and she asked to see our dad, but as usual he wasn't in and no one had seen him for about a week. So, we told the woman that he was out at work and that he would be back after five o'clock and we told her to come back then.

And she did, but he still wasn't back, so we kept the front door locked shut and we all kept very quiet, hoping that she would go away and leave us alone. But she didn't leave and she just kept knocking on the door; so eventually, Ted opened the front door and he went outside. He told the woman that he was our dad and then he asked her what she wanted; he was only thirteen and straightaway she told him that she wasn't stupid and that we had all better go to school or she would be back with more people who would make us go to school, and then she left. Ted came back into the house and he said that she was a bitch and that he had told her that he was our dad; and he said that he had told her to fuck off and she did and that was the end of it.

Ted then said that he was now the boss of the house, he was going to be our dad from now on and he was going to look after us. We all looked at him and then we all fell about laughing and I said that if he was now our dad, then he would help us; and because we were all starving hungry and we had no food in the house to eat, then he needed to get some for us. Ted looked at us all and then he said, 'Ok, go sit down in the kitchen and I will be back in a couple of minutes with some food for you all to eat'; so we all went into the kitchen and we sat at the table and waited for him to come back.

And within a couple of minutes, he was back holding a frying pan with what looked like a long sausage sitting in the middle of it. He then put the pan onto the stove and began to strike some matches and within a couple of minutes he had the stove lit and we all sat patiently waiting for the food to cook. But within a couple of seconds of the heat reaching the frying pan, the sausage began to smoke crackle and stink all at the same time, and we all began to choke as the kitchen filled with thick smoke. The smell was so strong that I turned around to ask him what it was that he was cooking, but he had gone red in the face from the smell and smoke and he was choking too.

Then the smell got so bad that we all had to run out of the house and Ted ran out behind us, and he was chasing after us with the frying pan and he was shouting that we had to come back and eat our dinner. But the smell was so strong that even the outside of the house stunk, and thick brown smoke was still coming out of the sausage. 'No', I shouted, 'it's disgusting. What is it?' 'It's a shit', said Ted. 'I done it', he said; then he shouted that it went in one end and it came out of the other, so it must still be good for you to eat.

Suddenly, he coughed again and he began to choke, so he stopped running and he slung the lot into the air and we all ran out of the gate screaming as he ran after us, shouting and laughing that we had to come back and eat our dinner. But I shouted, 'Eat it yourself, we're not hungry anymore' and we just kept screaming and running as Ted fell to his knees choking.

We all stayed out for the rest of the day and we sat amongst some tall grass in a field, hoping that Ted would not be able to find us and make us eat the shit. But after a while, it began to get dark so we decided to head back to the house; we all got up and Daisy, Simon and myself slowly walked home, still laughing about what had happened earlier in the day, and hoping that the smell would be gone by the time we got back. No one was around when we returned to the house, so we went straight inside and off to bed; the last thing we wanted was to see Ted when he got back and it worked and we were left alone for the rest of the night.

However, the next morning, when the three of us kids got up and went downstairs, Ted was waiting for us in the living room and he told us that we couldn't go outside until he did something. And then he made us stand in a straight line in front of him and he told us to hold out our hands as he took a big flat stick out of his trousers, and within a second he began to slap our hands with the stick. But before he could finish hitting us, dad walked in through the front door and he saw what he was doing. And without making a sound, he walked up behind Ted, leant over and gave him a huge slap around the head and told him to fuck off outside before he gave him a whipping around the head with his belt. Ted lifted his hands up to protect his head from dad and then he shouted at dad, telling him that we had no food and that he was hungry, then Ted ran like hell out of the house and as far away from dad as possible.

But Ted was right, we had no food in the house and we were all starving with the hunger. Dad looked down at us and then he said that he was going to get some food for us. But once dad left the house, we never saw him again that day and he never came back for a week. Ted did eventually come back and he decided that he had to do something fast or we would all die from starvation, so he gathered us all up and he told us all to go out and to do our best to find something to eat. We all walked off in different directions, hoping to find food; and within a couple of hours Daisy, Simon and myself had managed to find some apples and potatoes in a field, so we gathered them up and we headed back home, feeling very happy with ourselves.

As we walked towards the house, we could see that it was quiet and no one was around. But as we got closer, I could see a filthy pillowcase lying on the ground at the foot of the front door and it was moving. I slowly walked up to the pillowcase and I poked at it with a stick that I was playing with and the pillowcase stopped moving. I could see that the open end of the pillowcase had been tied up with string, so I undid the string and I looked inside; and just as I put my face into the pillowcase, out jumped two chickens and they fell to the ground. And as I stood back, they began to run around, but they had nowhere to go so I ran after them, chasing them in and out of the house and trying to catch them, but they were too fast for me and I fell over.

Then Ted came out of the house and he asked us why I was playing with our dinner, but I just looked at him, not quite understanding what he had just said to me and then he just laughed at me as I continued to chase the chickens around the yard. Then Ted grabbed one of the chickens by its head and within a couple of seconds he twisted its neck until it snapped, and he pulled the chicken's head clean off its body with his bare hands and dropped the chicken's body to the floor. Straightaway, the headless body began to run around and the chicken was flapping its wings like mad, and then without warning it stopped moving and collapsed to the ground, dead.

So Ted picked the chicken up and walked back into the house, with it swinging by its headless neck. We all ran into the house after Ted and I asked him if he could do it again to the other chicken.

'Please', I begged him, but he said to shut the fuck up and then he put the chicken into a huge metal pot. He said that he was going to cook it for us and he began to light the stove; but he had not taken any of the feathers off its body, so I told him what to do. 'Pull the feathers off it first or it won't cook.' However, he only pulled some of the big feathers off and then he filled the pot up with water again and put the pot back on the stove. I walked over to the stove and I looked inside the pot; some feathers and blood were floating around in the water and more blood was coming out of the chicken's neck that was turning the water red. It looked a mess and I felt sick just looking at it, so I walked away and I went outside.

And by now, all the others had come back and they had seen the other chicken still running around the yard. I told them what Ted had been doing and then we all sat down in the yard and played with the chicken, while we waited for Ted to come out of the house and break the chicken's neck. We sat waiting patiently with the chicken, and eventually Ted came outside and within a few seconds it was all over and the decapitated body of the chicken lay still on the ground and then we just sat and waited for the dinner to cook.

We waited for what seemed like hours and when the chicken was cooked, Ted put the whole thing onto a big plate and placed it in the middle of the kitchen table. It was steaming hot boiled chicken and nothing else, and the skin was pale and it hung from the chickens' body as if it was too big and didn't fit. We couldn't wait any longer and we all grabbed and pulled at the chicken, breaking the legs away from its body and pulling at the skin to get at the meat inside.

Eventually, the chicken broke open and, as we continued to pull at it, the chicken split apart, steam rose up into the air and it smelt bad. Ted had cooked the chicken with all the guts and other stuff still inside and, as we pulled at it, the guts fell out of the body and spread over the table. We continued pulling at the chicken and, as we did so, the guts slipped down off the table and onto the kitchen floor and we all stepped in them as we continued to grab and pull at the chicken. We continued to pull at the chicken and we ate as much of it as we could, but the smell and slimy guts had put us all off and we couldn't enjoy it as much as we had hoped; so eventually, I gave up and walked away.

It had now become so obvious that we couldn't look after ourselves that people in the village had started to notice it too; we had done our best by scrounging food from people and from their rubbish bins, but it wasn't enough, so we began to visit the rubbish dump just outside the village to look for food. We would walk to the dump almost every day and we would look through hundreds of black bags full of people's rubbish, then we would go through all the rubbish bins we could find, searching for clothes and eating anything we could get our hands on. To us, it didn't matter if it was dirty, old, smelling or covered in mould; we needed to eat and we did. We would rub any muck off the food and then put it into our mouths, and one of the best things to find was packets of out-of-date biscuits that supermarkets had slung out, as they would always taste nice.

But the dump smelt bad and it was full of things like needles and cotton with blood on it and other strange stuff from the hospital that would make us itch if we touched it. We would get cuts on our hands and knees from all sorts of things almost every day and our mouths would become so dry that we had to keep them shut; otherwise, bugs and big blue bottles would fly into your mouth. Then they would stick to the roof of your mouth and you would have to dig them out with your fingers or try to make some spit in your mouth so you could swallow them, and all the time the flies would be making a buzzing noise inside your mouth until they were gone.

And every now and then, a rubbish lorry would pull in with a new load of black bags and we would be the first to get on top of them and rip the bags open. We used to see many adults doing the same thing as us, but they would always wait until we had finished and moved on to another lot of bags before they came over to look through them. I think it was because we were the youngest and smallest in the dump that they gave us a chance to eat before they went through the bags. Even dad knew what we were doing and, some days before we left the house, he would tell us to look out for scrap copper wire and if we found any, to bring it home for him to scrap; and we did, but he never said thanks.

All this was fine and sometimes it was even fun; plus, down by the edge of the dump, there was a small stream and during the summer months we would climb down to it and wash some of the smell and muck off our hands and faces. Plus we would wash and swap some of our old clothes for newer ones that we had found in the dump, and at the end of the day, we would head back home with bellies full and happy faces.

However, one day while at the dump, we must have forgotten about our baby brother Simon being with us, as it was only after we had arrived back home and it began to get dark that I asked everyone if they had seen him, but no one had. The last time anyone had seen him was earlier in the day when we were all at the stream by the dump; in a panic, we all jumped up and we went off looking for him and we ran almost all the way back to the dump before we found him.

He was walking along the road and he was all alone, and he was dirty and wet all over and he was wearing only his underpants and a pair of socks. I grabbed him by the arm and then I cuddled him and he told me that he had fallen into the stream and he had shouted for us, but nobody came. So, he managed to climb out of the stream on his own and he took his clothes off because they were wet and too heavy for him and he couldn't walk in them. I grabbed his t-shirt out of his hands, I rung it out and then I put it back on him; then Ted picked Simon up and put him on his shoulders and we all walked home happy that we had found Simon and that he was safe. When we got home, we never told anyone, not even our dad about what had happened to Simon, as he would have killed us if he had known what had gone on; anyway, Simon was ok and everything was fine now.

After a few weeks, the days began to get colder and darker and I began to feel ill, my skin looked pale and it was thick with waxy dirt, and red patches with rings and dots began to appear all over my body and I looked very sick. My hair had become so stiff with dirt that it just stuck up into the air, and my scalp hurt and it bled if I scratched it. So one of my older sisters, Jenny, who was ten years old, decided that we had to have a proper wash with hot water and soap, but I had forgotten what soap was.

Later that night, Jenny took Daisy, Simon and me, as we were the youngest and dirtiest, with her to an old people's home and she managed to lift us up through an open window on the ground floor and into a bathroom within the building. We could tell that she had done it before because she told us to be very quiet and she knew where everything was, and then she locked the bathroom door from the inside. We took our clothes off and we all stood still while she washed us all with hot water and soap and it felt so nice being clean; once she had finished, she helped us back out of the window and we all ran off back home.

After that, she would take us back to the home every couple of weeks and we would climb through the same window and into the bathroom to have a wash. But the red marks and rings that were all over my body never went away and my skin was still red and itchy. We managed to get away with using the bathroom for a couple of months, before Jenny realised that someone was leaving clean towels and medicated soap for us to use and the bathroom door had already been locked shut from the outside. We think it was so that we could take our time and have a proper wash and even wash our hair without having to hurry. But my hair had become infested with head lice and they would never go away no matter how much I washed it. Anyway, we all had head lice and they would just jump from one head to another and simple washing would have never gotten rid of them, so we gave up trying and accepted them.

Then one day, while we were having a wash, somebody knocked on the bathroom door and said, 'Be quiet and hurry up, the doctor is coming' and with that we looked at each other in shock and grabbed our clothes. Then we climbed out of the window and ran wet and naked into the bushes at the end of the home's grounds; and when we thought we were safe, we stopped running and turned around just in time to see a couple of nurses looking through a ground floor window and smiling at us.

We quickly put on our clothes, then we ran off, giggling to each other and, from that day on, every time we went back for a wash they would only knock on the bathroom door when a doctor really was coming or if we were making too much noise. Otherwise, they would leave us alone to get on with washing; and sometimes when leaving, we would look back and we would see them looking and smiling at us from the windows of the home. They were our friends and the only ones we had.

It had been almost a year since we had anyone take proper care of us and even after having a wash, we still looked bad, our skin was pale and we were getting sicker by the day. I had lost almost half of my body weight and Simon's belly and face had swollen from drinking dirty water and having no proper food to eat.

Then one morning, a woman from the social services came to dad's house and she asked dad if he could bring all of us for a medical check-up. At first, he said no; but after she had a another word with him, he agreed, and the following morning he got us all dressed in the best clothes that he could find and then he took us all off to the clinic for the check-up. It took hours for the doctors to check us all over and it was obvious to the doctors that we were in very poor health; and after they had finished, they had a quick word with dad and then they said we could all go home. We didn't know it at the time, but they had already made the decision to take us all into care. And within a couple of days, two police cars full of police officers and social workers turned up at the house.

It was early in the morning when they arrived and, as they all got out of the cars, one of the police officers walked up to the house and knocked on the front door. I looked up at dad and by the look on his face I could tell that he knew they were coming; and as he opened the door, the police officer told him that he had to get us all dressed and that we all had to go with them to the police station. Dad shouted at all the people and he told them all to fuck off and he tried to close the door, but the police officer told him to stop messing around or they would have to arrest him. Dad said ok and then he came back inside the house and he told us that we all had to go with them, then he got us all dressed and he walked us out of the house and into the waiting police cars.

Once we were inside the cars, dad went over to one of the police cars and he got in the front seat, next to one of the police officers that he knew. The police officer told daddy that he was sorry, but he could do nothing to help us and then he drove us all to the police station. When we arrived, they took us children into the police station, but they would not allow dad to stay with us; instead, they put him into the back of the police car and they drove him straight to the courthouse.

Once there, they put him into a room and they told him that he had to sit and wait until they had time to finalise his court case, and until then he could not leave the building or talk to anyone. He asked the police officer what was going to happen to his children and if we were ok at the police station, and the officer told him not to worry, as they were taking good care of us and they would bring us along to him shortly. And dad had no choice but to sit down and wait for us. Back at the police station, we all shouted at the police officers and we made a big fuss, telling everyone in the station that we wanted our dad and that we should not have to stay there because we had done nothing wrong; and we told them they were bad people for taking us to the police station. But it didn't make any difference; they just looked at us and tried to keep us quiet by talking to us.

Then, one of the police officers asked us if we were hungry and if we wanted something to eat, and we all said yes, so one of the older police officers who knew our dad put his hand into his pocket and pulled out a load of money. Then he told two of the other officers to go and get us some food, and he kept us occupied by telling us jokes and letting us play around with some of the things in the station. Then, after about half an hour, the police officers came back and they told us all to stop playing and to follow them. They walked out of the room and up some stairs with us following behind them, but as they got to the top of the stairs they all stopped and we all stopped behind them, but we didn't stop quick enough and we bumped into each other and then we accidentally pushed one of the police officers into his back. He turned, looked back and smiled at us and then he opened a door in front of him, while at the same time he told us all to go inside, but just inside the doorway stood six police officers.

We walked in and we all looked up at them as we walked past, thinking that something bad was about to happen to us; but as we got further into the room, we could see a huge table covered in food, 'It's all for you lot', he said. 'Now go over to the table and eat something.' We all ran up to the table and we looked at the food, there were cakes, drinks and food that we had never seen or tasted before and then one of the police officers poured me a drink of coke and he handed me a cake to eat. I was very excited about the food and I just couldn't believe my eyes; we shouted at each other and then we jumped up and down with excitement. I grabbed at the food and I began to eat, but it didn't take long before I started to feel sick and I wanted to vomit; I hadn't eaten so much food for such a long time that my belly couldn't cope with it.

I drank some coke, then I sat down and began to cry, and I told the police officer that I didn't want the food anymore and that I wanted to go home with my daddy; then my brothers and sisters began to cry and I shouted at the police to let us all go. So, they opened the door of the room, they allowed us to walk back down the stairs and they gave us the freedom of the police station, letting us play around with everything, just to keep us happy; but it didn't last long and soon they had run out of ideas to keep us quiet.

Then I noticed an old man sitting in the corner of the room and as I walked over to him, he shook his keys; I asked him what he was doing with the keys and he told me that the keys opened all the cell doors and that I could have them if I wanted. Without speaking, I grabbed the keys out of his hands and I ran over to one of the cell doors, I looked over at him and reached for the lock on the cell door and I put the key into the lock and I shouted to the prisoner inside that he could go home if he wanted to. But a police officer was standing right behind me and he was shaking his head from side to side, then one of the prisoners looked through the hatch at me and he told me that he didn't want to go home and that I should keep the door locked.

Then my brother Ted grabbed the keys from me and, one by one, he opened all of the cell doors, while telling everyone inside the cells that he was now in charge and they could all go home; but none of the prisoners came out of the cells. As some police officers were standing behind Ted and they were shaking their heads from side to side and indicating to the prisoners that they had to stay put. Then Ted moved along to an empty cell and we all followed him, and as he opened the door, we all stepped inside and we told Ted to lock the door behind us, and he did. Once Ted had locked the cell door, he told us all that he was going to run off with the keys and we began to shout and scream at him to let us out; but instead of opening the cell door, he went back to the other cells and he told all the prisoners to get out. And he told them all to swap places with each other and the police officers let him do it, and they were all smiling as he made all the prisoners swap cells with each other and then he locked them in again.

After Ted had finished messing around, he let us all out of the cell and one of the police officers came over to us and he said that he was very sorry but we had to leave the police station and go with him; and then he told us that he was taking us to see our dad. We all shouted and screamed at each other with excitement and we all ran over to the door to get out. We just wanted to get out and go back home with daddy, but instead they put us all into a couple of police cars and drove us to the courthouse where daddy was waiting for us.

Once we got to the courthouse, we were taken into a small room and sitting in the corner was daddy, and we were so happy to see him that we all ran over to him and we hugged and kissed him. We acted as if we had not seen him for years, and he began to cry and he gave us all a big hug back, while telling us that he was very sorry and that he loved us so much. Then a woman entered the room, she asked us all to follow her and she took us into the courtroom, where many people were sitting and waiting for us. They told us all to sit down, but Simon and I just hung on to daddy's legs and we wouldn't let go, so they let us stay with him while they talked to each other about us.

Then everyone in the courtroom went very quiet and a member of the court staff began to read out our names and our ages, starting with the girls first. Lily age five, Daisy age six, Karen age ten, Jenny age eleven; and then the boys, Simon age four, Chris age nine, Ted age fourteen. Then the judge told everyone that daddy was not a fit and proper person to look after us and that all seven of his children would have to go into care. Daddy began to cry, so did Simon and then I began to cry, so I climbed up onto daddy's lap and cuddled him, while some of the representatives from the social services gave evidence against daddy and the reasons why they should take us all away from him. They said they needed to put us into a children's home so that we could be well looked after.

The judge looked over at daddy and he asked daddy if he could think of any reason why they should not take us all away from him; but daddy just cried and, shaking his head from side to side, he told us that he loved us and that he was so very sorry for not looking after us better. Then the court staff all stood up and left the room, leaving the police and social service staff to sort things out with us. They told us they were very sorry, but it was time for us to go with them and that daddy could not come with us.

Then the social service staff escorted us all out of the building and, at that moment, we all began to cry and we shouted at them that we didn't want to go and to leave us all alone, as we wanted to go home with our daddy. But they just looked down at us and I could see that they were struggling no to cry, but they just couldn't help themselves and soon everyone was crying and sobbing and the people said that they were sorry, but they had to do their job. And the police officer who knew daddy began to cry, but he still had to take us away.

And once everyone was outside, the police had to take daddy to one side and hold him back while the social service staff put us girls into one car and the boys into another. Daddy then broke down and collapsed to the ground, he was shouting and begging them to stop and the police had to hold him up and comfort him, while we were all driven away, screaming and shouting at him from the cars' windows, and then we were gone. Leaving daddy standing at the side of the road emotionally devastated and he had to be taken to hospital. Sometime later, some people told us that daddy had suffered a mental break down and he needed professional help to recover, so they put him into a mental home for three months, until he was able to cope with losing us all and he was able to go home and look after himself again.

CHAPTER 4

The Convent Home

After leaving the courthouse, the police drove us around in the cars for hours. I think it was more to do with trying to wear us out rather than us having to travel very far, and by the time we pulled into a drive it had worked. Because all we wanted to do was to get out of the cars and be with each other; but as we drove up the drive, we went through a big set of iron gates and up towards a very large building. 'It's a convent', the driver said.

But as we pulled up, only our car stopped at the front of the building and the other car with the boys inside carried on past us and around to the back of the building and out of sight. It was very quiet and, as I looked through the car window, I noticed some nuns coming out of the convent and they were heading towards the car. As they approached the car, one of the nuns opened the car door and in a strange but soft voice she said, 'Welcome to St Joseph's convent. Please get out of the car.' I looked around and it was now getting dark and a misty fog had begun to surround the nuns and the building; the atmosphere surrounding the place was creepy and I felt like I wanted to stay in the car. But one of the nuns grabbed me by the arm and she began to pull at me, but I held onto my sisters tightly so she could not easily separate us. But the nun kept pulling at me until I was out of the car, then she did the same to the others and once we were all out of the car the nuns gathered around us and they led us up towards the building. While at the same time, they told us that everything was going to be ok and that they were going to look after us for a little while.

We all looked at each other and I asked the nuns what was going to happen to our brothers, and one of the nuns said that they had to go to another part of the building to stay with other boys the same as them. Then we all walked through the front door of the building and into a hallway; and once inside, the nuns shut the front door behind us and they led us through a large room and into a bathroom. They said that they had to give us a bath and that we had to take off all our clothes, but we didn't want to; the room was cold and I was shaking with fear, but they didn't mess around and they just pulled at our clothes until we were all naked and then I began to cry.

We all huddled together to keep warm, but the nuns soon pulled us apart, telling us that we had bugs crawling around in our hair and that we had to have all our hair cut off. I was frightened and I was shaking from the cold of the room. I tried to run over to my sister Daisy, but as I ran towards her one of the nuns grabbed me from behind and, within a couple of seconds, she had pushed me on to a chair; and as she stood behind me, she commented that I had lovely long hair. Then, just as she had finished stroking my hair, my head was pushed back and held tight while another nun cut all my hair off. Then they did the same to Daisy, Jenny and Karen.

After that, the nun told me to get into the bath, but I was freezing cold and I was crying as bits of my hair had fallen into my eyes, making it difficult for me to see. So, I put out my arms and I shouted to Daisy and Karen, hoping that one of them would grab me and pull me towards them. But they never did and all I could do was listen as Daisy and Karen shouted for each other and me, while the nuns told them to shut up.

Then suddenly, one of the nuns lifted me up and dumped me into a freezing bath of cold water, then she covered me in soap and immediately my skin began to sting and it hurt so bad that I felt like

55

I wanted to be sick from the pain. I shouted to the nun for help, but she didn't listen to me and she pushed my head under the bath tap to wash the soap off my head. But I had my mouth open and I almost choked and I went dizzy from swallowing some of the water from the tap. She quickly pulled me out of the bath and stood me up, and then she patted me on my back while telling me that I would be ok.

She then dried me off and told me to stand next to the wall and then she walked away. I thought it was all over, but she soon came back and she covered me in medicated oil, making my skin hurt again. I was now bleeding and the blood was running down my skin from where she had rubbed scabs away from my body, because she had rubbed me so hard. I turned around and, as I looked over at my sisters, Jenny was being slapped around the head and told to shut up, while Daisy and Karen had medicated oil vigorously rubbed all over them that was making them cry from the pain.

Once the nuns had finished covering us with the oil, they told us all to go into the next room while they cleaned up, but we were only in the room for a few seconds when one of the nuns came back and put pyjamas on us. 'Come on', she said. 'Now follow me.' So we all walked behind her. She led us back through the convent, out of the front door and into the cold night air; it was freezing and I pulled Karen close to me to keep me warm, and Daisy and Jenny did the same. Then the nun said, 'Quickly, quickly, hurry up. I haven't got all night', and she ran behind us, pushing us along, while telling us that she had things to do. I turned to her and I asked her where are we going. 'To your new home', she said. 'We call it Willows house, and you're going to live in it for a while.' I turned back around and I could see the house in the distance. 'Walk quicker, she said. 'Quickly.' And I ended up having to run the rest of the way until I reached the front door of the house.

She opened the front door and switched on the light, and we all walked in, not knowing what to expect. It was very quiet and I could see a staircase leading up to the top of the house. Shoes and a few coats lay scattered around the floor, but no one was around. Then the nun said, 'This way', she began walking up the stairs and we followed her. I can remember walking past large rooms, with rows and rows of beds on each side of the rooms, but there were no people around at all. The nun said, 'This way', and she led us up to the top of the house and into a bedroom in the attic. 'This is your room', she said 'and you better keep it tidy and make no noise or you will be in a lot of trouble. You all have a bed each, but you all have to share the wardrobe and the chest of drawers. I will be back later', she said. And then she left the room, closing the door behind her.

But as I went over to open the door and to follow her, she quickly locked the door from the outside and it wouldn't open. I shouted and kicked at the door, but Karen said, 'Stop or she might come back and kill us.' I looked over at her and said ok, but I put my ear next to the door instead, and I could hear the nun as she walked down the stairs. I tried the door again, but it still wouldn't open. 'Now what do we do?' I said. 'Nothing', said Jenny. 'Nothing but wait.' So we all looked around the room, we sat on the beds and we told each other what we were going to do when she comes back and opens the door. After a while, I looked up at the ceiling and above me was a small window. I hadn't noticed it at first because the top of the room was so dark, but the window was too high for me to reach, so I just sat on the bed and looked around the room again. I could see a chair, a small table and a cupboard that was painted white, the same as the walls, so it was difficult to notice. I got off the bed and walked over to the table.

I decided that I had to try and get out of the room, so I pulled the table over towards the window and I used it to climb on, hoping that I would be able to reach the window and get out of the room that way. But the window was still out of my reach, so I got back down and I placed the small chair on top of the table and I tried again, but the window was still too high and my sisters shouted at me to get down before I killed myself. I turned around and I shouted back at them that we were all going to die anyway, then I climbed back down and I put everything back into its correct place.

Next, I went over to the cupboard, but it was locked shut. Someone had put a big silver padlock up high on the doors and it was difficult to reach, but I was just able to pull the doors open a little and I looked inside. At first, it was hard to see inside, but as my eyes got used to the darkness I could see board games, balls and many puzzles stacked on some shelves; but then I heard footsteps, the nun was coming back. So I ran back into the middle of the room and then we all moved over on to one bed and we waited for her to open the bedroom door.

But her keys made a rattling noise as if she was teasing us and as the door opened we expected the same grumpy old nun, but it was a different nun and she was smiling. 'Hello, children. I'm Sister Ann and I have some food for you', she said, and then she sat down on a bed next to us. We all looked at her and I asked her if she was going to kill us. She smiled and then I told her that I wanted to go home. 'This is your home now', she said, while she placed the food on top of the chest of drawers. 'I will come back later to help you into bed', she said, and then she left the room, locking the door behind her. We knew we couldn't get out of the room, so after she left we all ran over to the food and we stuffed our faces until we couldn't eat anymore. Then we fell onto the beds, laughing at each other because we all felt sick, plus I still had some food sticking out of my mouth that began sliding down my face and onto the bed and was making us all laugh even more.

About an hour passed, then Sister Ann came back. 'Hello, children. Have you all finished eating?' she said. 'Yes, but I want to go to the toilet', I said. She led us all down the corridor to a bathroom and she waited for us until we had all finished. Then she led us back to our bedroom and, on the way, she made sure that none of us wandered off. 'It's late, so you must all go to bed now and I will be back in the morning to see if you are all ok', she said.

Then she turned off the light and locked the door as she left the room. It was still early and none of us could sleep, plus we had never slept in a bed on our own before, so we all jumped up and we all got into one bed and cuddled up together for the night. We told each other that it was going to be ok and that we will all go home in the morning and then I fell to sleep.

When morning came, I woke up early and my bed was wet, so I got up and I began pushing and shoving the others. 'Wake up', I said. 'Quick, it's all wet. 'The bed's all wet.' But then the bedroom door opened and in walked Sister Ann. 'Good morning, children.' I looked up at her. 'The bed's wet', I said. 'That's ok, just all get up', she said. Daisy, Karen and Jenny all looked up. 'Get out of the bed please, children. We have to wash you and you're going to see the doctor.' We all got up, she took us into the bathroom and she gave us a wash. 'Now put these on', she said, while handing us clean pyjamas. 'And then go back to the bedroom please.' I put the pyjamas on and, as I walked along the hall, I looked down through the banisters. And down on the ground floor, I could see two nuns walking around and moving bags across the floor. 'What are they doing?' I said. 'Nothing', said Sister Ann. 'Are you a nun the same as them?' I asked. 'Yes, now go to your room and sit down and wait for me.' So I did. Daisy, Karen and Jenny followed me back into the room and the nun followed us in. 'I am sorry', she said, 'but you are all sick and you cannot go out until you get better. The doctor will be here in a moment and he is going to give you some medicine to make you all well again.' Then she left the room and she closed the door, locking us in again.

We sat in the room and we waited all day, but the doctor never came; in fact, no one came, so when evening came we just went to bed feeling sad, sick and hungry. The next morning, Sister Ann came to our room, gave us some medicine and she said that the doctor had been too busy to see us yesterday. Then she gave us breakfast and she let us go to the toilet; and once we had finished eating, she left the room and locked the door behind her again.

For the next two weeks, she did the same thing every morning and in the evening she looked in on us to see if we were ok. It was hard for us sitting and sleeping in the same room day after day, never going out and never seeing anyone else. And on one occasion, I asked Sister Ann if we could play with the toys in the cupboard, but she said that no one had the key to the padlock and that she could not open it without one.

Over the next few weeks, we slowly got better, but every night one of us would wet the bed and we could tell that Sister Ann was becoming annoyed with us, because she began to shout at us. She said that we were very bad children for constantly wetting the bed and that she would have to do something about it. She would still only allow us out of the room to have a wash or go to the toilet; and once she trusted us to do what she said, she allowed us to go down to the kitchen with her to eat breakfast, but that was only because she didn't want to bring the food up to us.

For the first few weeks, we never saw anyone else in the house apart from the nuns; then one morning, while we were having breakfast, I became full after only two mouthfuls of food and I couldn't eat anymore. I sat back in my chair and puffed my face up to show my sisters that I couldn't eat another thing, then Sister Ann looked over at me, she saw what I was doing with my face and she said that I was an ungrateful little child for the food she was giving me. But I couldn't eat any more and I told her that I was not used to eating so much food in one go, and she called me a bad child.

Then after breakfast, Sister Ann told us all to go back upstairs and to get ready as we were all going out to play. We all ran up the stairs, we got changed as quickly as possible and then we ran back down the stairs and over to the front door. It was going to be the first time in over a month that we would go outside the front door and we couldn't wait. We jumped up and down with excitement, then Sister Ann walked up to the door and she told us that we could go out to play for an hour, but we must be good for her and not run off. We said yes and as she opened the door, we all ran straight out into the yard and we ran in all directions, not knowing what way to go or what we were going to do.

Then Sister Ann followed us out, shouting for us to stop and to get back over to her and we did. She walked us around to the back of the house and into a small garden. 'Have fun', she said. We all looked around, but there was nothing in the garden; no swings, no balls, no toys, nothing at all, just grass. We stood and looked at each other and then we walked around the garden, talking to each other and trying to think of things to do, but there was nothing. I couldn't even walk or run around for very long as I was still suffering from pleurisy that Daisy and myself had caught while playing in the rubbish dumps back home, in daddy's village. So, after a while, we just sat down and I tried to make daisy chains from the small flowers that I plucked from the grass around me.

And for a while, we talked to each other about how we felt and I began to think about what might have happened to our brothers, but then a man walked into the garden and interrupted us. He walked straight over towards me and he bent down in front of me and said, 'Hello, children', while spitting his words all over me. 'Hello, children. What are you doing? Would you like some clothes and shoes?' he said, as he dropped a pile of old clothes onto the grass in front of me, while all the time trying to keep his balance. Then he fell to his knees and leaned forwards towards me, as if he was going to grab me; but instead, he put his hands down onto the grass to stop himself from falling over onto his face.

I slowly moved away from him, pushing myself backwards along the grass with my hands. He smelt, he smelt disgusting from drinking beer and he was dribbling uncontrollably from his mouth and his saliva was dripping down on to my bare legs. He leaned towards me and he tried to say something, but all he could manage was to mumble, 'Pretty, pretty little girl' and then he rubbed one of his hands up and down my legs. His breath stunk and he had a bad look on his face, as if he was angry about something that I had done.

Suddenly, Sister Ann came running into the garden and she told the man to leave at once, but he told her to fuck off and to go away, calling her a stupid cow. And with that, she picked up the clothes and she went back into the house, leaving the man on the ground in front of me and he was still touching my legs. I began to shake with fright and I moved back again, but he moved closer to me and he began to grab at my clothes with both of his hands. I rolled to one side and then I got up and shouted, 'Run' to the others and we all ran back to the house and we stood next to the closed door, shouting for Sister Ann to open the door and let us back into the house. The door opened and we ran inside, while Sister Ann went back outside and walked back around to the man in the garden.

We looked out of the window and we could see that she was in a bad temper and we could hear her telling the man that he had to go now; but before he left, she told him to come back later when no one was around, then he left and Sister Ann came back into the house. Then she told us to forget all about the man and to go and find something else to do in the house and then she locked the door.

Later in the evening, when all the other nuns had left the house and it was our bedtime, the man came back and we could hear him with Sister Ann. They were both in the kitchen and they were laughing and joking together, and Sister Ann was telling him to stop it and to be quiet or someone might hear him. Then we heard the kitchen door close and the house went silent, so we all got into our beds and we went to sleep.

The next day, Sister Ann became very hostile towards me and, from that day on, she made my life a misery. Whenever she felt like it, she would slap me around my face and hit me for no reason at all and she would tell me that I was an ugly little child and think nothing of it. I hadn't done anything wrong to her, so I couldn't understand why she was being horrible to me and she made me very unhappy.

A couple of days later, we were all getting ready to go downstairs when we heard a car pull up outside the house and then we heard the sound of children's voices; so we looked out of one of the top floor windows and we could see children and some adults talking to Sister Ann. Then a nun came into the house and she shouted up to us to get downstairs and outside. We all walked down the stairs, looking through the banisters as we went, and we could see a few people standing at the bottom of the stairs and they were all making a lot of noise; then some children looked up at us and they began to talk to each other. We all held hands and we continued to walk down the stairs. And when we reached the bottom of the stairs, no one took any notice of us, so we walked outside and there were some nuns greeting more adults and children as they arrived at the house in their cars; and there were even more nuns walking up the drive, carrying bags and suitcases.

This went on for the whole day and in the evening Sister Ann told us to go into the dining room so we could meet all the other staff and children that had arrived throughout the day. She said that they had all been away for the summer holidays and they all lived in the house with us, so we went into the dining room and everyone said hello and one of the nuns told the children to tell us their names and ages. Then she told us to go upstairs and to bed, but we were hungry as no one had fed us all day. So I asked Sister Ann if we could have something to eat, but she said, 'No, just go to bed'; and then she pushed us out of the dining room and she closed the door behind us, and we went to bed hungry.

The next morning, the bedroom door opened and a new member of staff came into our room and the first thing she said was to get up; but Daisy was still asleep and she didn't hear her, so she walked over to Daisy and shock her bed while telling her to get up. Then she told us all to get dressed and to get downstairs fast; and once downstairs, another member of staff told us to go into the dining room and sit down for breakfast. But as we all walked into the room, there were ten other children all sitting around the table, and as we walked in they all looked at us and then they began to giggle to one another. We walked over to the table, sat down and we began talking to the other children. Then one of the staff came into the room and she put bread, butter and some cereals on the table and she told us to eat; but I wasn't hungry and I told her that I didn't want to eat today.

She looked at me, then she walked out of the room and within a couple of seconds Sister Ann came into the room and they both walked over to me. Then Sister Ann stood behind me and she put her hands onto my shoulders. 'Get up', she said and, before I could move, she pulled me out of my chair by my hair and she walked me out of the dining room, into the hallway and over towards the new members of the staff. 'This is what you do with them', she said and she began to yell and shout at me. And she told the new member of staff that if she wanted to continue working in the house, then she needed to be firm with us.

Then Sister Ann began hitting me around my head and then she slapped me around my face. I was shocked and my whole body flopped like a rag doll and, within a second, I collapsed to the floor. Sister Ann then turned and walked away, leaving me on the floor in the middle of the hall; and as she walked into the dining room, she shouted back at me to get up, to get back inside and to finish the fucking breakfast.

I had never been hit like that before, by anyone, and I was shaking like jelly. I got up off the floor, went back into the room and I walked over to the table. I sat back down and picked up a spoon, but I was still shaking and as I tried to eat my breakfast, it shook off the spoon and went all over the table. I began to cry and I picked the food up with my hands and put it into my mouth, hoping that she wouldn't hit me again, and none of the other children spoke a word until we had all finished breakfast. Even then, it was only to ask for permission to leave the table; and one by one, we all walked out of the dining room and into the hall where some of the staff were waiting for us. We all stood in front of the staff and they said that it was time for us to go to school and they told us to go and get our things. But then one of the staff turned to me and said, 'You and your sister Daisy can't go to the same school as the others. You're still too sick and you won't be able to walk all the way to the school, so you have to stay at the house and later a nun will take you to the convent with her and you will be schooled there instead.' She was right, I felt sick and I could hardly stand up, so I sat on the stairs and waited for the nun while all the other children got ready and then went off to the main school.

After a couple of hours, the nun who was going to take us arrived at the house and we went off to the convent with her. On the way, she told us that she would only be taking us today and from tomorrow we would have to walk to the convent's school on our own. So we had better remember the way and not mess around or be late, or we would be in a lot of trouble with the head nun. But she was walking too fast for us to keep up with her and we had to run along behind her. I was still feeling sick, and I began to cough and I told her that I had to stop, but she just kept walking and telling me to hurry up or we will be late and then we would all be in big trouble with the head nun.

Once we got to the convent, the nun took us into a room in the back of the building, and inside, sitting on one of the chairs in the room, was Simon, my baby brother. I shouted, 'Simon' and I ran over to him, throwing my arms around him and almost squashing him with joy. He shouted, 'Lily, Daisy' and then he began to cry and we cried too because we were so happy to see him. After a few seconds, one of the nuns came over to me and she said that from now on Simon was going to be staying with Daisy and me at our house. She said that he was too small to stay with the other boys and he needed us to look after him, as they did not have the time to care for him and she said that he was now our responsibility. Then she told us all to sit down and to start counting from number one, so I walked over to a chair, I sat down and looked over at

Simon and he was smiling. We began to count, one, two, three, four, five; it was great having Simon with us and he was smiling and counting at the same time. Simon continued looking over at me, then he wiped his lips and his face with his hands and he began to cry again. 'It's ok', I said. 'We won't leave you.' And from that moment on, he stuck to me like glue and he would never leave my side.

After school, Daisy, Simon and I had to walk home on our own, and off we went and it was great. We all held hands and we skipped along the road, while telling each other all about the things that we had done at school and about what had happened to us over the last few months. Then I asked Simon if he knew what had happened to our other brothers, Chris and Ted. And he said that the nuns had put them into two different houses, that he wasn't allowed to see any of them and that he didn't know what houses they were in. 'Ok', I said, 'It doesn't matter', and we continued to walk home.

When we got back, we met up with all the other children in our house and we all went into the sitting room and I told everyone about Simon my baby brother; then one of the nuns came into the room and she told us to do some homework. But it was only dinnertime and I could see bread, butter and some jam on the table; so instead of doing my homework, I went over to the dinner table and I sat down and began to eat. But for some reason, one of the nuns came up behind me and she gave me a terrible beating around my head, knocking me off the chair and onto the floor. I got up and I began to cry, and as I looked up at her, she told me to go to my room and to stay there until the next day. But my head was throbbing and I could hear a humming noise in my ears, so I told her what was happening inside my head; but instead of her helping me, she continued to shout at me and then she chased me out of the room and up the stairs until I got to my room. I screamed and I shouted back to her that I had not eaten a thing since breakfast when Sister Ann hit me around the head, and then I slammed the bedroom door shut and I sat on my bed crying.

It wasn't fair, I thought to myself, I had done nothing wrong, nothing at all. About half an hour later, my sisters and Simon came into the room and we all talked and played until it was bedtime; then Simon got into my bed with me and we cuddled up and fell asleep together, just like we used to back at daddy's and mummy's houses. The next few days were all the same; we got up, had breakfast and then we went to school. But one day, one of the nuns told us that we would have to go home for our lunch because we couldn't stay and have lunch in the convent anymore, as they didn't have the time to feed us.

So Daisy, Simon and I began to walk home on our own and about halfway home I walked across the road and Daisy followed me, then I turned to her and said, 'Where's Simon?' 'I don't know', she said. So we both turned around and looked for him. He was still standing on the pavement at the other side of the road. I shouted to him, 'Quickly, cross now while no cars are coming', but the road was wide and he kept saying no and that he was frightened. 'Quickly, now', I said. 'It's ok. Quick before it's too late.' He looked at me and then he ran, but it was too late and at that moment a brown-coloured car came along the road. I shouted again, 'Quick', but it was too late and the car hit him and then the car skidded to a stop.

I looked over at Simon and he was lying in the road and, all of a sudden, the road around him began to shimmer in the sunlight. I walked towards him and, as I got closer to him, I realised that it was a pool of Simon's blood that was shimmering in the sunlight and he wasn't moving. 'He's dead', I shouted. 'He's dead.' And then Daisy and I both ran over to him. I looked down at him as he lay in the road and his body was all twisted and he was covered in blood; and as I stood looking down at him, his blood began to spread along the road and around his body. I screamed and I began to shake with panic from the shock of seeing his blood drain from his body. 'Quickly', I said and we both ran up towards our house, screaming for help.

As I got to the house, I pounded on the front door and I screamed for someone to help us; and as I kicked the door, one of the nuns opened it. She shouted at us to stop and she screamed at us to be quiet and stop shouting, but I couldn't stop and I kept shouting and I told her that Simon was dead, 'He's in the road dead'. Then another member of staff came out of the house and she told me to shut up, then she grabbed me by my hair and dragged me into the house and I smashed my knees on the steps as she dragged me inside. 'Sit down and eat your dinner', she said. I looked at her in shock; I couldn't believe what she had just said to me.

So in a panic, I explained to her what had just happened to Simon and she told me to stay at the table while she went off to look for him. I got up and followed her to the door and I watched her as she walked past Daisy, who was still outside the house. Daisy looked pale and I tried to go out to her, but another member of the staff dragged me back inside and closed the door, and then she told me to sit down and to eat my dinner; but I couldn't, I was too upset. So I just sat and waited for the staff to come back and within a couple of minutes she walked back through the door saying that Simon was gone and that someone had taken him to hospital.

I began to cry, saying that he was dead, but the staff told me to shut up and to eat my dinner; but I didn't want the dinner and I told her that I couldn't eat it, and with that she turned around and gave me a wallop around the head. She shouted at me that the food was not to be wasted and that she had not spent all day cooking it just for the fun of it. Then she screamed out loud at me, saying that I was an ungrateful child and that I could not see Simon until I ate all my dinner. I felt sick thinking about what had just happened to Simon, and each time I put the food into my mouth I gagged and I had to stop; but she said eat, and with the next mouthful I vomited the food back onto the plate and all over the table. She was furious and she made me spoon the sick up off the table and put it all back onto the plate; then she made me eat it all again, and she stood watching me until the very last spoonful went into my mouth.

Then she told me to get back to school, and as she opened the door, she pushed me outside and I fell to the ground. I closed my eyes and put my face down against the dirt and I began to cry. I knew that I had to be strong for Simon, so I lifted my head and I looked around, and Daisy was sitting on the step next to me and she was still crying. I picked myself up off the ground, I walked over to her and then we cuddled each other and we both held hands as we walked off back to school.

As we walked along the road, I told Daisy that it was just the two of us now and we had to be strong and stick together. But on the way back, we had to walk past Simon's blood that was still in the road; and as we got closer to the spot where Simon had been lying, some people were standing there and they were talking about the accident. I walked up to the people and I asked them if Simon was ok, but they told me to go away and they just kept talking to each other. I walked back towards Daisy, shaking my head from side to side, and then we continued walking back to school; but we still didn't know if he was dead or alive.

When we got back to the classroom, I asked the nun if Simon was ok, but she just looked at me and said, 'Sit down, you have work to do.' And for the rest of the day, we just had to sit and do our work. We never knew if Simon was dead or alive and it was like nothing had ever happened; the nuns just got on with what they had to do and nothing else seemed to matter to them. They never showed us any feelings and they always made us feel bad if we showed feelings towards each other.

After school, we had to walk back past Simon's blood to get home and I was shaking with fear as we walked towards the spot of the accident; and as we got closer, I looked down at the road and the blood was still wet and sticky, and it had been splattered along the road, as cars drove through it. And I could see tyre tracks going up and down the road, where they had driven over the blood and spread the blood along the road surface, and I began to cry. Daisy held me tight, telling me that it was all going to be ok and that Simon was going to be at home when we got back, but I knew he wouldn't be; he had been hit so hard by the car that he was dead. I walked along thinking about what had happened at lunchtime and I wished that I hadn't shouted at Simon to run across the road, but I had and it was too late to change anything.

I cried all the way home and I was wishing that Simon would be at the door when we got back, but he wasn't. I walked into the house and I asked one of the staff if Simon was dead, and she looked down at me and she said, 'No, he's alive and he's in the hospital.' I was so happy, 'I want to see him', I said. 'No', she said. 'It's entirely your fault that he's in the hospital', and then she began to hit me around my head. Then Sister Ann came into the room and she told the member of staff to go out of the room. 'I'm in trouble', she said. 'It's all your fault that Simon got run over and now I have to explain what happened to the school governors. Now go to bed as I can't stick your crying all the time.'

Sister Ann called the staff back into the room and she told her to get me out of the room and to put me to bed. I walked out of the room and up the stairs to my bedroom and it felt like forever walking up the stairs on my own, and I kept turning around to see if Simon was behind me, but he wasn't. I walked into my bedroom and Karen and Jenny were sitting on one of the beds, waiting for me. I told them both about the accident at lunchtime and then they told me that the nuns had told them that Simon was still alive and that one of the nuns and a priest had gone to the hospital to see him. They said that he had broken his arm and he had hit his head on the road, but he was going to be ok. I was so relieved, I sat on my bed and I put my head down onto my lap. I was so happy, but also very sad because he was all alone again and I couldn't help him and I began to cry. It would be six weeks before Simon was able to come home from the hospital and in all that time the nuns never allowed us to go and see him and no one ever told us if he was ok or not.

And for the whole six weeks, Sister Ann and the staff told me that I was an evil little girl and that it should have been me that got run over and squashed that day and not Simon. They all made me feel very sad and my sisters tried to stick up for me; but if they said anything to the nuns, they would slap them around their heads with a wooden spoon, and then they would make them miss their dinner to teach them a lesson for butting in and getting involved.

When Simon finally came home, we all ran over to him and we began to examine him; he still had stitches in his head and mouth, a plaster cast on his arm and, in his hand, he had a container full of little stitches that a nurse had removed from a big scar on his leg. He looked broken and his hair had been cut short so that the doctors could drain fluid from his skull, after his head had hit the road. We all surrounded him, giving him kisses, and we told him that we loved him and that we were very sorry for what had happened to him. He just laughed and he said that he was ok, and we spent the rest of the day playing with him and giving him things that we had found around the house and school; 'little secrets' we called them, most of the stuff was rubbish, but to us it meant a lot because it was all we had.

CHAPTER 5

The Holidays Without Fun

Months passed and eventually I settled down in the house; then one morning, Sister Ann told me that it was going to be the end of school term soon and that all the children in the house, including me, would be going away for the summer holidays. She said that some people were going to come to the house and take all of the children away for the six-week holidays and that we must all be good with the people and behave ourselves, while staying with them in their homes.

I was very excited at the thought of going on holiday as I had never been on holiday before, but we had only been at the house a few months, so the nuns didn't want to split us up. But they had a lot of trouble finding a family that would take all three of us little ones away together as one family. All the other children in the house had already gone away and we were the last to leave; but eventually, the day finally came and now it was going to be our turn to go on holiday. A member of staff shouted up to me to get my suitcase and to hurry up. I looked over the banisters and a young nun was standing in the hallway at the bottom of the stairs looking back up at me.

I ran down the stairs and towards her, 'I've come to take you away with me', she said. I looked up at her and I told her that she had to wait as my sisters and brother were coming with me, but she said, 'No, only you're going on your own.' I looked at her and then

I ran over to my brother and sisters and I grabbed hold of them, but then Sister Ann came into the hall and she grabbed me by my hands and she peeled me away from my brother and sisters. 'Please don't take me', I said and then we all began to cry and my sisters shouted at her to stop pulling me, but Sister Ann told us to shut up and grow up. Then she told me that I was a stupid child, as she pushed and slapped me out of the house and into the back of a waiting car.

I began to cry and I felt frightened by what she was doing to me, but she was not bothered about how I felt, then she slammed the car door shut, just missing my fingers in the door, but hitting me into the face with it instead. I put my hands up and I held my face as I fell back into the seat, and the nun drove off, leaving Sister Ann standing in the driveway, smiling at me, as the car drove out of the grounds. I looked at the driver and it was the young nun. I shouted at her to stop the car, but all she did was tell me not to worry as it was only for six weeks, and then she would come and collect me and bring me back to the house. 'I promise', she said.

She drove for miles and I cried for the whole of the journey, and I kept telling her that I wanted to go home, back to my brother and sisters, but all she kept telling me was that it was a holiday and that I was going to enjoy myself and have fun. After several hours, we eventually arrived at a farm that was in the middle of the countryside; and as we pulled into the drive, the nun told me that the woman of the house had three children all about my age. And she told me that I would be able to play with them every day and I was going to have a lot of fun during my six-week stay with them. We got out of the car and we walked up to the front door of the house, but she didn't stay with me; instead, she turned around and walked back to the car, leaving me all alone. I looked back at her, but she never turned around, she just got into her car and then she drove off.

I stood looking at the front door to the house, then it opened and a woman came out and she told me to come inside, then she closed the door behind me. The first day was fun and the woman was nice to me, and I played games with her children and, at the end of the day, I went to bed happy. The next morning, I got up and had breakfast, and then the children showed me around the farm and then they told me the names of all the animals they had.

But that night I wet the bed and the next morning the woman and her children all shouted at me and they called me names for wetting the bed. And from that moment on, they all turned nasty towards me and I could tell they didn't like me anymore. The children stopped playing with me and the woman allowed her children to tease and torture me, by calling me dirty and smelly, and they told me that they hated me.

After I had wet the bed, the woman said that I couldn't sleep in the clean bedroom anymore and I had to sleep in another bedroom away from her children, and she made me share a bedroom with an eighty-year-old man, who was filthy and smelt bad. She made me sleep at the end of his bed and all the woman gave me to cover myself with was an old army blanket, but the blanket made me itch and it smelt as if it hadn't been washed in forty years. The man was so old that he could hardly get out of the bed on his own and almost everything in his room was about the same age as him. The sheets and mattress were damp and everything in the room stunk of piss. I could hardly breathe and, at bedtime, I would almost choke from the smell of the piss lingering around the bed and I had to keep my head hung off the edge of the bed just to get some fresh air that was entering the room from a gap at the bottom of the bedroom door.

Scattered around the bedroom floor were pots and jugs that the man had been using to piss in, but no one ever came in the room to empty them, so they would just sit on the floor until he managed to get out of bed. Then as he walked around the room, he would knock the containers over with his walking stick, letting the piss run down through the gaps in the floorboards; and as the piss dried up, it left damp sticky stains scattered around the floor.

I had to sleep in the room with him for the whole of my stay with the family, and some mornings the woman's children would come into the bedroom and empty jugs full of cold piss all over the bed and me. Then they would run out of the room as fast as possible, while holding their breath and slamming the bedroom door behind them so that the door slamming would shake everything in the room and wake the old man up; and then the old man would shout at me and tell me to fuck off out of the room. Then the woman would open the bedroom door and laugh at me, while the old man tried to push me out of the bed with his walking stick. But she would make me lie in the damp bed until she said that I could get up, and I would be cold and shivering the whole time and she knew it.

Every morning, the woman and her children would call me names and tease me, by telling me that I would have to sleep in the bed with the old man forever and that I would never be going back home to see my sisters or brother. They would all sit in the kitchen having breakfast, but they would never offer me a place to sit down, they said that I had to go eat with the animals and then they would throw scraps of food onto the damp piss-covered bedroom floor for me to eat, while they made animal noises at me. This went on for the whole six weeks of my holiday and for all that time I stunk of piss and my clothes were constantly wet from it. So every morning, I would go down to the end of the farm and rest in an old caravan just so the sun could shine through its windows and warm me up and dry my clothes out; and while I was in the caravan, I would try and sleep without the smell of the piss choking me. But the woman never once gave me a wash and all the time she said that I was a worthless piece of shit and that I was never going to see my family again.

Then one morning, the woman came rushing into the bedroom and she told me to get up quick, she said that I was going home and that I had to get ready before the nun arrived. She quickly washed me and gave me boiled eggs for breakfast and then she put clean clothes on me and told me that the nun was coming to get me. I was so happy; for the last six weeks, I had thought that I was never going to see my family again, and this was now going to be my life forever.

When the nun arrived, I almost died with shock, I just couldn't believe that I was going back to St Joseph's and back to my family. I was so happy to see the nun that I began to cry, but no tears fell from my eyes. I kept a cold blank face, and I hid my emotions, not wanting the woman or the nun to think that I was weak and pathetic. The nun held my hand and she told me to thank the good family for looking after me so well. I looked at the woman and her children and they all smiled at me and they told the nun that they were all going to miss me and that I was now like one of the family. Then the woman walked me to the car and she gave me a big hug and smiled at me as she walked away.

Once inside the car, I put my face against the window and I looked out at the woman, as she stood waving goodbye, and before the nun got into the car, she looked over at me and she asked me if I was ok. But I never spoke and I just kept looking out of the window; so she got into the car, closed her door and drove off; and as we drove out of the drive, she asked me again if I was ok, but I never replied. Then the nun said, 'It's ok. You will never have to go back there again' and she drove away from the house. It started to rain on the way home, so I looked out of the car window and I could see faint flashes of light in the distance, and I could hear a thunderstorm as it rumbled above the clouds. And it sounded so nice that I wished it would come our way and blow the woman and her children up and send them all to hell.

It was dark in the back of the car and I could hardly see a thing, apart from the raindrops glistening on the outside of the widow. I put my face against the glass and I stuck my tongue up against its cold surface to catch the raindrops, knowing full well that I couldn't. And the water droplets ran down the outside of the glass like tears and past me like I was nothing, and that was exactly how

I felt, and it was as if the rain knew what I was thinking and it was crying for me.

I never spoke a word on the way back, but all the time I was thinking about my sisters and Simon and hoping they would be at the house when I got back, and I wished that I could be with them again. We drove for hours and eventually I began to fall asleep, but then the car stopped and the nun told me to get out. I looked up and I was back at our house, and I could see my sisters waiting for me by the main door of the house. I got out of the car and I walked up towards them; they looked at me and then they ran over to me and cuddled me, but I just stood looking at them. 'Lily', they shouted, 'what's a matter with you?' But I said nothing. They turned and asked the nun what was wrong with me and she told them that I was just tired and that I would be ok in the morning. Then she told us all to go into the house and up to bed, and as I walked away, she slammed the car door making me jump. That evening, everyone exchanged tales about what they had done while on holiday, but I just looked at everyone and said nothing, as I was too upset to talk to anyone about my nightmare.

For the next two weeks, I never spoke a word to anyone and my sisters kept asking the nuns and staff what was wrong with me, but they just said that I was exhausted and that I would be ok soon. But I had a sick feeling inside my belly, I had a pain in my head that wouldn't go away and I was unable to do anything for myself. And each morning, a nun or a member of the staff would come into my bedroom and get me dressed and then they would help feed me my breakfast.

But the nuns were becoming inpatient with me and eventually they told my sisters that if I didn't start talking soon, they would have to take me away and put me into a mental hospital and no one would ever see me again. And from that moment on, every night when we went to bed, Karen would get into bed next to me and she would talk me to sleep, hoping that in some way it would help me to get better, and it did. After about a month, I started talking again and I began to play with the other children in the house; and for a while, the staff and the nuns left me alone to be happy.

For the next couple of months, life went on as usual around the house, with all of us going to school and Simon sticking to us like glue and especially to me, as if I was his mum; but then the nuns began to hit me again and over time the beatings got worse. Then one day, a new member of staff arrived at the house. She was much older than most of the other staff and she told us that she had been working in children's homes for most of her life.

And the second she looked over at me, I could tell that she had taken a disliking to me, but I never understood why; and most evenings, when it was bedtime, she would play a game of hers with me. She called it the 'slapping game'; she said that it was my punishment for being a bad girl all of the time. The game was that if I ran up to bed fast on my hands and knees, I would only get a few slaps around my head; but if I was slow at getting up the stairs and I used only my feet, then she would slap me hard around my head with a slipper, hitting me until I got to the top of the stairs and into my bedroom. All of the staff knew what she was doing to me, but they never once stopped her or questioned her actions, as they were all as bad as each other, in some way or another. All the staff and the nuns had their own games that they would use to get at us, and I think that by hitting us it somehow made them feel good about themselves.

But one of the nuns was especially bad to me, and whenever she walked past me she would pinch me on my arms, while twisting her fingers at the same time so that she could do as much damage to my skin as possible. And once she had finished pinching me, my arms would hurt, my skin would turn black and blue and the marks on my arms would take about two weeks to fade away. You could see that she was getting pleasure out of it and she looked very happy with herself after she hurt me. Then one day after lunch, the new member of staff, who played the slapping game with me, told everyone that she was leaving and going to another home. I couldn't believe it, I was so happy; after everything she had done to me, she was finally leaving, but I didn't want her to know that I was happy so I just sat there and said nothing. But as soon as she left the room, we all looked at each other and said, 'Yes' and we were so happy that we slapped our hands together with excitement.

However, the day she left, a new member of staff arrived to replace her. Her name was Joan and she was going to be our cook. She was a very old woman and she seemed nice. The first day at the house, she gave us cereal for breakfast, a nice lunch and dinner; but the next day, when we all walked in from school and sat down for dinner, she was standing in the doorway and she was holding a large wooden spoon in her hand. I sat down at the table and I picked up a fork, I looked into my bowl and the food looked disgusting. It was mincemeat stew, but it was just a bowl of hot greasy water with a few pieces of mincemeat floating on the top, and a piece of black carrot floating just below the surface.

I put my fork into the bowl and I moved it through the liquid, making the grease part and then reform behind the fork in what looked like the colours of the rainbow. I was shocked at the thought of having to eat the thing and I turned around to tell the cook, but she was standing looking at me and she was slapping the wooden spoon against the palm of her hand. 'You eat the food', she said. I turned back around and I knew that if I didn't eat the food, she was going to slap me with the wooden spoon. I dipped my fork back into the bowl and I began eating the stew, but it was taking me ages with the fork and I felt like I wanted to vomit. But she was still looking at me, so I picked the bowl up and swallowed its contents as fast as I could, hoping that she would go away and leave me alone.

And as soon as I had finished, my belly began to rumble and I felt awful and I wanted to get up and run outside to be sick; but as I got up, she told me to sit back down and wait while the other children finished the food, she then went into the kitchen to fetch the dessert. I put my head down onto the table and I waited for her

79

to come back, and I was praying that I wouldn't be sick until I left the table. She soon returned and, as I looked up at her, my belly rumbled and my whole body shook uncontrollably at the thought of what was coming next; and as she put the desert onto the table, I could see that it was stewed, steaming hot rhubarb and nothing else. It looked disgusting and she had not even put any sugar on it. I was still holding my fork, so I dug it into the rhubarb and then I put some of the rhubarb into my mouth. It was nasty and bitter and it hung on my fork like a thick piece of old rope, but she made everyone eat it, while she stood looking over us with her arms folded and the wooden spoon sticking out from between them.

My belly rumbled again and I could hear creaking noises coming from inside my belly and I had to keep my mouth shut to stop myself from vomiting the mixture of oil, water and meaty rhubarb across the room and over the other children. But I couldn't help myself and I began to laugh and some of the mixture came out of my nose, but I tried to control myself and I managed to hold the rest of the mixture in my mouth, and I sat at the table until she told us to go back to school. I got up and walked out of the house, and as I turned the corner and walked out of sight of the staff, I came across all the other children; and they were all bending over, spitting and vomiting their guts up at the same time. I took one look at them all and then I joined them, and we all kept vomiting until nothing more came out of our mouths and our bellies were empty.

But now we were late for school and we had to run all the way back, and when we arrived the nuns told us all off; we tried to explain to the nuns why we were late, but they didn't want to listen to us and because we were all such bad children they made us all pray for forgiveness. After school, we returned to the house and our evening meal was no better, but we still had to eat it; and once we had finished, we all got sick again. She had only cooked us a decent meal on her first day at the house, just to impress the head nun; and after that, the food that she cooked wasn't fit for pigs let alone us, but it was all we had and, after a while, we got used to it.

It was now winter and the nights were getting longer and, as the weeks passed, the house got colder and colder, but the nuns never put the heating on in the house. They said that it would cost them too much money, so instead of heating the whole house and wasting money, they put electric heaters in their rooms only and left the rest of us to suffer in our freezing cold bedrooms. We were always freezing and our beds were made of metal, so if you touched off the bed frame with your body, the cold steel frame would make you shiver, and the nuns only gave us one blanket each, so every night we would have to wrap ourselves tight in our blankets to keep warm, but we were still freezing.

The nuns never gave us coats, hats or any other type of winter clothes to wear and no matter what the weather condition was we still had to walk to school; and for most of the time, they made us walk around in thin cotton clothes. And if we complained about anything, the nuns would just slap us around our heads, telling us that we were the lucky children and without having them to look after us we would all be dead from neglect. Maybe we would be dead, but the way they treated us was no better than being in hell, and most days I wished and prayed that I were dead anyway.

I knew it was going to be Christmas soon, because the nuns wouldn't stop going on about it and they behaved as if it was the best thing that ever happened to them. Then one night, one of the nuns put plastic figures of Jesus and Mary on the side in the living room, and when she had finished setting them up, she sat us all down and told us all about Jesus again and why they celebrated Christmas. And once she had finished, she told me that I would be going away for Christmas and that I would be staying with some nice people over the holiday season.

I looked at the nun and I thought back to the last holiday that I went on and I began to shake at the thought of what might happen to me. Then I shouted at the nun and I told her that I wasn't going on my own like last time, and then she told me that my brother and sisters would be going with me. She then smiled and said that we would have a lovely time staying with a nice family, and then she walked away. I went up to my room, I sat on my bed and I began to cry. The next day, I tried to stay out of everyone's way and I tried to hide from the nuns, I was hoping the nuns would forget all about me and send all the other children off for the holiday, leaving me all alone in the house until they all came back. But it didn't happen and once the nuns found me, they sent Daisy, Simon and me off on holiday with an elderly couple.

The next morning, the couple came to our house and they drove us away in their car and it took hours for us to reach the village they lived in; and throughout the whole journey, they never once spoke to us. When we arrived at their house, the man and woman got out of the car and walked off towards the house, leaving us still sitting in the back of the car. We looked at each other and giggled at what they had just done. We thought they had forgotten all about us, but they never stopped and they continued to walk away, so we got out of the car ourselves and we walked up towards the house.

As we reached the front door, the couple opened the door and stood next to it as if they were waiting for us to enter. We stopped for a moment and we looked at the house, it was very old and it looked broken. We looked at each other and then we held hands and stepped inside, hoping everything was going to be ok. And as we walked in, we could see that most of the things inside the house were either old and dirty or old and broken. I looked at Daisy and Simon and I felt like I wanted to run back outside, but as I turned around the man stood in my way and he quickly slammed the door shut. Then, without warning, he shouted at us to get under the kitchen table. I grabbed Simon and Daisy and I ran towards the only table in the room and stood next to it, then I turned around and looked back at the man and woman. And the man ran towards us and he kicked us hard in our legs until we got under the table.

Frightened, the three of us screamed and huddled together

under the table, but I was shaking so much that I wet myself; then Daisy and Simon began to cry, so I shouted, 'What have we done?' and the man shouted back, saying that we were dirty little gipsy bastard tinkers' kids, and beggars, and that we had better stay under the table or he was going to kill us all. 'And if you think you're going to have a nice Christmas, think again. You're going to get nothing from us, no toys, no presents, nothing at all, not even food. And you better not make a single noise for the next two weeks or you will be sorry.'

We huddled up to each other under the table, hoping the man would leave us alone, but then he walked over towards the table, bent down and spat into our faces; then he walked away, sat down in front of the television and glanced over at us again. So I put myself between Simon and the man, as I thought he was going to come over again, but instead he turned away and began to watch the horseracing on the television. I sat there for hours before I moved, but as I moved one of my legs forward to reposition myself, the man shouted at me and then he told me to kneel up under the table. I moved back and did what he said and he made me stay in a kneeling position for the rest of the afternoon. And once again, he said that he would kill all of us if I moved an inch; so I stayed still, but the pain in my legs became unbearable and my legs went numb from the knees down.

After a few hours, I asked him if I could get up, but he said no, and we had to stay there until bedtime. Then the woman came over to the table and she told us to get up and to get into the bedroom. I asked her if we could have some food, but she said that we didn't deserve food and that we had to go straight to bed, she would not even allow us to go to the toilet. Our legs were stiff and we couldn't walk into the bedroom as our legs had gone numb, so we had to crawl along the floor; and once in the bedroom, the woman put us all together in the same bed and it felt nice, we all cuddled up together and we quickly fell to sleep.

The next morning, the woman came into the bedroom and one

of us had wet the bed, so she grabbed the three of us by our hair and she pulled us out of the bedroom and she told us to get under the table again, and to kneel on the floor until she said otherwise. She said that if we tried to sit instead of kneeling, she would kick us all to death, so we did what she said. Then the woman made the man breakfast and they both sat down at the same table, as we were kneeling under, and the woman told us to be very quiet while they ate breakfast. I looked up at her and I asked her if we could have some breakfast too, but the man said, 'Shut the fuck up, you little bitch' and he kicked me until I moved back under the table.

He continued calling me names and he said that I had to wait while he ate his bacon and potatoes, and if we were lucky, he might throw us some scraps of food when he was finished. About thirty minutes later, they finished breakfast and the man threw us some fat that was left over from the bacon and the skins from the potatoes. He said that it was all we were getting for the day and that we had better eat it all, as he did not want to see any of it left on the floor. I grabbed the scraps and gave some to Simon, but he couldn't eat the bacon fat, so I had to chew it for him, and then I put the fat into his mouth for him to swallow and I gave him a potato skin to suck on, so that he got as much food as possible into his little belly. Then Daisy and I shared the remainder of the potato skins between us, as we never knew if they were going to feed us again.

After breakfast, the man and woman both got up from the table and they told us to stay under it, but I wanted to go to the toilet and I asked the woman if I could go. The man shouted at me and he said that I couldn't and that I had to hold it in all day. I started to cry and I told him that I needed to go now, but he looked at me and said, 'No, you have to hold it.' I begged him, telling him that I couldn't hold it any longer, but he walked away and after about ten minutes he returned and he said, 'Ok, but you only have ten seconds' and then he began to count. I got up and ran to the toilet, but I had trouble going and I couldn't because of the pressure he was putting me under. He had frightened me and he had made me wait for such a long time that I was now unable to relax and I had to run back and get under the table again without going to the toilet, and then I wet myself, but I never told the man or woman. Simon and Daisy were too scared to ask if they could get up and go to the toilet, so they just wet themselves under the table.

And we all spent the rest of the day kneeling under the table and getting long marks along our knees and shins from the floorboards that we were resting on. When evening came, we were ready to collapse from exhaustion and we desperately needed food and water, but all the man and woman said was get to bed. And they did the same thing to us for the next few days, only feeding us scraps from the table and a drop of water before we went to bed.

Then one morning, while they were having breakfast, the man said to his wife that he didn't think the nuns were paying him enough money to look after us and he said that he wanted to send us back to the home. But the woman told him that it was too late and that no one would be at the house on Christmas day. He looked down at us under the table and then he told us to get up and to go outside and play; we jumped up, hitting our heads on the edge of the table as we ran for the front door, but the door was locked and we couldn't open it. The woman looked over at us and then she got up and walked towards the door and we moved out of her way while she opened it for us; and once it was open, we all ran outside.

It was freezing, but it was the first time that we had been outside in almost a week, so it didn't matter about the cold. It was great being outside, and around the back of the house was an old caravan, and we played in and around the caravan for the rest of the day, pretending that we were back at daddy's house. And during the day, we used the caravan as a toilet, as we didn't want to go back into the house and then made to hold our wee for the rest of the night, but the man had been watching us through the window and he caught us using the inside of his caravan as a toilet. He came running out of the house, shouting at us and he ran into the caravan and he began kicking us, and he kept kicking us until we all fell onto the caravan floor screaming with pain. Then he dragged us by our clothes out of the caravan and back into the house and he made us kneel under the kitchen table for the rest of Christmas day, while he got drunk. And for the rest of the day, he called us all the names that he could think of and the woman said nothing.

A few days later, the woman said that it was the end of the holiday, and she told us to get into their car and they drove us back to the nuns; and on the way, they never spoke a word to us. When we arrived home, we got out of the car and the man and woman told the nuns that we had been very bad children and we had caused them nothing but trouble for the whole two weeks. And that we behaved like pigs every day, calling him and his wife names that he could never repeat in public and that we had ruined their Christmas. Sister Ann apologised to them, saying that she would punish us in the appropriate manner for what we had done to them. After the man and woman left, Sister Ann hit us as hard as she could and then she sent us to bed, but we were so happy to be back that we went to bed smiling to ourselves.

A few days after the Christmas holiday, we all went back to school; and after a while, I noticed that all the girls in my class were having birthday parties, but for some reason I was never invited to any of them. I was so desperate to have a birthday party that I would have done anything to have one, so I told one of the staff, Cathy, who had always been nasty to me, about all the girls having parties and she suggested that we should have a birthday party for me. As she knew, it was going to be my birthday soon, so she said that she would bake me a big cake and that I could invite all my friends from school to the house if I wanted to. I was delighted and I couldn't wait to tell my friends; I had never had a birthday party before and I knew it was going to be great.

As soon as I got back to school, I told a couple of my friends all about the birthday party I was going to have and the next day they came back to the house with me. I was so excited, and as I walked into the house, I looked around and I could see some bread and butter laid out on the table, but no cake. I went over to Cathy and I asked her about my cake and my party; but as I spoke to her, we were interrupted as the other children came in from school and pushed past me. After a few seconds, it was all calm again, so I asked her again, 'Where is my party? My friends have come home with me for my party.' She looked at me and then she shouted, 'What party? Who said you was going to have a birthday party? Who do you think you are asking for a birthday party?' Then, in front of my two friends, she raised her hand and slapped me around the face as hard as she could. While shouting, 'Why should we bake a cake for you? Now eat your bread and butter' and she gave us one slice each.

My friends were in shock and they just looked at me; they couldn't wait to get out of the house and as far away from me as possible. I started to cry and Sister Cathy grabbed me by my hair and swung me around the room, pulling chunks of hair out of my scalp and then dropping me to the ground and humiliating me in front of everyone. My friends backed away and they ran to the front door, desperate to get outside and as far away from me as possible. The nun, Cathy, had set me up on purpose, she had set it all up just to make me look bad in front of my friends and to put me in my place. What she did to me was so cruel and it was probably one of the nastiest things she could ever have done to me. She had taught me never to ask for anything else again, as all I would get was a beating.

I celebrated my birthday in my bedroom with my sisters, brother, a swollen head from the beatings, a handful of my own hair in my pocket and a pain in my head that stayed with me until the next morning. The next day, I went back to school, but none of my friends spoke to me; they stayed away from me for months and they made me feel very unhappy and alone and I never wanted to go back to school after that.

However, soon after, I got the measles, and I was able to stay in bed for a couple of weeks and that got me out of going to school. But Sister Ann had to give me medicine three times a day and she hated it. So whenever she came up to my bedroom, she would bring a member of staff with her and she would tease me by thumping the stairs with her hands and stamping her feet as loud as possible, pretending that she was in a bad mood and that she was going to kill me when she got to my bedroom. And when they came into the bedroom, Sister Ann would get the member of staff to sit on my chest and hold my mouth open while she poured the medicine into my mouth, chocking me and making me almost vomit. Then she would get up and walk out of the room, laughing and slapping the staff on the back, while telling her that they had both done a good job, and she would turn around and look at me before she slammed the bedroom door shut.

Once I had recovered from the measles, they sent me back to school with Simon and Daisy; but when I got into the classroom, the nun told me to stand at the front of the class and to wait there for her while she went to get me a uniform to put on. But when she returned, she had with her a thick woollen dress that was the old school uniform from about thirty years ago. She told me to put it on and I did, but it was itchy and I became very hot in the dress, and the nun told me that I had to wear it every day from now on, so I sat down and got on with my work.

I couldn't read or right very well as I had never been educated to that degree in the past. I was only six years old and I had hardly ever gone to school. So, whenever I got something wrong, the nuns would shout at me and make me stand in the corner of the room with a hat on my head that had a big D for dunce on it, so that all the other children could see that I was stupid. And the other children would make fun of me, by calling me stupid and thick, and it made me feel sad. The nun would make me stand there for the rest of the day, until it was home time, and at the end of the day my feet would hurt and my legs would shake from weakness as I walked all the way home.

I spent the next six months going through the same routine week after week and the nuns made me dress in the same woollen dress every day. Even after school, Sister Ann made me keep the dress on until it was bedtime and, when I finally took it off, my skin would be red from the heat and the scratching that I had done all day from wearing it.

One day, Simon, Daisy and a few of the other children got the flu, so the nuns made me walk to school on my own; and when it was lunchtime, I had to walk all the way back home on my own and it was horrible walking by myself. However, as I arrived home for lunch on the second day, I walked into the dining room, and a small boy was already sitting at the table and he was eating his dinner. I could see that he was sick with the flu, because his eyes were red, he had green mucus dripping from his nose and it was running down his face, and a member of staff was feeding him his dinner with a big tablespoon that was so big it could hardly fit into his mouth.

As I sat down to eat my dinner, the boy began to vomit and he vomited his food all over the table and on to his plate. The member of staff became angry with him and she began shouting at him and the boy began to cry, and then she screamed at him that she was tired of feeding him and then she slapped him around the face. She then turned around and shouted at me, telling me to eat my dinner; but just as I was about to, she got the spoon that she was feeding the boy with and she mixed all the sick and dinner together on his plate and then she fed it to him. Then she scooped up more of the sick from the table and mixed it in with his food and the boy vomited again, and then I gagged and I vomited too.

She went mad at me because of what I had just done and she spooned up more of the sick from the table and forced the whole spoonful into the boy's mouth, almost choking him; and he vomited again and the sick came out of his nose. She then ran around the table and hit me around my face with the boy's spoon and I vomited again, with the sick coming out of my mouth and my nose at the same time. Then the sick ran down my face and onto my plate and she hit me again with the spoon and she told me that I had to eat it all, and she began mixing my dinner and the sick together. Then she fed it to me, but I choked and I kept vomiting, with food coming out of my nose again as I tried to keep my mouth shut. So she ran back around to the boy and she put another spoonful of the mix into his mouth, and then she ran back to me and she fed me with the same spoon, while telling both of us that we had to eat it all and that she would keep feeding us until it was all gone.

The food stunk and it was sticky and slimy with green bits of sick mixed in with it, but I kept swallowing the mix and the boy did the same. She continued slapping both of us and I could tell by the look on her face that she was getting mad and crazy with us, and she was running around like the headless chicken did back at dad's house. She was running from one side of the table to the other and she kept it up until all the food was gone, then she told me to go back to school and to say nothing to anyone about what had just happened. I got up and I had to go, but the boy was petrified and he was shaking with fright; he looked over at me and he held out his arms while asking me not to go. 'Please', he said, but I had to leave and I headed out of the door and back to school, and from that day on I never saw the boy again.

Every day, the nuns would have fresh mincemeat and vegetables delivered to the house, but it wasn't for us, it was for them. The butcher's boy would peddle his bike up to the house and he would have the mincemeat sitting in a basket on the front of his bike, wrapped in white paper and tied shut with twine. But on this particular day, the road had just been re-laid with new tar and, as the boy rode his bike along the road, his peddle slipped and he fell over, dropping all the mincemeat across the newly laid road. It went everywhere, mixing in with little black bits of tar and small stones that lay on the road's surface. The boy got to his feet and in a panic he gathered up all the mincemeat, black tar and stones, wrapping it all back together and then delivering it to the nuns as if nothing had happened. But I had seen him do it, so I went along and I told the nuns and they said thanks.

Then that evening, when I went down into the dining room for dinner, the nuns announced to everyone that for a change they had made a lovely mincemeat stew for everyone and they asked us to thank the lord for the wonderful food we were about to have. I sat down and I looked into my bowl, and I could see that it was the mincemeat the boy had dropped onto the road earlier in the day and it still had all the stones and tar mixed in with it. And there was a small amount of oil seeping out of the tar that was floating on the top of the hot stew and it smelt strong and nasty, like the smell you get from a garage. I could see that the nuns were very excited with anticipation, and they were almost wetting themselves as they waited for us to put the first spoonfuls of the mix into our mouths. But one of the nuns couldn't wait any longer and she ran over to me and she began to feed spoonfuls of the mix into my mouth, just to see the expression on my face.

Straight away I felt sick, I tried to chew the mincemeat, but I couldn't because of the stones crunching against my teeth, and the tar was sticking to my gums and it was getting between my teeth and making it hard for me to open my mouth. So I had to swallow the mix, spoonful after spoonful, while all the time she stood watching me. And she was slapping a huge wooden spoon against her leg in a threatening manner, making sure that I didn't stop eating until it was all gone. She was just waiting for me to say something, so that she could slap me with the spoon, and she had a smile of pure pleasure across her face and she was almost jumping up and down with uncontrollable excitement while she watched me eat the food.

You could see that it was making her feel great as I swallowed every drop, leaving nothing, and I knew that she was going to punish me if I didn't finish it all. When I had finished, I turned to her and smiled, and I knew that she could see the black tar stuck between my teeth and gums and I knew that it would make her happy. I got up, I went up to my bedroom, I climbed onto my bed and I waited for the pain in my belly to go away.

Just after my sixth birthday, Sister Ann told me that, from now on, I would be going with a woman to her house every weekend, and she would be collecting me in the mornings and dropping me off in the evenings. I didn't understand what she was on about, but I soon found out what she meant. Every Saturday and every Sunday, the woman would turn up at the house in her car and she would pay the nuns some money, so that I could go with her to do all her housework for her. She would drive me to her house and, while I was there, I would have to do her cleaning for her, wash her clothes and polish all her furniture, then I would clean her toilet and do the washing up for her. She would make me sit on a high stool next to the kitchen sink so that I could reach down to all the plates and cups at the bottom of the sink, and not miss anything. Then, once I had finished, she would tell me to go and clean the bath, but the bath was always filthy and it always had thick scum lines all around the sides. I was only little and it hurt me to bend over the bath and I always got pains in my ribs from having to lean into it.

After I had been cleaning for her for a couple of weeks, she noticed that I was getting used to all the work and I was getting it done a lot quicker, so she gave me even more work to do. At first, she added the sweeping of the hallway and then the hoovering of the whole house; and then a couple of months later, I had three bedrooms and three bathrooms added to the cleaning list. Every Saturday and Sunday, I would clean for the whole day until about eight in the evening and when I had finished she would drive me back to the home and drop me off outside the gates, leaving me to walk the rest of the way up to the house on my own. Sometimes when I got back, Sister Ann would be waiting for me at the back door and she would smile at me as I walked past her and into the house.

Then one day, the woman told me that her guesthouse was quiet and then I realised what I was, I was her little chambermaid. So, instead of going to her guesthouse to clean, she said that she was taking me to her friend's house, so that I could clean out the stables and pigpens on her friend's farm for her, and the work on the farm was just as bad as working for her at her guesthouse. Then one Saturday morning, just before she picked me up, Daisy asked me if she could come to Mary's house with me. Mary was the woman that the nuns made me work for as a chambermaid on weekends. I told Daisy that it was hard work and not very nice, but she wanted to come with me and the nuns thought it was a good idea, so they encouraged her to go with me. Daisy thought it was going to be fun cleaning all day, but she soon realised that I was being used as a slave and that I had to work all day long without a rest. As soon as Mary realised Daisy was with me and that she had nothing to do, she put her to work and she made us spring clean the guesthouse from top to bottom.

And when we had finished, she asked us if we wanted to make some cakes; it sounded like fun, so we said yes. And for the rest of the evening, she allowed us to make jam tarts and fairy cakes, it took us hours and when we had finished the whole of the kitchen table was covered in cakes and they looked so nice that we couldn't wait to eat them. However, Mary had other plans for the cakes and she only gave us one each, and she kept the rest to sell for profit in her guesthouse. We both felt like crying, we had not eaten a thing all day and we were hungry, so Mary said that we could make beans on toast if we needed to eat; it was now very late, but we made the food and then she drove us home.

The following weekend, Daisy said that she didn't want to go with me, but I begged her I didn't want to go alone, I had been doing the cleaning on my own for the last couple of years and I just couldn't do it anymore. I begged her to come with me and eventually she said ok. 'But I'm not doing the cleaning', she said. I said ok and I told her that we will have fun this time, 'I promise' and she came with me. But instead of Mary taking us to clean her guesthouse, she took us to her auntie's farm and, when we arrived, she told us that we had to clean the stables. We looked at each other and then she gave us Wellington boots, a wheelbarrow, a shovel and a fork to pick the muck up with. I looked at Daisy and then Mary walked off into the farmhouse to have a cup of tea while we worked in the stable. But as soon as she was out of sight, we dropped everything and we ran off to explore the rest of the farm, but as we ran off we left the stable doors open, allowing all the horses to wander off.

After a while, Mary came back to the stables to see how we were getting on with cleaning the muck up, but we had walked off and she couldn't find us anywhere. And she had to go around, gather up all the horses and put them back in the stables and it took her about an hour to gather them all up. As we were walking around the back of the house, we forgot all about the stables and at the end of the farm we found a donkey tied up in a field. The donkey was very calm and it seemed happy to have some company, so we untied the donkey and we both got on its back, and then we rode the donkey up and down the field. It was only a small donkey and, after a while, it began to get tired, so we decided to take turns sitting on its back, while the other walked the donkey up and down the field. We fed the donkey some grass, and playing with the donkey was much more fun than cleaning out the stables; but then Mary found us and she shouted at us to get back and clean the stables.

But as I was getting off the donkey, Daisy slapped the donkey on the bum and it ran off, with me still holding on for my life. It was scary, but I loved it; and when the donkey finally stopped, I fell off its back and on to the grass and we both couldn't stop laughing. Then Mary began laughing with us and it was the only time I ever saw Mary smile. Then she said that it was time for us to go home and we all left the farm.

On the way home, I thought Mary was going to have a go at Daisy and myself for not cleaning the stable, but she never said a word about it and she dropped us off at our house as if nothing had happened. For the next six years, I carried on cleaning her guesthouse for her all on my own, with me being her little slave and the nuns being paid money for my services.

At Willows, the nuns had an old sewing machine and occasionally they would let us play with it and I thought it was great fun messing around with bits of old material and I tried making things with it. Then one day, while I was playing around with the sewing machine, one of the nuns came over to me and she showed me how to use it properly and I seemed to pick it up easily, so she showed me how to make a couple of pillowcases and simple things like sheets and handkerchiefs.

And after a while, she showed me how to make patchwork quilts and even more complicated items, including clothes. And the nuns thought the things that I made were great and they allowed me to use the sewing machine every day. After a couple of months, the nuns and staff began praising me and telling me how good I was with the sewing machine, they gave me some pattern books, and they asked me to see if I could make a dressing gown from the patterns. So I had a go and it came out great, and the nuns allowed me to make things all day long; and after a few months, I had made hundreds of items, from pillowcases to quilts. And they were so pleased with what I had done that they allowed me to carry on making things for the rest of the year. The nuns and staff were very good to me while I was playing with the sewing machine and they never hit me once.

But then one day, they told me they were having a summer fair and all the things that I had been making were for them to sell on a stall at the fair. I couldn't believe it, they had used me to work for them again, making them even more money, but this time it was out of something that I liked doing. That was it, I gave up straight away and I never made another thing for them again. It was a shame because I was good at making things and I thought it was fun until then and I never once thought of it as work.

95

The only time I had a break from cleaning the guesthouse was when the nuns sent me away for the summer, Christmas and Easter holidays and on some of the half terms, when people would come to our house and take me away with them. The people who took me always pretended to be nice while at the convent, but once they got me away from the nuns, they treated me like shit until the last day of the holidays when they brought me back to the nuns. And they always acted as if they were angels and I was the evil one and the devil.

I remember one evening, just after I got back from one of the so-called holidays, daddy unexpectedly turned up at the house and he was drunk; and as he stood outside the house, he shouted at the staff that he wanted to see his children. But the staff and nuns told him that he was not supposed to be there and they told him that if he did not go away, then they would have to call the police to remove him from the property. But he continued shouting at them and we all watched him through a window as he became angry towards them and then he looked over in our direction.

He could see us at the window waving at him and he waved back at us, so the staff went outside and they told him that if he could just shut up for a moment, then they would go and get us. He agreed and the staff let us all go outside to see him for half an hour and then he had to go, but he had upset us and now we wanted to go home with him. The staff told him to go away and then they dragged us all back inside and they locked all the doors and windows, so we could not get out and follow him.

Once inside the house, I shouted at the staff, telling them that I was not happy; and as I was walking away from them, one of the staff grabbed me from behind. She grabbed me by my hair and dragged me into the living room, then she hit me around my head so hard that I collapsed to the floor and she just left me there, closing the door behind her as she left the room. I can remember feeling very drowsy and sick and I had the smell of blood in my head, but I managed to get up, out of the room and back up the stairs to my bedroom. I walked towards my bed and I collapsed face first onto the bed; and as I tried to turn myself around, the room began to spin. I can remember having a severe headache and that was the last thing I remembered, until I woke up half way through the night vomiting all over myself and the bed, then I flopped over onto my face again and I fell back to sleep. When morning came, I was woken up by two members of staff who were looking down at me as I lay on the bed, they grabbed me by the arms and then dragged me into the bathroom and cleaned me up, then they sent me off to school and I felt sick for the whole day.

When I got home in the evening, Cathy, a member of the staff, told me to go into the living room and to wait for her there. I walked into the room and, as I turned around, she was standing right behind me; she must have followed me straight into the room. At first, she never said a word, she just put her hands together and she began to play with the rings on her fingers. I looked up at her and I asked her what she wanted, but she said nothing, then she turned and locked the door, then she clasped her hands together and she swung them up into the air. I looked up and I could see that she had turned the rings on her fingers around so that all the sharp bits that kept the diamonds in place were pointing inwards and down towards me. And with a big grin on her face, she smiled at me and then she brought her hands down and slapped me into my head.

With the first slap, I fell to the floor and everything went black; my head went dizzy and it felt like my head was spinning. She followed me down to the floor with another slap into the back of my head and I felt her rings sink into the back of my head and my neck twisted as my head dug into the carpet. But she never stopped; she just kept slapping me and hitting me into the head. Again and again she hit me and I could feel spit from her mouth dripping down onto my face. I couldn't get up, so I opened my eyes and I looked up at her; and each time I moved my body to get away from her, she would bring her hands back down and into contact with my head and the pain became unbearable. So I pulled myself together into a small ball and I waited for the slapping to stop, but it didn't and she was using the rings on her fingers to do as much damage to my head as possible, knowing that when she was finished, no one would be able see the marks that she had left through my hair.

She continued hitting me and, after a while, I began to see red flowing inwards from the corners of my eyes and the pain in my head went away and everything began to go dark and fuzzy. And even though she was still hitting me and I could still just about see her hands raining down on me, one after the other, it didn't hurt me anymore and I began to feel warm and peaceful inside. I felt my head as I lay against the carpet, but it didn't hurt anymore, so I closed my eyes and I fell to sleep.

The next thing that I remembered was one of the nuns telling a doctor that I must have hyperventilated and blacked out at the top of the stairs, and then I must have fallen all the way down the stairs to the bottom, and that's how I got all the lumps and cuts on my head. He looked at me and he thought it was a bit strange that I only had lumps and cuts on my hands, head and neck and on no other part of my body, but he was a friend of the nuns and staff, so it didn't really matter to him how I got the marks. I can remember him telling the staff to keep me away from other people and not to send me to school for a couple of weeks until the marks on my head and neck went away, and they did exactly that.

I was able to stay in bed most of the time and the nuns gave me a lot of food and attention, but I was not allowed out of my room and I never saw anyone apart from my sisters and brother. All I could do was to get up and look out of the windows on the top floor of the house and I could see that the weather was getting warmer outside and I wanted to go and play. And once the nuns realised I was getting better, they allowed me to spend some time outside, playing on my own while all the other children were at school, but I never had any toys to play with. I had to make up my own games and I spent as much time as possible in the fields behind the house on my own, and I began making crop circles in the long grass by lying down and rolling around in the field. Then, when I was well again, everything went back to normal with them hitting me again as if nothing had ever happened.

At the bottom of one of the fields behind our house was a stream, and we would all go skinny-dipping in it, but we never told the nuns or staff what we were doing, as they would have hit us and punished us by sending us to bed. And one day, on the way down to the stream, Simon found a box of matches, lying next to an old jacket that someone had left in the field; so he picked the matches up, he put them into his pocket, and he soon forgot all about them.

The next day, while Simon and I were walking in the field, Simon put his hands in his pockets and, all of a sudden, he pulled out the box of matches. 'Look what I found', he said, while holding up the matches. I looked at him and I told him to throw them away as they were dangerous, and he did, but not before pulling all of the matches out of the box and striking them against its side. I shouted at Simon to stop, but it was too late; he slung all the lit matches up into the air and they landed on some dry grass and, within a few seconds, the grass went up in flames.

We quickly ran off back to the house and we ran inside closing the front door behind us. Then we ran up to the top floor of the house and we looked out of a window, and for the next five hours we both stood watching as one of the fields went up in flames. The whole sky lit up with the colour of orange from the flames and it went on all night, and about fifty people stood watching as the field burned to the ground. No one got hurt, but the smoke made everyone in the house cough; and for the rest of the week, all the staff and the children kept talking about what happened. We never did tell anyone that we did it and the next day we had to walk past the field to get to school and some of the field was still smoking, with little patches of grass still on fire from the night before. Simon held my hand tight and he looked up at me for reassurance, and then he smiled and shrugged his shoulders at me as we both looked straight ahead and just kept walking past the field, not once looking back, just in case someone caught us looking and then blamed us for what had happened.

After school, Simon and I took the long way home, so we didn't have to walk past the burnt field, but the walk back took much longer than we thought and it made us late. When we finally arrived home, Sister Ann was waiting at the front door for us. I looked up at her and I held Simon's hand tightly as we walked slowly past her, and once inside I dragged Simon along as fast as possible, so that she couldn't hit him or trip him up just for spite. But as I walked along the hall and towards the stairs, she called me back and she asked me to go into the living room with her. I looked at Simon and I told him to run up the stairs and to hide in the bedroom until I get back, and then I walked into the living room and stood in front of her.

'Sit down', she said, and then she held up a hairbrush in front of me. 'I want to brush your hair.' I looked at her confused, she had never brushed my hair before, so I hesitated for a moment and then I sat down on the chair and I faced the wall. I tensed my shoulders as I waited for her to hit me with the brush, or for something else bad to happen to me; and sure enough, she dug the brush into my head and then she pulled down on the brush as hard as she could, pulling my head back as far as it would go. She hurt me, but I said nothing and she kept tugging at my hair until the brush came loose, then she did it again. 'It hurts', I told her. But she said, 'Good, that means it's working.' Then she slapped me into the back of the head with the brush and she continued brushing my hair for what seemed ages. Then suddenly she stopped and she told me to go away. I got up and I walked out of the room and up the stairs to my bedroom; and as I walked in, I told Simon that he could stop hiding. Then I lay on my bed, crying to myself until I fell asleep, and all the time I was wishing I were dead, but in the morning I woke up and I knew my life would be the same as usual and I felt sad for myself.

One lunchtime, while on the way home from school, I stopped to play in the garden outside the house with Karen and another child; and while I played with them, a big brown car pulled into the drive of the house. It was Sister Ann's man friend, the one who touched me in the back garden when I first arrived at Willows a long time ago. He got out of the car and he began to walk towards me. I stopped playing and I looked over at him; and as he walked up to me, he bent over and grabbed me by my arm and he began to pull me towards his car.

I struggled and I tried to get away from him, but he held onto me tight, he pushed me into the back of his car and then he slammed the car door shut, he went around to the driver's door and he got into the car. His clothes smelt old and strange and he stunk of alcohol and cigarettes. I tried to get out of the car, but he had locked the door; then he turned around and pushed me back into the seat and he handed me a packet of sweets, while telling me to shut the fuck up and to stay in the car. I looked at him and he was so drunk that he had trouble putting the key into the ignition to start the car, but he eventually got the car started and he began to drive away, with me in the back.

But Karen had seen what he was doing to me and she began screaming at me to get out of the car, but I couldn't. She ran in front of the car, 'Lily', she shouted and she banged her hands on the bonnet of the car, then she ran to the window and thumped the glass as hard as she could. I moved over to the window, I shouted back and I grabbed the door handle, but the door wouldn't open Then one of the nuns came running out of the house shouting, 'He's taking Lily, he's kidnapping her' and she ran in front of the car and the man had to stop. She had managed to stop him before he drove out of the gates with me and she shouted at him to open the car door.

But she did not wait and she ran around and opened the car door herself, while the man continued to drive the car slowly forward and towards the gates. Still screaming at the man, the nun pulled me out of the car and then he stopped the car at the gates. He looked over at the both of us, and we could see that he was fed-up and angry with the nun for what she had just done, and because he didn't get away with kidnapping me. He got out of the car and he shouted at both of us, and then he called the nun and me bastards as he got back in the car and then he drove off.

God knows what he was going to do with me; but for the next six weeks, he continued to harass me from his car, and every time I walked home from school, he would be parked by the side of the road with his car door open wide. And as I walked past the car, he would offer me sweets to get inside and to go with him, but I never stopped to talk to him and I would run past the car as quickly as possible, not giving him a chance to grab me.

Sometimes, he would turn up at our house and just walked straight in through the front door, he would be drunk and, as he staggered through the house, he would try to grab me or one of the younger girls, and he would try to drag us away with him and into his car. But the nuns would turn up just in time and tell him to go away and then they would push him out of the house and lock the door.

He eventually stopped harassing me for a while; but as I got older, he started again and he harassed me for years, by pulling up in his car and offering me things to get in it with him. I never did, and I never spoke to him, I just ran from him. But I watched him for years while he harassed and talked to the older girls and offered them money, fags and gifts, to get in the car with him for a few hours, and some of the older girls did.

CHAPTER 6

I Want To Die

The smell of fresh air woke me early; it was summer and the air was warm, and as I lay on my bed I could hear the birds whistling, and I was daydreaming, pretending to be one of them. My window was open, so I whistled back at the birds, but it wasn't the same and the birds just kept whistling; never once bothered by my attempts to copy or communicate with them. I looked up at the window and then I covered my eyes, wishing that I was one of them.

But all of a sudden, my concentration was broken by the sound of Sister Ann shouting at me to get up. I felt sad for myself and I wished I had been dead. I lifted my pillow and I placed it over my face and held my breath, but then Sister Ann came into the room and she pulled the pillow away from my face. 'I want to die', I shouted. 'Good', she said. 'But you will go to hell if you do it that way.' 'Will I go to heaven?' I asked. She looked at me and then she said, 'No, you will be going to purgatory.' 'What's that?' 'It's not heaven and it's not hell, only good people go to heaven.' 'Will you go to heaven?' I asked. 'Of course I will. I am a good person and I am married to god,' she said, showing me a gold ring on one of her fingers. 'You're a bad girl, so you're going to sit in a room all on your own forever, and you won't go to heaven or hell, nobody wants you. You will have to sit in the room until you can prove that you've been good or bad, and then you will go to hell. If you want to go to heaven when you die, you will have to pray every day; in the morning and then again in the evening before you go to bed, and only then might you have a small chance to go to heaven.'

But I was sick of praying. The nuns at school had me praying all day and the nuns at our house had me praying every day after school and again on weekends, and the only thing that I would pray for was to die; so the last thing I needed was more unanswered prayers. I got up out of the bed, had breakfast and went to school. Then in the evening, Sister Ann told me that the following morning I would be going away for the summer holidays. I told her that I was sick of going away with bad people and I said that I wasn't going and that she couldn't do a thing about it, 'I'm seven years old now and I don't need to go away anymore.' She looked at me and, saying nothing, she walked off and I went to my room. I knelt down at the end of my bed and I prayed for God to let me die, but nothing happened. So that night, when everyone was sleeping, I went down into the kitchen and I took a packet of Anadin painkillers out of the first aid box and I hid them down my knickers, and then I went back to my bed.

The next morning, I got up early while everyone was still sleeping and crept out of the house. I was going to kill myself before anyone got up. I ran off to the fields at the back of the house and I ran down to the stream that ran along the bottom of the fields. I knelt down by the stream and I opened the packet of tablets, then I put some of them into my mouth and I cupped my hands together to drink some water from the stream. But as I lifted the water to my mouth, some of the tablets fell out of my mouth and into my hands, and then they fell into the water. I quickly grabbed as many of them as I could and I pulled them out of the water; but as I lifted them up, they melted away and slipped through my fingers and then they were gone. I remembered that from my bedroom window I could see an old carven in the field next to our home, so I headed for it; I had decided that I was going to hide there from Sister Ann.

When I reached the caravan, the door was unlocked, so I

stepped inside and I lay down on the floor, and it felt cold. I wanted to die. I shut my eyes and, within a couple of seconds, my head began to feel dizzy and strange, and I began to feel sick, so I lifted my head and vomited onto the floor next to me. My belly felt strange and I began to get pains inside my body that I hadn't had before. I thought I was dying and I wanted Simon and Daisy with me. I wanted to get up, but whenever I moved, my belly got worse, so I stayed on the caravan floor and shut my eyes again. I don't know how long I was in the caravan for, but it felt like hours and eventually I drifted off to sleep.

And the next thing I can remember fuzzily was being woken by someone lifting me up and talking to me. I don't know who it was, but they must have brought me back to the house and put me into bed. When I woke up, my whole body felt stiff and weak and tingly and I had to stay in bed for the next two days. I was glad that I didn't die, but at the same time I still wanted to, because my life had always been horrible and nothing was worth living for. While I was ill, the nuns tried to feed me, but I refused to eat and I tried to starve myself to death, so the nuns sent for a psychiatrist to find out what was wrong with me.

When he arrived, the nuns told him that I had gone mad, that I had run away and I had tried to kill myself, and now I wouldn't eat anything. But after the psychiatrist had a chat with me without the nuns in the room, he knew that I was fine. And he told the nuns that there was nothing wrong with me, and then he left. The nuns were disappointed, and once he had gone, they told me that if I did not start eating, they would send me away to a mental hospital and I would never see my sisters or Simon again. I didn't want them to send me away, so I began to eat again and the nuns left me alone for a few days until I got better. They still had plans to send me away for the summer holidays and they were only waiting for me to get strong enough before they did so; and a few days later, two nuns walked into my bedroom and grabbed me by my arms. I didn't stand a chance, they grabbed hold of me and they dragged me down the stairs, slapping me into my back on the way.

And once downstairs, they dressed me and then marched me out of the house and into the back of a waiting car. I shouted at them to let me go, but they slammed the car door shut and the car drove off; they had locked the car door, so I lay across the seat and I kicked at the windows as hard as I could, but my plimsolls just made a thudding noise as they thumped against the glass. I tried again, but nothing; it was no use, so I shouted at the driver to stop and then I screamed as loud as I could, but the driver took no notice of me and she continued driving.

Then a couple of seconds later, she turned around and I could see that it was Sister Ann and she was smiling at me with excitement. 'You wait', she said, 'you just wait.' I leaned forward and I tried to hit her in the face, but as I moved to the edge of the seat, she swung her arm around and she knocked me back against the car window. My head hit the glass and the pain I got was so bad that I had to hold my head with both hands, as my head felt like it was going to explode. She continued driving and, as the hours passed, I still felt sick; and when she finally stopped the car at our destination, I was still holding my head. 'Get out. Get out now before I hit you again', shouted Sister Ann, as she opened the car door.

I got out of the car and I looked around. I could see an old house sitting in the middle of a farm. 'This is where you're going to be staying', she said as she slammed the car door. I felt sad, I was missing Simon and Daisy terribly. Suddenly, a group of children ran past me and up towards the car and they were shouting; and as they got to the car, they climbed all over it. Then a scruffily clothed woman, with a fag hanging out of her mouth, walked up to us and she shook hands with Sister Ann. I could tell that they had known each other for some time; and after shaking hands, they both walked off, leaving me on my own and the children to play with the car.

I looked over at the children and I counted them; there were five children, all acting as if they were mad animals. The oldest, a boy, opened the car door and he sat in the driver's seat. He then began pulling at the steering wheel and moving it from side to side as if he was driving the car, then he got out and he slammed the car door shut as hard as he could. Then he walked over to the car aerial and snapped it clean off and, as he looked around, he began to walk towards me. And then he asked me, 'Who are you?' 'Why?' I said. 'Because I'm going to hit you with this.' I looked at the piece of car Ariel in his hand and then I ran off after Sister Ann and I ran in front of her. 'He's going to hit me', I shouted. 'Go away before I hit you', she replied. The boy soon forgot about me and he ran off after one of the other children.

I walked back to the car and I got inside, but Sister Ann came back and she told me to get out. 'You're going to be staying with this woman for the next two weeks and you had better be good for her,' she said. Then she got into the car and drove off, leaving me standing next to the woman. 'Don't worry', she said, 'come with me and we can make the dinner together.' And we walked into the kitchen together and I sat and watched her as she boiled cabbage and potatoes for dinner. While I sat with her, she told me that I was going to be sleeping with all her girls in the big bedroom; then she told me to go and play, so I got up and went outside to look for her children, but they had all gone off out of sight. So I wandered off and I began to look around the farm. Everything lying around the farm was very old and most of the things I looked at were broken, and in a barn was an old tractor. The wheels were all rusty and the seat was lying on the ground, broken.

I looked around, then I left the barn and I headed back to the house. But on the way back, one of the boys came up behind me and he shouted at me, making me jump. 'You're stupid', he said. 'No, I'm not.' 'You come from a nuns' home and you're stupid.' I felt like crying, but instead I walked away and I went back into the house. The woman came over to me and she gave me my dinner. 'It's only me and my children', she said. 'I have no husband, he's dead, so tomorrow I have to go to work and the children will look after you and feed you.' All the children soon came back into the house and after dinner we played around for a while and then we all went to bed. I lay down on the bed and thought to myself that this was not that bad and then I fell to sleep.

The next morning, I got up and I went into the living room, but no one was around; so I went outside, it was very quiet and I could not see anyone. I walked around for a while, then I went into the barn and one of the woman's sons was standing next to the tractor. It was dark in the barn and, as I stood at the entrance, I could see the boy looking over at me, then he walked over to the barn door and closed it, locking himself and me inside. 'I want to go outside', I told him. 'Shut up. You can't', he said. 'I will tell your mum', I said. 'No, you won't, she's gone to work. Now get on the floor.' 'What?' 'Get on the floor.' 'Why should I?'

Then he pushed me hard into my chest, 'Stop it', I said, then he hit me into my face with his fist and I started to cry. 'Kneel down on the hay', he said. I did what he said as I didn't want to get hit in the face again, and then he stood in front of me. He looked down at me and he began to undo his trousers. I looked up at him and he had no pants on. 'Touch it', he said. 'No.' 'Do it or I will kill you and feed you to the pigs. I've done that before you know.' I tried to get up, but he grabbed me by my shoulders and he pushed me back down, then he grabbed one of my hands and put it on his dick. I didn't want to touch it and I tried to pull away, but he pulled my arm even harder and then he moved my hand along his dick, moving my hand up and down it until it went hard. Then it made a mess all over me. 'Now get up and get out, and if you tell anyone, I will kill you and feed you to the pigs.' I got up, he walked over and opened the barn doors and I ran outside and back up to the house. When I got back, I went straight into the bedroom and I never told anyone, not even his mum about what he had done to me.

The next day, I tried to stay away from him, but eventually he came looking for me; and when he found me, he grabbed me by my neck and then he forced me back into the barn again. I was frightened and I began to shake at the thought of what he might do to me, then he pushed me into the corner of the barn and he told me to take my clothes off and to lay down on the floor; but I said 'No, I won't.' 'Do it or I will kill you', he said. I had no choice, I started to cry and then I lay down on the hay next to the tractor.

He walked over to me and he started to touch me, he moved his hands all over my body, moving his hand over my clothes and around the top part of my legs, then he made me take all my clothes off and open my legs in front of him. I felt cold and sick and I was shaking with fright, but it did not bother him and he began rubbing his hands all over my body. I started to cry because of what he was doing to me, but he kept touching me, while at the same time telling me to be quiet. Then he stood up, undid his trousers and wanked himself off in front of me, and he kept doing it until he had finished and I had to lie there, covered in his mess. I was too scared to move an inch until he said I could, and then he told me to get dressed and to go play with his brothers and sisters. I got up, but I felt sick and I wanted to go home; but I knew no one could help me, so I just walked away and I said nothing to anyone.

Every day, I would try to hide from the boy, but he would still come looking for me and, when he found me, he would do the same things to me. Day after day, it went on for the whole of the holiday and all of the time I was too afraid to tell his mum, just in case he killed me and fed me to the pigs. He said that the pigs would eat every bit of my body and my hair and no one would ever know what happened to me. All I wanted was to go home and eventually one of the nuns came back to pick me up. I knew it wasn't worth telling her about what had happened because she would just hit me for telling lies, so I said nothing and I went home with her in the car.

However, about a week later, I told my sister Karen about what had happened to me while on holiday and she went and told Sister

Ann. I was frightened that Sister Ann was going to beat me to death. But instead, she asked me about what had happened to me, and she made me tell her every single thing that the boy had done to me; making me repeat it to her again and again, until I got so upset that I couldn't tell her anymore.

Then she left it at that and I thought no more of it until later in the year, when the nuns decided to send me back to the same family again, for another holiday with them. And the same things happened to me all over again, with the boy making me touch him and do things to him that made me feel sick; and at the end of the holiday, I left the farm saying nothing to no one. And the following year, the nuns sent me off to them again, but this time it was for the whole of the six-week summer holidays and by the end of the holiday I felt like I wanted to die. The boy had abused me every day for six weeks and sometimes he had done things to me that still upset me today. He treated me as if I was nothing, worthless, and as if I had no feelings at all; the boy treated the animals on the farm better than he treated me, and all the time his mother never once asked me if I was ok. Her son was happy, and what he was doing to me was keeping him out of her way for hours, so she was happy too.

When Sister Ann came to pick me up, she could tell that I was unhappy and that something had happened to me, but she said nothing to the woman or me. On the way home, she looked at me and she promised me that I would never have to go back to the family again and that made me happy. Later that evening, one of the staff came to my room and told me that one of the nuns had spoken to the woman and her son over the phone, and they all knew about the abuse I had suffered, and now that would be the end of it; then I realised they had known all along.

A year passed and I forgot all about the boy and the things he had done to me. I was nine now and Simon was seven. The summer holiday had started again and the nuns began to send all the children off on their holidays, and they split Simon and me up again, sending Simon away with my sisters to a place by the sea and then it was my turn. Sister Ann told me to get in the car; she said that I was going back to the same family that I went to last year and the year before that.

I could not believe it and I went crazy. I told her that I could not go back to them anymore, but she said that she had no other place or people that she could send me to and I had to go. I began shouting at her, telling her that she had promised me that I would never have to go back there again. But she shouted back at me and then she pulled me over to the car, 'You're going and that's that', she said. I was frantic and I began shaking from the shock of the thought of going back, she opened the car door and she pushed me inside, locking the door so that I couldn't get out. Then she stood against the car with her back against the window; she was breathing heavily from struggling with me, with her body moving up and down until she got her breath back.

After a few seconds, she moved around to the other side of the car and she got in the front seat. 'What's your problem', she shouted. 'I hate them. Don't you remember?' I said. Then she turned to me and said, 'You should have been good the first time you were at the house and none of this would have happened.' 'What are you talking about?' I said. 'You shouldn't have touched the boys.' 'I didn't', they did it to me. The big boy touched me. He touched me bad, all over my body.' She looked at me in shocked amazement, and for a moment I thought she was going to let me out of the car, but then she said, 'You're still going anyway' and then she drove off. I sat back in the seat and I stayed quiet. I knew that nothing would stop her from taking me to the house, so I just sat back and waited for my fate.

When we arrived, Sister Ann got out of the car first and then she walked around and opened the car door for me, as if I was royalty. I got out and I looked up at her and she said sorry, and we both looked over at the house. 'Go on then', she said. But, instead of shouting at me, she spoke to me in a soft and gentle voice, and as I walked towards the house, the oldest son, the boy who had been abusing me for the last few years, walked out of the barn and towards me, with the woman, his mum, following close behind him. As they approached us, the boy said, 'I'm going shooting in the fields and you're coming with me.' Sister Ann gently pushed me towards him and said, 'That's a good idea. Go with him, it will be fun.' I looked at him and he had a shotgun slung across one of his arms. I had no choice and I followed him off into the fields, leaving Sister Ann talking to the woman.

The boy walked into the middle of the biggest field on the farm, with me following behind him, and then he stopped, turned around and faced me. The grass in the field was tall and thick and he had made sure that no one could see us. Then he looked at me and said, 'You told them, didn't you?' and then he pointed the gun at me and again he said, 'You told them what I've done to you.' I took a step back, I brushed my hands against the tall grass to make myself some space and then I said, 'No.' 'I'm going to shoot you and feed you to the pigs', he said. 'I've done it before and I know how to do it and no one will ever find you.'

He then poked me in the ribs with the shotgun and he told me to walk back towards the barn. I was shaking and I had no choice as I didn't want to die, so I turned around and I slowly walked in front of him and I headed towards the barn. I looked around for help, but there was no one around; the nun and the woman had vanished. I continued towards the barn and, when we got to the barn, I walked inside and he closed the door behind us. 'Lie down', he said. 'No, I won't', I said. 'Lie down.' 'No, I won't and I'm going to tell everyone what you're doing to me', I said.

He looked at me for a few moments and the moment felt like forever, then he pointed the shotgun towards my chest and pushed the barrels into my ribs. I stood still and stood my ground, then he pointed the shotgun down towards the ground and took a step back away from me and, without saying a word, he opened the barn door. I took a deep breath and stood up straight, and then I began to walk towards the barn door, thinking to myself that he was going to shoot me in the back. I kept walking, praying that he wasn't going to shoot me and I managed to walk out of the barn without making eye contact with him.

And then I slowly walked away from the barn and up towards the house. I knew he was behind me, watching me from the barn door, but I never looked back; and with every step I took, it felt like the house was getting further and further away from me, but eventually I made it to the house and I went inside. To this day, I do believe that if I had not stopped him then, he would have had full sex with me and then he would have killed me and fed me to the pigs.

After that incident, he left me alone for the rest of the holiday and all I could do was sit and wait for one of the nuns to come and take me home; and after six weeks, one eventually did and she took me home, back to my brother and sisters. The nuns sent me back to the family one more time after that; I hated going and I was frightened at the thought of what the boy might do to me when I arrived at the farm. However, the boy never came near me or touched me again and I spent most of the time hiding out in the fields, as far away from him as possible, waiting for the time to go home. And I never went near the pigs, just in case he shot me in the back and then fed me to them.

CHAPTER 7

Getting Older

I was getting older now and for some reason Sister Ann began to show some interest in me; she still hit me every day, and pulling my hair and calling me names was the normal thing for her to do. But now that I was older, she would spend more time talking to me and she just couldn't stop looking at me. And she would talk to me about things that I didn't understand and I had no idea why she was being my friend, and I always felt strange and uncomfortable when she was around me.

Sometimes, she would rub her hands gently down my hair, showing me kindness and affection, and I felt sick when she touched me. But then a slap on the back of my head with a hairbrush would show me that she had not changed and everything was still the same between us. One day, I became ill and she seemed to be genuinely worried about me, then Simon became ill too, so the head nun took a look at us and she decided that we needed to go to the hospital. The nuns treated us as a burden to them and they hated having to take us to hospital.

When we arrived at the hospital, the doctors looked at us and they said that we had whooping cough and they said that we both had to spend a few weeks in the hospital. Well, it was the best time of our lives; we both had to be isolated from all the other children in the hospital and we had an entire ward all to ourselves. It was great being in hospital and we spent hours every day jumping all over the beds. We swung on the curtains and Simon would swing from one bed to another, screaming as he held on for his life, as he pretended to be Tarzan of the jungle. The nurses even allowed us to play with some of the instruments they left lying around the ward and it kept us occupied for most of the time; and occasionally, the nurses would walk in and check on us, to make sure we were ok.

Then one day, I decided to play doctor and I pretended that Simon was the patient and I was the doctor; and because he was sick, I needed to check his temperature for him. I told him that he had to lie down on his belly as he was very sick, and then I stuck a glass thermometer up his bum. But as I pushed the thermometer into his bum, he moved and the thermometer broke and half of the glass tube became stuck inside his bum. I shouted and I screamed for help, and I kept on screaming until the nurses came running in. Then I told them what had happened to Simon and they quickly rushed him away. Eventually, they got the broken pieces of the thermometer out and they said that he was ok, and they cleaned him up and took everything dangerous away from us and they gave us soft toys to play with instead.

For the rest of our stay in the hospital, the nurses allowed us to stay up for as long as we wanted and the doctors fed us food we had never seen or tasted before and we both felt happy. I got better, but Simon was still sick and he was vomiting all day long and he would use the metal bins around the ward to be sick in; but just as he was about to vomit, I would pull the bin away from him and the sick would go all over the floor. Simon would just laugh, thinking it was very funny as the vomit came out of his nose and mouth at the same time and then covered the hospital floor.

But the doctors didn't think it was funny; but they never shouted at us for what we had done, instead they gave us lots of attention and love, which was just what we needed. None of the nuns or staff at the home had ever treated us like kids and we liked it and we wanted to stay in the hospital forever, but eventually we got better and we had to leave. But before we left, the doctors gave us lots of toys and sweets to bring back to the other children in the home; but when the nun came to take us back home and we got in the car, she took everything from us and we never saw any of it again.

I was only home for about a week when I became sick with the mumps; I couldn't believe it and I must have caught them at the hospital. Then Karen got them and we both had to spend the next three weeks together in our bedroom, all on our own; and every day one of the nuns would come into the room and squeeze me by my neck to see if I was ok, and to get me to take my medicine. But as I was recovering from the mumps, I caught another infection and I became very ill. I got so bad that I could not even cope with any type of light, as it made my eyes hurt and it gave me a headache.

Then after a few days, my body became covered in red blotches and my whole body felt stiff. The staff became worried about what I had caught and they soon stopped coming into the room, as they thought they were going to catch something bad from us; and a few days later, a doctor came to the house, and he gave us some medicine. The nuns and staff would only come as far as the bedroom door, they would leave us food and drinks on the floor outside the bedroom door and we had to get up and go get it ourselves. We were so sick that we could not even walk and we had to crawl along the bedroom floor to get to the food and water. And just for spite, the staff and nuns would put the bedroom light on, so that we were in pain and we would beg them to turn the light off before they left, but they never did. They loved it and they could not get enough of being spiteful to us; and just when we needed them most, they showed us their true colours.

Then one night, Sister Ann came into the bedroom and she sat next to my bed. I was still awake, but I had my eyes shut, so she had no idea that I knew she was there. At first, I thought that she was going to hit me and I got myself ready to protect my head; but instead of beating me, she just sat in the room and stared at me. Then, after a while, she got up and left the room and I fell to sleep. The next night, she did the same thing. I thought it was a bit strange that she was not hitting me, but I didn't care what she was doing as long as she was leaving me alone.

The third night that she came into my room it was very late; I was exhausted from praying all evening and I was just about able to stay awake. She came in, she sat down on a chair next to my bed, then she bent down and picked my knickers up off the floor, and she put them against her face and then she smelt them. Then she put her other hand on top of my blanket and she began to move her hand up and down over the blanket, rubbing my whole body through the blanket. I stayed still and I kept my eyes shut, hoping that she would stop what she was doing and go away; but she didn't, she just kept rubbing her hand up and down my body. I was waiting for her to move her hands up to my neck and strangle me or for her to do something horrible to me, but instead she just kept rubbing her hand up and down over my body. I felt strange and I didn't know what to do, so I just pretended that I was asleep and she continued smelling my knickers for a few more seconds, then she threw them to the floor, got up and left the room. I didn't know what to do, so I just pulled my night clothes and my blankets back into position and then I went to sleep.

When morning came, I thought to myself that she must have wanted to be my friend. But as I walked into the dining room for breakfast, she was standing by the door and as I walked past her she gently slapped me around my head and I knew that everything was the same as usual between us. After breakfast, I went off to school and, on the way, I told Daisy what Sister Ann had done to me for the last few nights and she said that she thought it was a bit strange, but she told me to forget it. She said that if Sister Ann was not hitting me in my bed, then it must be ok for her to touch me and I thought no more of it.

However, that night when I went to bed, she did the same

thing to me again and she kept doing it to me for the next few weeks; and each night, she would spend more time touching me through my sheets and blanket. I felt bad for letting her touch me, but I knew that if I had said anything to her, she would hit me and then she would tell the other staff that I was lying and making things up to get her in trouble, so I said nothing to her. I did, however, tell some of the older girls about what was going on and they told me that all the staff and nuns had been doing the same thing to them for years and it was nothing to worry about and they just laughed at me. They said that I had to accept it, as it was normal for the nuns and staff to touch all the children as they got older, so I left it at that and I never told anyone else again.

Days led into weeks and weeks became months and then years went past. I still looked thin and I was nearly always sick; the nuns never gave us much food to eat and it was the same thing for all of us children living in the house. We had very little to do all day, we had nothing to play with and the nuns and staff kept anything given to us, like birthday presents, gifts, nice clothes and anything of value, all locked away in cupboards around the house. Then, after a while, everything in the cupboards would all just disappear and whenever we asked to play with toys, they would say that we did not deserve nice things and that is why they kept them from us.

Then one Saturday, Sister Ann told me that it was going to be sports day and she said that I didn't have to go to work and in the afternoon the nuns gathered us all up into age groups and then each group had a colour and my colour was red. We all went into a field at the back of the house and we began to play games; it was a lot of fun and because I was the oldest in my team, I was stronger than all the other girls were and I kept winning. When we all finished playing, the nuns gave out prizes and we had a choice of what we could have and our house, Willows, picked footballs because we had never had one before. And by the time the nuns had finished handing out the prizes, we had a lot of balls. When we got back to the house, the nuns brought all of us into the hall and they told us that we were allowed to keep the balls and they never took them away from us. But once all the balls had broken, they never replaced them either. It was a lot of fun that day and I will never forget it.

Sometimes after school, the nuns allowed us to play outside in the garden, while some of the staff and nuns cooked food for themselves; it was their way of getting us out of the way for a few hours, while they spoilt themselves with good food. On one particular day, the smell of the food coming from the kitchen was so nice that I just had to see what it was that they were cooking, so I made an excuse to the other children and I went into the house to go to the bathroom. Then, on the way back, I stopped at the entrance to the kitchen and I just stood and looked inside. One of the staff was sitting at the kitchen table eating a pork chop with fried onions and gravy, and it smelt so nice that I just stood looking and smiling at her. She looked over at me and, in a nasty voice, she told me to go away, but I just stood looking at her. 'Go away', she shouted, but I could not move, I had been sent into a dazed trance by the gorgeous smell of the food.

Before I knew it, she jumped up out of her chair, she grabbed the biggest wooden spoon I had ever seen from the table, and she ran towards me with it. I quickly realised what she was doing, so I turned around and I ran off through the house and up the stairs towards my bedroom, but she soon caught up with me, and she hit me as hard as she could around my legs with the wooden spoon. I kept running, but I tripped on one of the stairs and she landed on top of me, then she held me down with her body while she hit me on my legs again and again with the spoon. And she kept on hitting me until my legs were black and blue and she only stopped hitting me when she could not lift her arm anymore from exhaustion, and I had stopped moving.

My legs were so badly beaten that they were almost bleeding, but I never made a sound, until I told her that I only wanted to see the pork chop that she was eating because it smelt so nice and because I had never seen one before, but she said nothing. She just got up and walked back to the kitchen, leaving me lying on the stairs, and my legs had swollen so much that they didn't look like my legs anymore. And I had to crawl the rest of the way up to my room on my hands and knees. It took over two weeks for my legs to get better and all the time I had to keep them covered up so the nuns and staff wouldn't shout at me for showing the marks off to the other children.

Everywhere we went the nuns were praying, and Sister Ann wanted us to do the same. She would tell us that we had to pray to be forgiven for all our sins, but by now I knew I wasn't going to hell, they were and no amount of praying was going to save them from their fate. In the evenings, Sister Ann would sit on the floor in the middle of the hallway of our house and she would make us all sit around her like she was the queen bee, and we would all have to do the rosary, and say Hail Mary's and lots of other praying stuff that I hated. We all had to take it in turn to say our prayers, but every time someone got a prayer wrong Sister Ann would give them a slap in the face; and when it was Sister Ann's turn, we would all end up laughing at her.

The whole situation was so funny that we just couldn't help laughing, the thought of us all sitting there and her being serious in the middle, praying like it was going to save her, was just too much for everyone and we couldn't help but take the piss out of her. I hated her for making me pray and she knew it; but to get her own back on me for laughing at her, she would make any excuse to cut my fingernails, and she would cut them down so close to the base of the skin that my fingers would bleed and throb with pain for days and days.

So, to stop her from hurting me, I began to bite and chew my nails until they were so short that she couldn't cut them anymore. And on other occasions, she would tell me that I had head lice in my hair and she would use a metal tooth comb to get them out of my hair. She would dig the comb hard into my scalp, making my head bleed, then she would pour the lice lotion onto my head and she would allow the lotion to run into the wounds on my scalp so that the lotion would sting and hurt me. I seemed to be the only one getting head lice at the time, and the excuse was very convenient for her to use against me.

In St Joseph's, there was a hall and at Christmas, before they sent us away for the holidays, we would have to perform a Christmas play and the nuns would have us perform the same play every year. However, before we could do the play, we would have to practice it; and for weeks, the nuns would make us do our homework first and then in the evenings they would send us out into the garden at the back of the house to rehearse the play. It was like more punishment to me, so instead of rehearsing the play, I would run off into the fields and try to hide from the nuns; but after a while, they would come out and look for me, and they would try to catch me and then bring me back into the house. However, I would run for miles up into the apple orchards, I would stay there for a couple of hours and then, on the way home, I would eat the apples that I had found lying on the ground and I would laugh to myself, thinking how great it had all been.

Once the Christmas nativities were over, it was time to go away on holiday again, but I didn't want to go on holiday anymore; almost every time that I had been sent away, someone had either physically or mentally abused me, people touched me, hit me and called me names and I didn't want any of it anymore. So when Sister Ann said that it was time for me to go on holiday again, Karen and I decided to run away and we decided to run back to daddy, and that day we began our plan.

Karen said that if we covered our faces with red spots and we pretended that we were sick, the nuns would not be able to send us away. I knew she was right, so I agreed with her and the next day she took a red pen out of her school bag and she spent about two hours covering our faces, hands and necks in red spots and then she put some white powder over our faces to make us look pale and sick. We had the measles. The children in the house always had the measles or chickenpox or some other disease that had red spots connected to it, so to us it was the perfect plan. After we had finished, Karen went downstairs and she told one of the nuns that I was sick and I could not get out of my bed as I had red spots all over my body. The nun said ok and then she came up to our room and looked at me; at first it looked like we had fooled her, but as she got closer to me she put her hand on my face and she rubbed the spots. The red ink smudged all over my face and she began laughing at me, then she said, 'Wash your face, you're going on holiday. The car will be here in a few minutes.' I had no choice and I had to go away, like she said.

This time, I was sent to stay with a family that I had never spent time with before. They had six children and my stay with them wasn't that bad; but when I got up on Christmas morning, none of the children were in their bedrooms. It was still early and the house was very quiet and I thought they must have all gone for a walk, so I walked down the stairs and towards the living room; but as I walked into the room, the whole family turned around and looked at me. It looked like they had forgotten all about me being in the house and the children were standing next to a heap of presents sitting under the Christmas tree.

I was so excited, but as I walked towards the tree the woman told me to go away as none of the presents were for me. So I sat on the stairs and I watched through the living room doorway as the children's mother handed them their presents and I never got a thing, not even a bar of chocolate. When the woman had finished handing out the presents, I was so upset that I went back to my room and I never bothered coming out again until the next day; and throughout the whole time I spent in my room, no one ever came up to see if I was ok. I never got a chance to celebrate Christmas and I was treated like I was nothing; it was as if I had no feelings and I didn't matter to anyone and I was nothing for them to worry about.

Over the years, the nuns continued to send me on the so-called holidays; and the next time they sent me away, they sent me to a man and woman who were very good to me, and they treated me like I was their own child. They lived on a farm and they had many other children staying with them, but none of the children were their own, 'lost souls' they called them, but everyone seemed to be happy. My Christmas with them was fantastic, I never thought Santa Claus would ever come to me as I came from a children's home and he never visited children's homes; well, at least that was what the nuns had always told me. I always thought Santa never liked me because he never gave me anything. But this time it was different, all the children and I got presents, I even got what I wanted; it was a pram and a doll and I was so happy, I just couldn't believe I got presents. I loved the family and I wished that the man and woman had been my mum and dad.

We played all day long and all the children were nice to me, apart from one boy who resented me and hated me for being there. He was jealous of the attention that the man and woman were giving me and, whenever no one was around, he would thump me into my back with his fist; day and night, he would pinch me and pull my hair and he would do anything he could to make me unhappy. However, I loved it there and no matter what he did to me, I didn't want to leave them.

The day after Christmas, it snowed and we all went with the man and woman to their granddad's house; and while we were there, we used the bonnet of the old man's old Morris minor van to slide down the hills. The hills were big and sliding down them was great and the best fun I had for years; but every time we went down the hill, we had trouble stopping at the bottom and we almost went into a stream. The whole day was fun and I never even missed my own family. When the holiday was over and I went back to my home, Willows, and I told Sister Ann all about the fun that I had had and she said that she would try to send me to them again. But before the chance came, the man and woman moved away, and I never saw them again.

Instead, Sister Ann found a nice old couple for me to stay with and their names were Alice and Terry. They had never had any children and Alice used to be a teacher and her husband, Terry, still worked in a bank. They were good people and they never once raised their voices to me. Alice had a little dog and, whenever I went to stay with the couple, I was allowed to keep the dog with me for the whole time; and even when I went to bed, I was allowed to have the dog cuddle into me. The dog was the only friend I had and she never left my side. Alice and Terry were just crazy about me and from then on the nuns allowed me to go and stay with them on almost every holiday I had. They even allowed me to stay with them on the Christmas and Easter holidays and Alice even had presents kept for me, so that we could celebrate my birthday together, and they gave me more presents than I could ever have wished for in my life. It took me a while before I could fully trust them both, but once we all got to know each other it was great, and eventually Alice and Terry instructed the nuns never to send me anywhere else for my holidays again. They insisted the nuns send me only to them and to no one else, and for some reason the nuns agreed.

Alice and Terry treated and loved me as if I was their own child and Alice did as much as she could to make me feel happy. Alice even made clothes for me and she always took me with her when she went out shopping; and every summer, she would take me to the Dublin horse and dog show with her. She even arranged for me to have horse riding lessons, so we could both go horse riding together in the fields at the back of her house. And on some of the holidays that I spent with her, she took me away for long weekends to Northern Ireland, to see her family; introducing me as a member of Terry's family. Then back at her house, we would cook together and we would sit and play for hours, never once getting bored with each other's company.

It was the only time that I ever felt normal and a part of something, it was my first taste of normality and they spoilt me so much that I liked it. Terry also had a family and, whenever we visited them, he would introduce me as a member of Alice's family and no one ever said a word about whom I was or where I came from. Terry also had a brother, who was a priest; he was forty-five years old, his name was Father Brien, and he was a nice man, and from the first time I met him he seemed to take a liking towards me. Every time I went with Alice and Terry to visit Terry's family, his brother would be at the house and for some strange reason I always felt as if he was waiting there for me.

I remember one weekend, Terry's brother spent all of his time following me around the place, he was always trying to get my attention and he would give me sweets while he talked to me. Then after a while, it became impossible for me to be at the house without him being around me, like my shadow. After I had visited them a few more times, he began to touch me as we took walks through the garden together. At first, he would just brush up against me as we walked together; but then one afternoon, while walking on our own, he hugged me and he told me how lovely he thought I was and how proud he was to have me as a part of his family. I looked up at him and he smiled at me and then he let me go and we continued walking; but he had made me feel uncomfortable, so I made an excuse and I ran back to Alice and Terry, who were up at the house and, in the afternoon, we went home.

Then one morning, while I was staying at Alice's house, she asked me if I would like to go with her to a local dog show and I said yes. But on the way to the dog show, she suggested that we stop to see Terry's brother Brien, as he had moved closer to them and he was now teaching at a local boarding school not far from where we were going. I said, 'Yes, great, it would be nice to see Father Brien again,' so we both agreed and we headed off to see him. When we arrived at the school, Father Brien was already waiting for us at the entrance and I thought it was a bit strange, but then I thought to myself that Alice must have rung Terry and told him about our change of plans, and then Terry must have rung Brien to let him know we were coming.

Alice and I got out of the car, we walked towards Father Brien, and he greeted us with open arms, but he hugged me so tight that I could hardly breathe and I had to struggle to get free from him. Then he suggested that we all sit down on the grass together and have a picnic within the boarding school's grounds. It sounded fine and he said that it would be nice, as everyone else from the school had gone away for the holidays, so we had the whole school to ourselves. We walked around and we found a nice quite spot overlooking a pond and Alice and I sat down, while Brien went and made us something to eat. When he came back, we spent about an hour talking.

Then all of a sudden, Alice looked at her watch and suggested that I should stay with Brien while she went to the dog show on her own as it was getting late, and she said that she would pick me up later, on her way home. I said ok and Alice wasted no time, she got up and walked off, leaving me sitting on the grass with Brien. But as soon as Alice drove out of the school gates, Brien looked at me and said that it would be nice if we went for a walk down to the pond. I said ok, so we both got up and walked off towards the pond; and when we got to it, I fed the remainder of the food to the ducks.

Then, once I was finished, he said that we should leave the pond and go inside the school as it was getting late, and I agreed. He looked at me and smiled, and then he led me up towards the school. I thought to myself that it would be nice to see inside such a big school and I continued following him up towards the school. However, as we got closer and I headed for the main entrance, he said, 'No, not that way' and he began walking away from the main entrance and around towards the back of the school, and I continued to follow him. As we walked around the corner, he stopped next to a small entrance and then he told me that as well as teaching at the school he also lived at the school and that his

126

room was inside. 'That's nice', I said. Then he opened the door and said, 'Come on' and we both walked in and he led the way up towards his room. The school was huge and it was very quiet inside and every step I took echoed along the corridors, and it sounded creepy as if someone was following me.

After walking for several minutes, he eventually stopped and opened a small wooden door and inside was his room. I looked inside and all I could see was a small dark room with a bed, a chest of drawers and a table; humble things, just right for a man of God. The room was simple and, as I entered, he told me to sit on the bed while he closed the door. I looked around, but there were no chairs so I sat on the bed as he said, and he continued closing the door. However, as he closed the door, he also turned the key, locking the door shut, and then he walked towards the window and closed the curtains. And within a couple of seconds, the room become dark and I could just about see Father Brien's silhouette as he stood in front of the curtains.

I called to him for reassurance and I asked him to turn the light back on, but he said, 'It's ok, Lily, I'm here' and then he leaned forward and grabbed me by my hands. 'Why have you made the room dark?' I asked, but he said nothing and then he sat down next to me on the bed. I moved back along the bed to make some room for him; but at the same time, he moved with me. He was still holding my hands and I began to tremble, then he moved closer and grabbed me by my arms.

I tried to get up off the bed, but I couldn't; the force of him holding me was stopping me from getting up, so I moved my body back and away from him, but again he moved his body towards me, but this time he got even closer to me. I asked him to stop messing around and to turn the light back on, but he said nothing; so I tried to wriggle off the bed, but his grip on me was too tight, so I leaned my body back as far as I could go, but my head hit his pillow and I had nowhere else to go. I began to tremble and I asked him what he was doing, but still he said nothing; then he leaned towards me and moved his face against mine, and I froze with fright as he put his mouth against mine and began to kiss me. I couldn't do a thing to stop him as he was too strong and I was unable to move my body away from his, so I moved my face to one side, doing my best to avoid his kisses.

Then he moved his whole body closer to mine and then he climbed on top of me, while he moved me into the centre of the bed. And he began to kiss me on my face even harder and then he kissed me on the lips again and he told me that he loved me and had always loved me. I didn't know what to do; I was shocked, frightened and afraid at what he was doing to me and at the thought of what he might do next. I wanted to scream, but as I opened my mouth nothing came, I could not make a sound and I felt like I couldn't breathe.

My heart was pounding like it was about to come out of my chest and he continued to smother my whole body with his, while he continuously told me that he loved me; it was as if he was trying to reassure me that everything was going to be ok. But it wasn't and he began to move his body between my legs, spreading my legs open wide with his and I knew that he wanted to have sex with me, but I didn't want any of it. I wriggled, then suddenly someone knocked on his bedroom door and he stopped.

He jumped up off the bed and I felt as if I could breathe again, he quickly turned on the light and I could see a look of shock spread across his face. I got off the bed and I felt happy as he walked over to the door and unlocked it, and as he done so, I looked over his shoulder and I could see that it was Alice. She had come back. I looked over at her and she had a puzzled look on her face, then she asked me if everything was ok and I said yes. Then she looked around the room and she asked Brien why his light was off and why had we been sitting on the bed in the dark, as she had heard the noise of the light being switched back on. His face went red as blood; suddenly, he looked very guilty and he had trouble replying to her, as his words came out of his mouth all mumbled up. I could see that the situation was tense and I felt awkward for all of us, so I interrupted them and I said that he closed the curtains and turned off the light to have a sleep. I just wanted to get out of there as quickly as possible and I would have said anything to do so.

Alice still looked puzzled and Brien's face was even redder than before, but then she said ok and she told me to leave the room and to go outside and wait by the car while she spoke to Father Brien. I ran outside and I waited by Alice's car; and about ten minutes later, she came out of the school and she told me to get into the car. I did what she said and, as we drove off, she told me that there were roadworks on the way to the dog show and it was taking too long to get there, so she had changed her mind about going and instead she had decided to come back and spend a little more time with Brien and me.

However, now she said that it was getting late and we had to go home. I looked over at her and I wanted to tell her about what had just happened in the room, but I knew that if I said anything to her, it would cause a lot of trouble between everyone and I would probably be the one to get the blame for it, so I said nothing. But I had a strange feeling that she already knew something was wrong and that is why she had come back to check on me. As we drove off out of the gates, we both looked back at the same time and we could see Father Brien standing alone in the drive; and then, as we drove away from the school, Alice asked me again if everything was ok. I said, 'Yes, fine', and during the journey home she quizzed me over and over again, why was the door locked and why were the curtains pulled shut, and why was the light switched off, and did he do anything to me.

And all I could tell her was that Father Brien was tired and he wanted to lie down for a moment. But she knew that something was wrong and she never let him near me again; and soon after our little incident, Father Brien was assigned to a church in Australia and I never saw him again. I didn't know it at the time, but for many years after Brien was sending me letters, telling me how he felt about me. However, the adults around me were keeping the letters from reaching me and it wasn't until about six years later that I found out, when a bunch of letters were handed to me and I just threw them all away, never reading one of them.

Whenever my stay with Alice and Terry ended, I never wanted to go back to the home, but I had no choice. But Alice always promised me that she would always come back to get me on the next school holiday, and she did, and she would never send me back to the home empty-handed. She would always give me bags of stuff to bring back for the other children, she would give me clothes, toys and ribbon for them; and when I got back, the children loved it all. They would play with the things all day until the nuns got fed up with it all and then they would take it all away from them, saying they were going to keep it all safe for them, but the children would never see any of it again. I continued going back to Alice and Terry every year until the day I left Willows and the convent, and I miss them both very much.

CHAPTER 8

Time To Leave

I was getting older now, and the nuns began to give me pocket money each week, so I could buy myself sweets from the shops on the way home from school. But they also had a little black note book that they kept the names in of all the naughty children, and my name was always in the book. The trouble was that the nuns always used the book against me and they used it against me to keep me from having my pocket money each week. If I had been bad during the week, then my name went into the book and I never got my pocket money. I got so used to them waving the black book in my face and telling me that I was not getting any pocket money again, that in the end I told the nuns to stick the book up their ass, and I never saw the book or any pocket money again.

It was only five pence a week anyway, plus I had my own way of getting money. As at the back of St Joseph's was a field where every weekend men played football, and they would use one of the rooms in the convent as a changing room, leaving all their clothes lying around the room as they played football. Then me and some other kids would sneak into the room and go through their pockets, looking for money. And we got more money in a month than we would ever have gotten from the nuns in a whole year. We would all get a couple of pounds each, then we would sneak off to the shops and buy ice cream, sweets and even fags and matches. It was great; but after a few months, the nuns found out about us stealing the money and they locked the changing room door and that was the end of that.

One morning, I came down from my bedroom and I told the staff that I had wet the bed again and she told me not to worry, and that she would change the bed sheets later in the day. So I sat down, ate my breakfast and then I went off to school, but she never changed my sheets, she just pulled the covers back into place and then made the bed, leaving it wet. Then in the evening, when I got back from school, all the staff in the house were rushing around and cleaning the house, putting clean towels, soap and shampoo in the bathrooms and even fresh food into the kitchen cupboards.

Then the staff gathered us all together in the dining room and they told us all to be good, because some people from the health service were coming to see us and they were going to check over the house. The staff cleaned us all up and, just as they had finished putting clean clothes on us, two men walked into the house and the two men introduced themselves as health inspectors,. Then they asked us children many questions about the house and the food that the nuns had been feeding us. Once they were finished talking to us, they walked around the house, checking on the condition of the kitchen and looking in all the food cupboards; then they went into all the bedrooms and took off all the blankets and sheets from the beds to check the condition of the mattresses.

Everything was fine until they went into my bedroom and pulled back the covers on my bed; it was still wet and the sheets smelt, and they had stains all over them. The two men were very angry with the staff and they left the house complaining to the nuns that they would be making a full report about what they had found. Sister Ann said goodbye to them and then she closed the front door, walked over to me and slapped me into my face. 'That's for wetting the bed', she said, and then she asked me why I never told the staff about the wet sheets. I tried to explain to her that I did tell the staff that morning, but the staff said that I was lying and she told Sister Ann to leave it at that; but she didn't and she kept slapping me and shouting at me for not telling them about the sheets and she blamed me for everything that went wrong. In fact, I do believe to this day that the staff had set me up that day, just to get me the beating from Sister Ann.

As time went on, I began to notice more things going on around the house and some of the strange behaviours going on between some of the nuns and staff. Over the years, people would come and go and so would some of the children; and if you asked the nuns if they were coming back, you would be told to shut up and to go away. I also noticed that some of the nuns had become very close to each other; they had been working and living in the same home and convent for so long that some of them had become almost inseparable, sticking to each other like lovers or conjoined twins. They always walked around in pairs and never ashamed of showing affection to one another in front of us. I will never forget two of the staff that made me feel very uncomfortable when they were around me. They were always playing with each other, touching and fondling each other's bodies and they never stopped. They would constantly touch each other's tits and put their hands up each other's dresses and touch each other between the legs. And they would use a long wooden spoon while they were in the kitchen to poke up each other's knickers and then they would use the same wooden spoons to stir our dinner while they prepared our food in the kitchen.

Then at mealtimes, they would sit next to each other at the table, smiling and giggling at one another while they put a hand down each other's knickers and rubbed each other's private parts under the table. They were disgusting, but I could never say anything to them, and if I looked at them, they would stop for a moment and then give me a dirty look as if I had interrupted them while they were doing something very important; and I always felt embarrassed and uncomfortable while they were around me.

Over the years, I would see and hear things that I could never speak about to anyone, and many of the staff and nuns would touch the children and each other as if it was normal and nothing to worry about. And while I was in the same bedroom as them, they would get into bed with each other and rub each other's bodies; and they made me feel sick, but to them it was fun having someone in the same room with them while they played around with each other.

Between all the beatings, I did have a few nice times playing like a child, but my fun would always be interrupted by a nun or a member of the staff calling me names or hitting me for some unknown reason. But it wasn't just me they abused; all the children in the home suffered in one way or another and, over the years, the constant abuse began to take its toll on everyone. Over time, some of the older girls were sent away to workhouses and the only reason the nuns sent them away was to keep them away from the boys; and some of the other children just disappeared over night and no one ever saw them again. I had not seen or spoken to most of my brothers for years and the only one I managed to have some kind of contact with was Chris, as he still lived in a home not far from ours. The nuns ran that home as well as ours, and occasionally I would pass Chris as I walked to school, as our schools stood right next to each other. But the nuns would never allow the boys and the girls to mix, so he would be standing on the corner waiting to go into school, and as I walked by we would have just enough time to say 'Hi' to each other, before he went inside the building.

Then one day, I managed to get to the school a bit early and Chris was standing on the corner, hoping to catch a glimpse of me as I walked past; and I had just enough time to ask him how he was, and he said that he felt sad at being separated from us and he felt lonely. He said that our older brother Ted was old enough to leave and he had gone back to live with daddy at the house. He looked sad and I wanted to cuddle him, but I had to go and we both went our own ways to our schools. I knew then that the same thing was going to happen to Simon and me, as we were a lot younger than our other sisters were and soon they would be old enough to leave our house, and they would go home to daddy, leave us behind to suffer at the hands of the nuns.

I felt sad and sorry for myself; and sure enough, three months later, they sent Jenny away, but not because she was old enough to leave, but because she was a bad girl and she had caused a lot of problems with the boys from one of the other homes. She had been caught kissing and messing around with the boys, so the nuns sent her off to a workhouse in Dublin; but I heard that a few days after she got there, she escaped and she had run away to London, to our mum's house, and she was never coming back.

Now Karen was the oldest and it wasn't long before she started to take an interest in the local boys; but she wasn't allowed to have a boyfriend, so she had to sneak out of the house late at night to see the boys. Every evening, she would open a second floor window and then climb down the drainpipe and sneak off for an hour or two; and then Daisy and I would have to stand by our window and wait for her to come back and then we could help her back into the house.

But the window was high off the ground and we had to tie three bed sheets together for her to climb back up to the window. Daisy would tie one end of the sheets around her waist and then I would pull on the sheets, but Karen was fourteen years old and too heavy for us to pull her up on our own. And as she grabbed hold of the sheets and she began to climb up them, we would slide along the floor and slam up against the wall and almost fall out of the window as she climbed up the bed sheets. She was so heavy that we had to sit on the floor below the window and wedge ourselves against the wall, while Karen climbed up, laughing at us as she climbed through the window and fell on to the floor from exhaustion. Sometimes, we had very little strength to help her, so we had to tie one end of the sheets to the legs of one of the beds; otherwise, we would never have been able to hold her weight.

After doing this for months, I got sick of Karen keeping me up all night, just so that she could go and see the boys. So one night, I said to Daisy that when Karen gets back and climbs to the top of the sheets, let's drop her; but Daisy said, 'No, we might end up killing her and then what will happen?' I said, 'Well, she might just get hurt.' Then Daisy said that she might just get back up and then she would beat us up for dropping her. We spent ages laughing and plotting what we were going to do to her when she came back and grabbed hold of the sheets. And in the end, we decided to drop her; and when she came back, we waited until she was halfway up the sheets, then we let go and, a few seconds later, we heard a loud thud as she hit the ground. We both looked at each other, then we got up and looked out of the window, and as we leant over and looked down, we could see Karen lying on the ground and she said that she had hurt her back. But after a couple of seconds, she got back up and we gave her another chance; and as she got to the top, we helped her through the window and into the room. When she got back inside the room, she stood up and then she beat us both up, by whacking both of us around the head with the lid of the rubbish bin that was in our room; and after that night, she never trusted us again.

A couple of months later, the nuns told us that Karen was now old enough to leave the home, and they sent a letter to our mother, explaining that Karen was now old enough to leave and a week later my mother sent my sister Tracy's boyfriend, Fred, over to Ireland to take her back to London. The nuns couldn't wait to get rid of her, but the paperwork wasn't ready, so Fred had to spend a couple of days waiting around while the nuns prepared Karen's leaving papers. And while Fred was waiting, he spent a lot of the time hanging around the home and playing with me and giving me a lot of attention.

Then on his last visit to the home, before he left, he played with me as usual, but then he grabbed me by my leg and pulled me towards him, and I suddenly remembered whom he was and what he had done to me back at my sister's house in London. I quickly pulled away from him and ran off up to my bedroom and locked the bedroom door. I knew Karen was going away with him the next morning, so later that evening I told her about what he had done to me back in London when I was a baby and I told her to stay away from him and to stay around as many people as possible. So that he could not get her on his own, otherwise he would do things to her that she wouldn't like. She was afraid, but she understood what I was telling her; and the next morning, I helped her put three sets of clothes on, one layer on top of the other, making sure he would never have enough time to take all the clothes off and touch her. I cuddled her and we said our goodbyes and the nuns gave her a strange look, as they could not understand why she was wearing so many layers of clothes and why she was acting so odd, and then she left with Fred. I was so upset; I turned around and went back into the house.

Now it was only Daisy, Simon and me, with Chris still on his own in the boys' house; one by one, all the others had left and now we had no one to protect us from the nuns. I told Simon and Daisy that we will never be split up or separated. But because we had no one to protect us, the nuns took advantage of us and the beatings they gave us became more frequent and more severe; and day after day, I was sent to my room and I never got a chance to see or mix with the other children in the house again.

I became depressed and I felt sad for myself. I told Daisy that she would be the next one to go, but she said, 'Don't you worry, I won't leave you.' Then we both went looking for Simon and when we found him we said that we were the three musketeers and that we would stick together forever and we all promised each other that we would never leave the home without each other. I looked at Simon and Daisy, and I said all for one and one for all, and then we all shouted it out together as loud as we could, letting all the staff and nuns know how we felt about each other. Then we marched through the house, shouting out as loud as we could that we would never leave without each other.

But the next day, one of the nuns came into our room and she told us that Chris was going to be leaving the institution soon and then she left the room smiling. At that moment, I decided that I would run away, I just couldn't stick it any longer, but Daisy didn't want to go, so I decided to take Simon and another little boy and girl from the home with me. And the next morning, we left early, we should have been going to school, but I knew it was my only chance to get away before anyone realized we had gone. I had decided to head home back to daddy, and as we walked along the road, we all held hands and we headed up along the Waterford road and in the direction of daddy's village. I had decided that we would hitchhike, as daddy's house was a long way away, and I knew that by just walking it would have taken us a whole day to get there.

We walked and walked; and after a couple of hours, a car pulled up and a man gave us a lift part of the way and eventually we made it to daddy's house. We walked up along the cobbled path towards his house and I couldn't believe it; he was there and he was as shocked to see me as I was to see him, and he cuddled Simon and me. We went into the house and we sat down, then I began telling him all about the nuns and staff and what they had been doing to us over the years; but within a couple of hours, the police came knocking at the door and daddy hid us all in the kitchen. They had come to the house to tell daddy that we were missing, but as they entered the house, they realized that they had found us; and after they spoke to daddy, they took us all back to the home.

As soon as we got back, a member of the staff took me into the dining room and gave me a beating that I will never forget and I thought I was going to die. However, I was so used to the beatings that she had to hit me harder and harder so that she could get some kind of reaction from me and the satisfaction of seeing me twitch with pain. After the beating, she dragged me to my room and she left me lying on the floor. I was too upset to get up and I just lay there for hours, trying to think of ways that I could get them back. But it didn't matter as she had locked the door and I couldn't get out of the room. And I had to spend two weeks there, with all the windows and the door locked shut, and I had no company. The air in the room was hot and stale and for days I tried to open the window, but I couldn't as they had screwed wooden blocks to the window frame so that I could not open it and run away. And they kept the bedroom door locked shut from the outside and they only opened it to allow my brother and sister in at bedtime, so they could sleep; and then in the morning, after they went to school, the nuns would lock the door again and I would be all alone once more.

One day, while I was locked in the bedroom, I began to have pains in my belly and, as the pains got worse, I shouted for the staff to open the door and to help me. I banged on the bedroom door, but no one came, so I lay on my bed and I waited for the pain to go away, but it never did. And within a couple of hours of me lying down on my bed, I fell asleep; and when I woke up, I thought I had wet my bed, but as I looked down I realised that I had started to bleed from between my legs. The bed sheets were soaked with blood and I became frightened and scared, so I got up and I ran over to the bedroom door; again, I shouted for the staff, but still no one came. I sat back on my bed and I prayed to God, but nothing happened.

I sat there and I thought I was going to die, the blood kept dripping out of me and I used my clothes to soak it up, and I kept my legs closed together, hoping it would stop the bleeding. I screamed out loud, begging for someone to help me, but still no one came and I began to cry, as I didn't want to be alone when my life finished; but I was alone, so I curled up on the floor and I waited for my life to end. Hours passed and it was now evening and I was still alive, but my hands were covered in blood, I looked a mess and my clothes were covered in blood too. I looked up at the window and it was now dark outside, then I heard the noise of keys rattling as a nun came to the door to give me my dinner.

And as she opened the door and walked in, she dropped everything; all she could see was me standing in front of her covered in blood and she thought I had done something to myself. I stood looking up at her and then I told her that I was dying, and she almost fainted as I explained to her that I was bleeding from between my legs and that it wouldn't stop. She looked at me and then she said that it was nothing and that I was a stupid bloody girl and then she walked away.

I begged her to stay and help me, but she just walked away, locking the bedroom door behind her. And all I could do was listen through the door as she walked down the stairs. I picked the food up off the floor and ate what I could and then sat on my bed, not knowing what to do. I was still bleeding when one of the nuns came back and opened the door again, and as I looked up, Daisy came into the room and, as she looked over at me, I began to cry and all she could see was my blood-covered body and clothes. I told Daisy that I was bleeding and that I was going to die, but then she smiled at me and she told me all about periods. I had no idea what she was talking about, as no one had ever told me about periods, growing up, having sex or even about where babies came from, and most of it was all a big shock to me.

Daisy then left the bedroom and when she returned she handed me a sanitary pad, and she said that it was the only one that she had and that the staff and nuns would not give her any more for weeks. She said that I had to put it between my legs and, when it was all wet and dripping with blood, I had to keep using it again and again. 'That's disgusting', I said and I told her that I couldn't, but she said that the nuns and staff would get angry if we asked them for more pads, so I used the pad and it felt strange; and when it got all wet, I put it on the side to dry out and then I used it again. But after a couple of days, it fell apart, so Daisy had to go and steal one for me.

I couldn't believe what I had to do and I was so embarrassed about my periods that I hid them from the staff and nuns for almost a year, before finally telling them that I needed pads. But they already knew and they didn't care if I asked for a pad or not. I was too embarrassed at having to wash out the pads that I just couldn't do it any longer, and even then they only gave me one a month and I had to steal more if I needed them.

CHAPTER 9

Getting Them Back

Now the time had come for me to go to secondary school and the only school available to me was an all girls' school run by the nuns, but I didn't want to go as I hated school and everything to do with it. I hated the place, the people and even the lessons; no one had ever tried to educate me properly, and I was always behind in lessons and the nuns always made me sit at the back of the classroom like a dummy, ignored by everyone and out of the teacher's way. And now it was too late for me and I was not interested in school anymore; I still had to go to school, and once there I still had trouble sitting at the back of the classroom all day with nothing to do and it was driving me mad. Plus the nuns were getting fed up with me and they made it obvious, with them giving me dirty looks whenever our eyes would meet in the class.

The only two men allowed inside the school grounds was the maintenance man and the headmaster Mr Williams, and Mr Williams absolutely hated me and every single girl in St Josephs. Over the years, everyone had forgotten that I had parents and it seemed like everyone around me hated me and thought of me as an inconvenience to them, and no one ever had time for me. I had been put in the home and in my position because of my parents' inability to look after me and not because I was a bad person, but no one seemed to understand that, and they all blamed me for the position I was in. Mr Williams especially hated me, because I didn't care about anything or anyone anymore, and the fact that I had no respect for him or his school made my situation even worse.

Every morning when I arrived at the school, the nuns would make me pray. They would make me pray for forgiveness, for all the sins that I had committed against them, and they would tell me to stand up and pray, but I wouldn't; I would stay sitting in protest against all the praying they made me do over the years. I was sick of praying for myself and I was sick of praying for them, I had been praying for the last eight years and now I was sick of it. So I decided that the day had come and I was going to tell everyone what I thought of them, and I did. I told the nuns that I was not going to pray for them anymore and I told them that I hated them and their school, and their stupid way of life.

The nuns were shocked and furious with me and, from that day on, they would find any excuse, no matter how small, to send me to Mr Williams; and it was just so they could get their own back on me. And once I was alone in Mr Williams' office, he would shout at me, saying that I was an ungrateful, worthless little girl that didn't deserve anything, and he would make me write lines as a punishment, knowing full well that I was unable to read or write properly. And if the nuns told him that I had been a very bad girl, he would take me into his office and lock me in a broom cupboard for the rest of the day that was in the corner of the room.

I would have to stand in the small dark space and I would have to knock on the cupboard door if I wanted to go to the toilet; and if he didn't answer or open the cupboard door, I would have to stand and wait in the cupboard until home time. Then, just before he left his office to go home, he would unlock the door and let me out and I would have to run to the toilet before I wet myself. Almost every day the nuns would tell him that I was a bad girl and I just couldn't take it anymore.

So, one day at lunchtime and before they sent me to Mr Williams again, I decided that I had had enough, so I got my bike out of the bike shed. I was going to ride out of the school and home; but as I got my bike out of the shed, Mr Williams ran towards me, shouting at me as he got closer, 'Where do you think you're going, Lily?' And he shouted at me to put the bike back in the shed and to get back inside the school. I didn't reply to him and I kept walking with my bike, as if I hadn't heard him, and he shouted again, 'If you walk out of that gate, you're going to be expelled.' I smiled to myself. I was so happy to hear him say that, that I almost turned around and said thanks. But instead, I just kept walking out of the schoolyard, pushing my bike with me.

He was furious and he shouted at me again, 'Stop', but I didn't; I got on my bike and I began to peddle. He was in such a temper that he ran over to the car park and then he got into his car. I looked back at him and I began to peddle as fast as I could, as I knew he was going to come after me. I managed to get a head start on him and I rode along the road and through some red traffic lights, knowing that he couldn't follow me until the lights turned green.

Then I rode between two cars and they skidded to a halt, just missing each other and me as I cycled between them and out the other side, without them squashing me. The two drivers shouted at me and beeped their horns, but I just kept peddling. I knew Mr Williams was close behind me, but I never looked back, I just knew I had to get away from him as fast as possible. I rode up and over the pavement and I cut across the corner of the road, trying to get some distance between us and I could hear his car skidding as he turned the corner and began to gain ground on me.

So I rode through another set of red lights, peddling even faster and he had to stop for the traffic lights again. I carried on peddling and I could see the convent up ahead. I knew that if I just kept going, I could reach the gates before he could catch up with me and I did. I rode through the open gates and I headed for the front door, dropping my bike and running the last few yards towards the front door, screaming as loud as I could for the nuns to open the door. I never looked back, but I heard his car pull up and then him running up behind me. But as he got closer to me, the front door of the convent opened and I ran inside.

He was furious and he wanted to kill me, but one of the nuns stood in front of him and she politely told him to step away from the door. He went crazy and pushed his way past her and then he ran inside, chasing me through the hall and into the kitchen, then he ran around the kitchen table after me. I stopped at one side of the table and then I made horrible faces at him, sticking my tongue out at him and laughing up into his face from across the table, while the nun shouted at him, 'Mr Williams, you can't do that to a child. Get out now', she said.

Then I shouted to the nun, telling her that he was locking me in a broom cupboard at school and he was keeping me there all day every day. He looked over at me and he shouted at the nun that I was a horrible, nasty little girl and that I was now expelled from the school. She said, 'Yes well, good, that's fine and now get out of the house.' He was furious and he continued shouting and swearing at the nun, telling her that I was the devil's child and that he wanted to kill me. However, the nun shouted back at him and eventually he had to leave the convent, and I never went back to school again and the nuns gave up on me ever going back again.

Now that the nuns couldn't send me to school, I was constantly under their feet all day, and I was always hanging around the institution and Willows; and now that I was bigger and older, the nuns couldn't get away with hitting me as much as they used to. Plus I was now able to stand up to them and I was able to fight them back if they laid a hand on me; and if they shouted at me, I would stand in front of them and shout right back at them and they hated me for it.

I didn't want to stay at the house anymore and I began to venture out more and more each day, and I began to hang around with some of the children from the village and some of the bigger kids from the institution. But the nuns didn't know everything about what I was up to and, in the evenings, I would sneak out of my window to be with the other kids. The nuns would have me and all the other children in bed by 9 pm and the whole house locked up for the night by 10 pm. But once everything went quiet and the nuns had gone to bed, I would open my bedroom window, climb out onto a ledge and then close it behind me so that it wouldn't be noticed; then I would shimmy down the drainpipe, making sure I didn't disturb any of the pipe fittings on the way down, so that I could use the same escape root night after night.

Then, once on the ground, I would run around to Simon's window and wake him up by knocking on the glass. He would open the window and I would tell him to leave it open all night, so that when I returned later I could get back in, rather than me having to climb back up the drainpipe and then climb through my own window again. I did this for months, with Simon leaving his window open for me night after night.

But one night, when I returned and I tried to get back in, Simon's window was locked and no matter how much I rattled and knocked on the glass, he wouldn't open the window, he wouldn't even walk over to it. I looked through the glass and I could just about see him and the two other boys that slept in his room through the net curtains, and they were all hiding under their blankets. I couldn't understand why he never had the window open for me, because he always did, so in the end I had to climb up the drainpipe and over the roof, entering the house through an open skylight.

I climbed in and then I dropped down on to the floor; no one had heard me, so I crept downstairs to Simon's room, I opened his bedroom door and the room smelt of fags. I walked in, switched on the light and walked over to Simon, and I tried to pull the bed covers away from his face, but he held on to them tight, and so did the other two boys in the room. I tried again, while I asked him why he didn't open the window for me, but he never answered me. Then I got angry with him and I pulled at the blankets hard and pulled them away from his face and he began to cry. He then told me to go away and he shouted at me to leave him alone. 'What's a matter, Simon?' I said, as he held back his tears just long enough to tell me that three of the older boys who used to live in the home had come back during the night and climbed in through the open window.

He said they sat in the room and they made him and the two other small boys smoke fags with them, and then the older boys began hitting them and they all took turns in raping him and the two other boys, one at a time, while the two other big boys held them down. He said they had big kitchen knives with them and they held the knives against their throats while they raped them, one after the other. I was shocked and I could see that Simon and the two other boys were very upset and frightened, so I walked out of the room and I walked towards the staff's bedroom. I was getting ready to tell her about what had happened to all of them. But then I stopped. I knew that the staff would only say that we were all telling lies and making things up to get her in trouble, so I turned around and I went back to Simon and I comforted him until he fell to sleep. I stayed there all night, watching over him and the two other boys, making sure no one entered their room that night.

The next morning, Simon was very quiet and he pushed anyone who tried to talk to him away, and even I had trouble getting close to him; and getting a word out of him was almost impossible, he had become a withdrawn shell overnight. Simon was never the same person after that night; he became a very sad little boy and from then on he became very angry towards everyone and he would lose his temper quickly. He would slam and kick doors and shout at people, causing himself many problems with others around him and he would have terrible nightmares about what had happened to him. After that terrible night, I promised Simon that it would never happen to him again and I spent months sitting and sleeping on the floor outside his bedroom door, so that he could sleep in peace. And throughout the night, I would go into his bedroom and check the window, making sure it was still locked shut.

He was only ten and I knew that he was feeling very alone and ashamed about what had happened to him. Some nights, I would sit on the floor next to his bed and I would hold his little hand all night and occasionally I would get up to kiss him on his face or cuddle him like a mother would, until he fell to sleep. Some mornings, Simon would wake up and find me still holding his hand or asleep on the floor next to his bed, and he knew that I had been keeping him safe all night by watching over him and he liked it.

The staff knew that something was wrong with Simon, but they never knew what was bothering him; so whenever Simon lost his self-control and went mad with everyone around him, the only way the nuns knew how to cope with the problem was to hit him and punish him, and that is exactly what they did to him, day after day. Whenever he got angry with himself and caused problems, two of the nuns would gang up on him, with one nun holding him down while the other nun hit him in the head until he collapsed and fell silent to the floor. Then they would drag him into his bedroom and leave him there until he woke up again.

He never did tell the nuns what the boys had done to him, as he knew the nuns wouldn't care and they would push him away, saying that he was a liar. But one day, his anger and temper towards everyone got so bad, that while the staff were cooking a mincemeat stew for dinner, he went into the kitchen and slung the saucepan of stew onto the floor. That was it, the staff couldn't take any more of Simon's tantrums, so the next day they sent him away; they didn't give a shit about Simon or his problems and they sent him to Dublin for six months to a reform school for boys. And that was probably the worst thing they could have ever done to him; I was the only person he had, and he needed me even more than ever now, but he was all alone and faraway, with no one to turn to.

I was so upset with the nuns for sending Simon away that I

couldn't get it out of my mind, so I ran away and I headed toward Dublin to find Simon, but the nuns found out and they sent the police after me. And it didn't take the police long to catch up with me, and once they found me they took me back to the nuns; and once I was back in the house, I tried to explain about what had happened to Simon and why he was behaving the way he was, but they were not interested. They just didn't give a shit about his problems, all they wanted was for me to stop running away as it was causing them problems, and they were sick of having to explain to the police why I was running away all the time.

After that, the nuns tried to keep me locked inside my room and out of the way, but I protested and I starved myself for a whole week. However, they said that if I didn't start eating again, they would call the mental hospital and have me committed as a mad person for the rest of my life. I knew they were telling the truth and they would have me committed, as they had done it to other children before. So for a while, I did what they said and I did my best to behave myself, but I still told them that the only way I was going to eat properly again and not run away was if they got Simon back. But they said no, so I decided to play them at their own game and I behaved myself for a couple of weeks until they let me out again.

And straight away, I took the opportunity and I ran away. But the police found me again and they brought me back, and the nuns gave up on locking me away and I spent the next six months running away almost every week, until they eventually gave in and they brought Simon back to me. But it was too late. When he arrived home, I looked at him and he had changed; things had happened to him at the reform school that he would not even tell me about and it had changed him forever. His heart and spirit had been broken, he was an empty shell and his soul had gone forever, but I still loved him and I told him so every day. 'Simon, I love you and I always will.' But he just looked at me with empty eyes and I felt sad for him. He might just as well have been dead as his life was over, but I continued looking after him and I never gave up on him.

In the last few years of my stay at St Josephs, fewer and fewer young girls arrived at the house. Times were now changing and the church no longer had the iron fist hold on the local community as they used to have and even the police began to question the church's actions. In the old days, the church had more power than the police did, and no one ever questioned the church or their actions and the nuns and staff got away with murder; they answered to no one but God, and only God.

But now people were asking questions, and many of them had less and less respect for the church and their actions were becoming questionable. They were losing their grip on the power they once had and now only stupid and corrupt people stayed close to the church for its protection. Girls still came and went at the home, with the occasional girl sent to the home by her out-of-date family, who still had some kind of loyalty towards the church, rather than towards the authorities.

And as I got older, some of the nuns left the institution and they were never replaced. So now, there was only a handful of nuns and a few staff left running the house; and for us girls still living there, it was great. We began to get our own back on the nuns and staff; we caused them as much trouble as we physically could. The tables had now turned and, whenever the nuns attacked me, I attacked them back and I liked it. And if they shouted at me, I would shout right back at them and they were now scared of me. I was getting the convent, the nuns and the complete church system back for what they had all done to me over the last nine years, and I was retaliating against them all. I had never forgotten about all the beatings they had given me, or all the times they had locked me up in rooms and cupboards, and all the times they let people in and out of the institution sexually and mentally abuse me. So now, I was doing every bad thing that I possibly could, just to upset them. And I began to have a lot of fun causing trouble for them.

I remember one night, three of us girls from St Joseph's

decided to run away with some of the local boys and girls from the village for the night. There were about ten of us in total and we all met outside our school, we spent a couple of minutes talking and then we all walked off down the road and past an old pub that we all knew well. We had a shopping trolley with us that we used to carry all our stuff in and on the way past the pub; we tried to steal a keg of beer from the back yard. But we made too much noise and the owner of the pub heard us and he ran outside and chased us up the road, but we couldn't push the shopping trolley fast enough, so we had to leave the trolley and beer keg behind and run.

It was funny, but now we had lost everything we had, as everything was all in the shopping trolley and we could not go back for it; so we carried on, running up the road, and we headed into the countryside. We walked for miles, looking for a place to hide and sleep for the night, but we couldn't find anywhere safe. Then one of the local girls told us about an old caravan that her father had at the bottom of one of his fields, so we all headed towards the field and we had to walk back past the pub. It was quiet now and everyone had gone home for the night, so we continued on past the pub. And it was late and dark when we eventually arrived at the caravan, so we all went straight inside, with the girls down one end of the caravan and the boys went down to the other end. The caravan had partitions inside that we used to make separate bedrooms, one for the girls and one for the boys, with us all staying down our own ends; and after spending a few hours talking to each other, we all went to sleep.

We all behaved ourselves that night, but in the morning we were woken by the girl's father who owned the caravan. He had walked down to the caravan, looking for his daughter, and found us all sleeping in the caravan together. He went mad at us all, telling us to get up and get out of the caravan, but we just laughed at him, so he went off and he called the police; but before they arrived, he came back and took his daughter away with him so that she would not get in trouble.

The police soon arrived and they surrounded the caravan, and they all stood outside and looked in through the windows at us. We tried to hide by getting into the cupboards and under the folding beds, but they came in and arrested us all. I found the whole situation funny and I began to laugh at the police as they dragged me out of the caravan. And I shouted at them to let me go and to go away, because we had done nothing wrong. They said that we were all in trouble for staying out all night with the boys, then they put us into police cars and they drove us all to the police station.

Once there, they brought us into an interrogation room and they asked us what we had done all night while in the caravan. We told them that we had all just had fun talking, and then we all fell asleep, with the girls and boys at separate ends of the caravan. Then the door of the interrogation room opened and in walked the head nun from St Joseph's, and she had a member of the social services following close behind her. They both sat down and then she asked us question after question and the police officer kept quiet. And because she never got the answers she wanted, she said that all three of us girls from St Josephs would have to go to the hospital, because everyone thought we had all been raped by the boys. They said that we had to have an internal examination as they thought the boys had raped us during the night. I went mad, telling them that we had all slept at different ends of the caravan all night and that nothing had happened between us. Then the police said they would have the boys from the village arrested and they would charge them with rape if we refused to go to the hospital for the examination. We had no choice but to agree under protest; we didn't want to go to the hospital as nothing had happened, but we had to, so that the boys wouldn't get charged with raping us and put in prison.

When we arrived at the hospital, the police took us into a room and we all had to take our clothes off and lie on beds with our legs open wide. It was horrible, and there were lots of other people standing in the room looking at us, and I knew they all didn't need

151

to be there, but they were and they all stood watching the three of us, as we lay on the beds next to each other with our legs open wide, waiting for the doctor. We waited for what felt like hours, with everyone taking turns to walk past and look at us, and then a doctor came into the room and everyone in the room stood around as he examined us, by putting his hands up between our legs and giving us an internal examination with something that looked like a long ear bud.

Within seconds, it was all over, but everyone still kept looking at us and then the doctor told us that we could get up and we closed our legs and got off the tables. Then the nun began to speak, and she told the doctor that we had all spent the night in a caravan with a group of boys and that we had sex with the boys. But the doctor could see that we were all still virgins and he knew that nothing had happened between the boys and us, and he told the nun that everything was ok and that we could all go home.

She looked disappointed and she was furious with the doctor for not finding anything wrong with us. She shook her head in disappointment as she left the room and, as she walked away, all the other people in the room followed behind her. The doctor looked over at us and he smiled, then he told the nurse to help us all get dressed while he went outside to speak to the nun; and when he came back, he said that everything was going to be ok and that we could all go home.

We were so happy to be getting out of the hospital, but then the nun came back in with some of the people and they all quickly surrounded us and escorted us out of the hospital and into the back of waiting cars. They were stopping us from talking or mixing with other people on the way out of the hospital, and then they drove us home.

The next day, the nuns began telling everyone in the home that I had gone mad and that they needed to call a psychiatrist to come and see me; now they wanted to get rid of me and put me away forever. So they began to fabricate things up about my behaviour, just to get their own back on me for wasting their time and making them all look stupid in the hospital, and they did everything possible to get me put away. They even called doctors and psychiatrists to have me physically and mentally examined, and they were going to use all the reports they got to have me taken away and locked up forever.

However, halfway through their examination schedule, I ran away again; and this time, I hitchhiked all the way to a place called Tramore, where the nuns had a beach house next to the sea. I knew they were not using it at the time, so when I got there I broke a window and climbed inside and I had an old sleeping bag with me, so I made myself a home. I was going to stay there for as long as I could, but I still wanted Simon and the nuns to know that I was ok. So every day I would get up early and thumb a lift about fifty miles away from the house and then I would call the nuns by reversing a call from a phone box, letting them know that I was ok and still alive, then I would thumb a lift all the way back to the house. The nuns were furious with me on the phone, calling me names and telling me they were going to kill me when they got hold of me.

However, I still rang them every day for the next four days, until eventually the police found me and took me back to the nuns, and they did their best to have me put away for good. They even sent Simon away to another institution just to get at me, but it didn't work and they had to bring him back again as the other institution could not control him. I knew this was my last chance to keep Simon and me together, so I made a plan to run away with him and never come back.

However, the nuns never gave me a chance to escape again. They kept Simon away from me as much as possible and they concentrated on getting psychiatrists to commit me to a mad house; and after a couple of weeks, the reports flooded in. The nuns wanted everyone to think I was nuts, but it would have been much quicker if they had just bribed someone to take me away, but they were too tight with money to pay someone to do it. That's all they wanted, power and money.

REPORTS

Report 1

ST. XXXXXXX. RESIDENTIAL HOME
XXXXXXXXX ROAD
KILKENNY.

<u>Dear. Xxxxxxxx xxxxxxx</u>   Date.<u>xxxxxxxx83</u>

<u>REPORT ON LILY O'BRIEN. D O B. 4-1-197X</u>

Lily commenced secondary school in September, but as a result of her troublesome and disruptive behaviour, she was dismissed after six weeks.

Lily can be withdrawn at times. She seems to live for the next cigarette.

She is full of self-pity, easily offended, and sulky. Her use of abusive language is sex-orientated. Her dress sense is also sex-orientated, she is vain and figure conscious.

Since September, she has absconded on a few occasions overnight, and once for a period of four days. This would appear to be a cry for attention. She could not understand why people would be annoyed with her for doing same. When in the presence of Garda, she is aggressive and uncontrollable, tearing, biting, and kicking. She likes to believe she is untouchable in this situation.

Regarding her brother Simon (who is in care in St. XXXXX) she is warm towards him, and he is quite often her 'partner in crime'. Her sister Daisy is held at length. She is very unlike Lily, in that she is cool and calculating, and knows where her comforts are. Lily has no real friends as she has little respect for herself or anyone else. She feels very much rejected. In the past, there has been little or no contact with her family in England. At present, there is a renewed contact, but this can have an upsetting effect on her. She would like some contact with her father, but would not like the staff or any of the other children to see him. This would embarrass her.

When in good form, Lily can be very pleasant. She is gifted with her hands, and has made some beautiful patchwork items. Her cooking skills are very good, and she is particular about cleanliness as she cooks.

The resident manager.
Xxxxxxxxxxxxxxxxxxxxxxxxxxxx

Report 2

Xxxxx xxxxxxx health board.
Case conference report: Lily O'Brien. Xxxxxxxxxxxxxxxx
Date of Case conference report   7.1X.1983

A case conference was held today involving myself, Mr. Xxxxx, sister superior, and one of the care staff from St. XXXXXXX. Lily had been seen on 2Xth XXXXX 1983, which I suggested that she be psychologically assessed and have an E.E.G. xxxxx xxxxxxx psychologist saw her on 4.1X.83, with a finding of a full-scale I.Q. of 74, which places her in the borderline range, and she felt that she was in need of remedial work, as well as a therapeutic programme. The E.E.G. has been done, and the report is due, but is not yet received. Application has been made to facilitate her in Cork, but there is up to one month's waiting list including a brief visit by Lily. In the meantime, attempts will be made to try and engage Lily in a series of activates which will allow her to look forward to further developments, e.g. a visit to her father this week, horse riding at the weekend, and the possibility of a weekend with a staff member. At the moment, she is a bit withdrawn, sleeping in, and doing little beyond smoking. There is really no programme easily at hand to inject her into in the short-term; the same would apply to any consideration of Sarsfields court, which would be for a three-week assessment only. And there is little likelihood that she will be got in there quickly, and I would think that the recommendation would probably be much the same as is ordinarily planned for her. Generally, it is agreed that Lily is an acting out angry girl who behaves, rather than discusses or engaging in any kind of interception. My own estimate is that six months of a programme would be an absolute minimum, and would probably constitute the adjustment period before anything meaningful would go on with her. In answer to the specific question, I feel that she should be permitted some kind of contact with her brother and sister who should continue on in St. XXXXXXX. Finally, the results of the E.E.G. may have some real bearing on possible therapeutic interventions here. I trust that most points were raised.

Dr. X. XXXXX.

Consultant psychiatrist.

Report 3

Report from doctor xxxxx xxxxxxxxxxxx to social worker.   1983

Dear Mr. XXXXX,

Thank you for your detailed social report on Lily, which I received at St. Patrick's in time for seeing her on Thursday evening. I'll not restate the details of history, which are well known to you, but would like to add just a few items that came out in my conversation with her. She regards her earliest years in the family as the best in her life and, by her reminiscences, makes it sound very like the freedom of the open road with little discipline, but a strong family feeling. Further, she gave me a history of a significant head injury leading to hospitalisation. She placed this at about age three years, and she gives a history of lifelong headaches since then. Her most significant emotional attachments appear to be to her brother, Simon, and an older brother in England. For assessment she was interviewed in a sitting room/office and was noted to be casually dressed, not an unattractive young lady, but one who presented herself as older, worldly wise and hard. Initially, she reviewed some of her recent escapades in a rather defiant manner, showing the tattoo on her arm and making her dislike for the personnel at St XXXXX very apparent. Interestingly enough, she caught herself up on the verge of using various profanities without actually saying any. Having gotten this out of the way, she settled a bit and we were able to talk in more give-and-take fashion. She came to the point of acknowledging that there were some personnel that she did not get along with, but would always get more animated when talking about the trouble she has been in. Pursuing some of these events, it became apparent to me in her telling that when she loses her temper, she sometimes has no recollection of what went on thereafter. Her thought process is not bizarre, although it is coloured by her anger at not getting her way, that is, freedom to do what she wishes. She seems prepared to fight any restrictions, even the reasonable. She seems oriented. Her judgment is impaired, both historically and at the time of interview in that being a little less hostile might have served her cause a little better. She has little insight and projects most of her difficulties onto others, taking little responsibility for her own actions, believing them to be provoked by others. In short, she presents the sort of mental status that one would expect from a conduct-disordered child and she is best labelled as an un-socialised aggressive reaction. It is further my impression that she probably cannot be coped with in St XXXXX and I would make the recommendation that she be considered for a smaller hostel-like setting for pre-delinquents; the good shepherd in Cork may be such a facility. I am further concerned about her angry episodes coupled with a history of injury, headaches and suggestive amnesia and on sight made the recommendation that she be sent for an E.E.G. If it were positive, it just may be that medication might be a partial answer to her problem in controlling her aggressive outbursts. Finally, in view of the fact that it has been over four years since she was last psychologically assessed and this might be essential to any placement attempted, I would further recommend that she be reassessed in the near future. At the moment, I do not see her as a candidate for medication. The treatment of such children lies in the area of greater control, smaller setting, positive role model and a fairly stringent program.

Yours truly. Consultant psychiatrist. Xxxxxxx xxxxxxxx

Report 4

Report - Lily O'Brien. D.O.B. 4-1-1970. Today's date 26-1X-1983

Since arriving back in September, Lily's behaviour has constantly deteriorated. She started with what appeared to be good intentions with regard to school. This turned out to be 'the sooner we get started, the sooner we finished'. She is just putting in time in school, and the sooner she reaches sixteen, the better is her attitude. In school, the teachers find her quite troublesome and abusive at times. She constantly seeks attention and can be very cheeky, so much so that the other girls tell her she should not act as she does. To gain attention, she might start to say the prayer (at beginning of class), just as everyone has finished. Or answer out of turn, or answer after the question had been answered. The teachers she likes most are those she is most troublesome with. She seems to be aware that these teachers would like to do something to help her. The teachers who pay her no attention, but just get on with the business of teaching, are the ones she hates.

Signed key worker. Xxxxxxxx
House parent. Xxxxxxxx

However, all the reports had no effect, and the nuns' plan didn't work, as I knew how to play them all at their own game, and I did my very best to behave myself while I was being interviewed by all the doctors, and I never told the doctors as much as I really wanted to. I did my very best to hold back on the obscenities and eventually the nuns gave up, and all they could do was pray for me to quickly grow up and to get as far away from them as possible, and all I wanted was the same thing. God, they hated me and I hated them.

CHAPTER 10

Going Home

I was going to be old enough to leave the home soon, so I made the decision to go back home to London England, as I wanted to be with my mum, and I asked the nuns if I could send a letter to my sister who lived in London and they said yes. I couldn't send a letter to my mum, as she couldn't read. I was sending a begging letter from me to her, begging her to take Daisy, Simon and me into her house if we left the institution. And the other reason I sent the letter was because the nuns were at the point of splitting us all up, and I was afraid that I would never see Simon alive again.

In the letter, I pleaded with my sister to send a letter to the nuns if she agreed to take us, and I wrote to her once a week every week for months, hoping she would reply; but nothing, no letters, no phone calls, not a thing from anyone in my family. In my last desperate attempt, I wrote to my mother, telling her that I hated her for sending us away when we were small children and I said that I never wanted to see her again, but it didn't work and no one ever replied.

The penny finally dropped, no one wanted us, and I felt so sad and I did not know what to do next. We were abandoned, unwanted children. Finally, I approached the head nun of St Joseph's and a member of the social services, to see if they could do something for us and they said yes. They said they would send my mother an official letter on headed paper, asking her if she would take us in, as we were now at an age to be considered for release. God, it made us sound like prisoners and it was not far from the truth. The nun sent the letter off to our mother in London, explaining that her three children were now twelve, thirteen and fourteen years old and they were now ready to go home to her.

My mother received the letter and after getting someone to read it to her, she thought it might be a good way for her to get more money out of the government, London's Brent council and the social services. She thought she could get more child benefit and a raise in her unemployment benefit and income support if she brought us over, and then told the social services that we were staying with her. So she took the letter the nuns had sent her, she went to Brent social services with it and she asked them if they could help her and they said, 'Yes, of course we can'; they said that if we were all staying with her then they would arrange all the extra benefits for her. And because she was unable to read or write, she asked London's Brent social services to send a letter back to Ireland, and she asked them to arrange everything for her and they did. They sent letters to the head nun at the institution, and between all of them they made the arrangements with the courts for us to be released and sent to England, and all done without anyone ever stepping a foot inside a courtroom or speaking to us.

We never knew a thing about what was going on, until two days before we left the home when the nuns told us that we were all leaving together. God, we were so happy. I had always told Simon that I would never leave the home without him and now I was going to keep my promise to him. The nuns were happy we were leaving, so they gathered up all the children that were left in the home and they had us all stand together while they took a group photo of us. And we could tell that the nuns and staff could not wait to get rid of us; and for the rest of the day, the nuns walked around as if God himself had arrived.

The day came and at 6 am a social worker arrived at our house; the staff had already packed our bags and the nuns were all waiting downstairs for us, while a member of the staff got us ready. After almost ten years at the home, we were finally leaving and I had butterflies in my belly. I was so excited, but also afraid at the thought of what might happen to us when we walked outside. We slowly walked down the stairs and towards the front door and, as I got to the door, one of the nuns handed me a small single suitcase; after all those years, all I had was a single suitcase that was half-empty, I didn't even have enough belongings to fill it. I didn't even want the thing, but I took it, just so that I could get out of there as quickly as possible.

I looked at the nuns and I laughed at them as I walked past them and out the front door to freedom; and once outside, even the morning air smelt different. I know it was probably because it was six in the morning, but it didn't matter to me; it still smelt different and I liked it. I screamed as loud as I could and then Simon, Daisy and I got into a waiting car and, within a couple of seconds, the car drove off. I looked back through the car window and I could see all the nuns walking back into the house and not one of them bothered to turn around and wave goodbye to us; and I was so happy as they walked back into their prison.

On the way to the ferry, the social worker drove like a lunatic. He could not have gone much faster without causing an accident and we all slid from one side of the car to the other as he drove around the corners like a mad man. Then we all fell back into the seat as he sped up and headed towards the docks; he was driving like he had the devil in the back of the car, but it was only us and we all thought it was funny. God only knows what the nuns must have told him, because all he kept doing was to look at us through the rear view mirror and then mumble to himself something about the devil, God and late. And he clung on to the steering wheel as if his life depended on getting us to the docks and out of Ireland forever and he never once spoke to us.

It took a while to reach the docks; and when he finally pulled up, he swiftly opened the door and told us all to get out. The nuns had given us absolutely nothing, no money and no food or water, only the tickets for the ferry and the train back to London England, but we didn't care, we were so excited about getting on the ferry that we forgot all about everything else going on. We moved out of the way of the car and the driver got back in and then he drove off, leaving us standing in the middle of the dock road.

We didn't know what to do, so we walked up towards a big crowd of people that were standing around and I spoke to a man in a uniform who was a boarding officer. I showed him the tickets the nuns had given us and he allowed us to walk on to the ferry. Once on board, Simon and myself spent most of the journey playing tag, running around and causing a nuisance to all the other passengers; and after a while, the ferry staff asked us to calm down a bit and they kept an eye on us for the rest of the journey. Daisy just sat down for the whole journey, as all the things Simon and I got up to were embarrassing her.

When we arrived in England, we had to go through customs and it was all a bit too much for us; we got confused with the whole situation, and a couple of police officers noticed us. They walked over to us and they took us out of the queue and over to one side, then they helped us with our things until we got out of the departure area and into the exit hall, where we met our sister's husband Fred and one of our brothers, Chris. They had both travelled from London to pick us up and to take us back to our mother's house in London. I was so happy to see Chris, but I hardly recognised him as he had changed so much and grown up.

After we all said hi to each other, we headed towards the train station and we got on the next train to London. The journey was going to take over seven hours, so we all sat down and we talked for a while, then I told Chris and Fred that we had not eaten all day, so they both got up and they went and bought us a few bits to eat from the buffet car on the train. Then Fred came and sat down beside me, he took out some playing cards from his pocket and then, smiling at me, he asked me if I remembered him. I looked at him and I said no. We played cards together and he gave me a lot of attention playing tag and had, with him chasing me up and down the length of the train. I was having a lot of fun, but Chris just sat on the seat with a very serious face and he hardly moved an inch.

After a while, I sat back down again and Fred and I played snap with the cards again, then Fred went and got me a hot chocolate drink. I thought it was nice of him and I continued playing cards with him, while he moved closer to me and eventually he sat right next to me. He was very nice to me and I could not remember the last time anyone gave me as much attention as he gave me then. After a while, I got up and I headed to the toilets; but as I walked off, Fred got up too, and he followed me along the train, trying to play had with me as I walked through the carriages.

Then he ran in front of me and he began to run in and out of the toilets, opening and closing the toilet doors and just playing around, and as I got level with the toilet, he pushed the toilet door open and then he pushed me inside. He then ran into the toilet and forced his body up against mine, forcing himself between my legs; and before I had a chance to push him away, he stuck his tongue into my mouth. And with that, I just stood back and looked him straight in the face and suddenly it all came rushing back to me, and I instantly remembered who he was and what he had done to me many years before back in London, when I was a child.

The very second his hands touched me, everything started to rush back and I was shocked and I felt sick. I moved back away from him, thinking this is the same man that abused me. Oh my God, I could not believe it, I had only been out of the institution for a few hours and already someone was trying to touch me and sexually abuse me all over again. Words could not explain how shocked I felt and I had trouble speaking. I pushed him away from me, I opened the toilet door and I ran back down the train towards Chris, Daisy and Simon, and I sat down next to them. Chris looked at me with a very serious face and I could tell that something must have happened to him on the journey up to meet us.

My mind was racing and all I could do was think back to what Fred had done to me when I was a child, all those years ago back in London; it was the same person and he had tried to touch me again, here right now on the train. What the fuck's going on? I thought. Why me, what have I done to deserve this? I sat on the seat, held my head with both hands, pushed my head back against the back of the seat and I took a deep breath; and I would not move off the seat and neither would Chris. The dirty bastard must have tried to do something to Chris on the train, I thought to myself, and for the rest of the journey I didn't move an inch.

I never once got off the seat and all I could think about was what he had done to me all that time ago when I was a little girl. It had all come back to me, every last thing that he had done to me. Straight away, I knew I did not want to go back to England and all I wanted was to go home back to Ireland and back to Willows. I felt sick and my belly felt like someone had just punched me hard into it. I had no one to help me, no one to turn to and all I wanted was to go home, but I couldn't. I felt like I wanted to pull all of my hair out of my head with frustration. And all Fred did was sit opposite me and look at me with a dirty smile on his face.

When the train arrived at Paddington station, my head was still hurting and it felt like it was going to burst, my mind was racing through all the things that had happened to me when I was just a baby. And as I got off the train and I began to walk along the platform, my head began to spin, I had to stop, and then I vomited. I stood still for a moment and everyone stopped and looked at me. I lifted my head and I told everyone that it was the lack of food on the train that had caused me to be sick and that I would be ok in a moment.

But all I could do was think about what was going to happen to me if I went back to my mum's house with Fred. I wiped the sick from my mouth with the back of my hand and, as we walked out of the train station, Fred said that we were going to get a cab to mum's house, as it would be quicker than taking the underground train. We all said ok and as we got into the cab, Fred sat next to me and I almost screamed; but instead I just froze, and I could feel myself turning pale at the shock of him rubbing his body against mine as he sat down next to me. Him sitting next to me was the last thing on earth that I wanted and all he did was go on about me coming over and staying with him and Tracy at their house. I said nothing and I never once looked at him; all I wanted was to get out of the cab and as far away from him as possible.

When we arrived at mum's house, we all got out of the cab and walked towards the house, not knowing what to expect. The door opened, and as I walked through the front door and into the living room, all my other brothers and sister were standing in the room waiting for us. And I could see Jim, my step dad, and his two children, my step brothers that my mother had given birth to while we were in Ireland, all standing in the middle of the room, waiting to greet us.

Then within an instant, everything that Jim had done to me came flooding back. I recognised him straight away and my heart almost exploded with the shock of having to face him again. My mind was racing and I was thinking through all the things that Jim had done to me when I lived with him and mum; and within a second, I must have gone through everything that happened to me a thousand times, everything flashed inside my head at the speed of light. And within that single moment, I had the sensation of my head being pushed under the water and the choking feeling that I felt as I swallowed water from the cold bath. Even the taste of the mustard that Jim had forced into my mouth all those years ago came rushing back to me and I felt sick.

I looked around for a place to sit down and in the corner of the room was a wooden stool. I walked over to it and sat myself down and looked over at Fred and Jim. Then my hands began to shake and I could feel myself turning pale again; cold sweat ran down my face onto my lap, and I felt like I was going to faint. I had completely forgotten all about everything that the both of them had done to me, but now I couldn't stop thinking about what they had done to me over ten years ago; I was right back where it all started in London, and now I was sitting opposite the same people who had abused me back then. And now they were both standing in front of me, telling me how happy they were for me to be back with them and how they had all missed me so much. I felt sick, I felt like I wanted to die, and I wished I had been back in Ireland with the nuns.

Then my mother came into the room and she gave me a big hug, whilst at the same time handing me a door key and whispering to me to lock my bedroom door when I go to bed later. 'What?' I said. I looked at her in disbelief at what she had just said to me and I closed my hand tightly around the key, before anyone noticed what she had just given me. I wanted to laugh out loud with the shock of what she had just said to me, but I just stayed silent. And I thought to myself, 'This can't be real, can it? Can this really be happening to me all over again?' She then let go of my hand and walked away, while smiling over in the direction of Jim. I quickly put the key into my pocket and then I walked around the house, looking at everything, just to stay out of everyone's way.

Nothing had changed, the situation I was in was like as if I had stepped back in time and I was looking at myself in the past. I felt like I was being abused all over again, and I was. Just the look on Fred and Jim's faces was enough to hurt me and they both knew it. It was getting late now, so everyone settled down for the night; I said goodnight to everyone and went upstairs to my bedroom, making sure that I locked the bedroom door behind me. Still feeling sick and wishing I were back at the institution in Ireland, I got into the bed and wished it had all been a dream and wished I had been dead. I still had all my clothes on and I wasn't going to take them off for no one. I thought to myself that in the morning I will get up and head back to Ireland, before anyone could stop me leaving, and eventually I fell to sleep, still holding the door key tightly in my hand.

However, when I woke up in the morning and even before opening my eyes, I could smell a stench of damp, stale air in the room and I knew that I was still in hell. I opened my eyes and I looked around the room, then I got up, walked towards the bedroom door and listened. The house was very quiet, so I walked closer and unlocked the door, hoping that I would be on my own; but as I walked out of the room and down the stairs, I could see mum standing in the kitchen, and she was cooking something.

I continued down the rest of the stairs and, as I walked into the kitchen, I could see that she had three pig's feet sticking out of a pot and the whole room stunk of cabbage. 'I'm cooking you a pig's trotter for your dinner,' she said, looking excited as she shook the pot from side to side and then dug at one of the pig's feet with a huge fork. I looked at her and I told her that I was not going to unpack my suitcase, and that I was going back to Ireland right now. But she just kept prodding at the pig's feet and she said that she wanted me to stay for a while as it would soon be Christmas, and she said that we would all have a great time being together as a family for the holidays. I couldn't stop looking at the pig's feet sticking out of the pot and, for some strange reason, I felt like I wanted to stay for Christmas; so I agreed and I told her that I would only stay until Christmas had finished and then I was going right back to Ireland. She said ok, but then she told me that I had no return ticket, so I would have to stay with her forever, unless I went to Brent council's social workers and ask them for a ticket back to Ireland. She seemed happy for me that I wanted to go back to Ireland, and she even told me where to find the social workers and how to get the tickets out of them.

So I put on my coat and I headed off, following her instructions; and after a couple of hours of waiting around the council offices, a social worker agreed to see me and because of my age he agreed to contact my social workers back in Ireland for me. And after an hour, both social workers agreed to supply me with the tickets to go back to Ireland, but only on the condition that all three of us who had come over to England went back to Ireland together.

I agreed and headed straight back home to tell Simon and Daisy, but Daisy said that she didn't want to go back to Ireland; she said that she was happy in England and she wanted to stay forever. But really, I knew that she was being pressurised by our older sisters to stay in England; that is why she said no to me, and that's the real reason why she wanted to stay in England. I told her that I thought we were only in England for a two-week holiday and not to stay forever, but she knew that I was lying, and that I knew we had to stay for good. Plus she said that she wanted to stay as she was having fun. I hated her for saying that and I went back to the council office, and I told the social worker that Daisy didn't want to go back to Ireland, but I still did. But he told me that we could only go back together or not at all, and his decision was final.

I headed home again and I gave up trying for now; and for the next few days, I just walked around the streets feeling sorry for myself, wishing that I were back home in Willows, safe in my bedroom. Nobody in London was bothered if I was around or not and I felt lonely because over here everyone just walked past me as if I was invisible.

Then one evening, while I was in the living room watching TV, Jim came in from the pub and he was drunk. He walked straight past me and went into the kitchen, and then he came back out and asked me to make him an egg on toast. I had never made egg on toast before, but it sounded like fun and I had seen the nuns back in Willows make it before; so I put water and then an egg into a saucepan, then I put it on the stove and I lit the gas. But as soon as the water started to boil, I took the saucepan off the stove, put the egg into an eggcup and gave it to Jim, but I had forgotten all about the toast. He grunted thanks at me and then he broke the top off the egg, but the egg was still like water and it splattered out of the eggcup and onto his clothes. He went mad and shouted at me, calling me all kinds of names and then he said that I was useless and no good to anyone.

I ran back into the living room, I hid behind the sofa, and I waited for a while until he had calmed down; then I got up and I sat back down. He then said to make him a cup of tea, so I got up and I went back into the kitchen, but I used the water straight out of the kettle without boiling it and it was only warm and I only dipped the teabag into the cup for about five seconds, so the tea looked like milky water. I had never made tea before and again he went mad when I handed it to him, calling me names and shouting at me like I was nothing; then he got up and chased me out of the living room and he shouted at me again. But this time, he told me to go away and to never come back, so I went up to my bedroom, locked the bedroom door and went to bed, hating all my family and everything about my life.

The next morning, I was woken by my bed shaking and I couldn't work out what was going on; then suddenly and even before I had a chance to open my eyes, I felt a hand move under my bedcovers and someone touched the top of my right leg and then they moved their hand over my belly. Quickly, I opened my eyes and it was Jim, he was kneeling down next to my bed and he was touching me; and even though he knew that I had woken up, he continued to move his hand down my belly and into the top of my knickers. I jumped up and, as I turned around, he was still kneeling next to my bed and he was wanking himself off. I shouted at him to stop and, without saying a word, he stood up, walked out of my room, and went down the stairs and into the kitchen; then he sat down at the table next to my mother.

I got up and followed him down the stairs and into the kitchen; I looked at him sitting in his chair as if nothing was wrong, then I stood next to my mother and I said to him, 'Jim, could you please keep your dirty perverted hands off of me please? You're a disgusting filthy pig.' Then I told my mother that he had come into my room and I had caught him kneeling down beside my bed, and he was rubbing his hands all over me and he also put his hand into my knickers and touched me between my legs while he had a wank.

But to my shock, she just smiled at me and she totally dismissed what I had said to her, as if I was telling her a joke, and Jim just laughed at me as mum took his side and told me to go away and to stop being stupid. I shouted at her and then I asked her how he got into my room as I had locked my bedroom door from the inside; but all she could do was smile and shrug her shoulders at me, while she ate a slice of toast. Shivers went down my spine and I felt like I wanted to cry. I was so upset that I just turned around and left the room, then I picked up my coat and I left the house without saying another word to them both.

My belly was empty and I was hungry, but I didn't want to stay in the house any longer. So I walked along the street and after a while I found myself walking towards my sister Tracy's house, and all the time I was thinking about how bad things were and I was wondering if everybody in the world was as bad as Jim, Fred and my mum. Then as I walked along the pavement, I heard someone shout my name from a distance; and as I turned around, I could see that it was Simon and he was running as fast as he could to catch up with me. I had forgotten all about him, I thought he was still asleep at mum's house; but as he caught up with me, he said that he had heard everything that I had said to mum and he said that he wanted to spend the day with me. 'Ok,' I said, 'but first I need to find a local doctor's surgery, as I have a bad pain in my head that won't go away,' and then we both went off looking for a doctor's surgery.

But it wasn't long before we found ourselves playing around in Queens Park underground station. We had never been in an underground station on our own before, so we decided to have a bit of fun and we went down the escalator and then we got on an underground train. We never intended to go far and the train was very shaky; so after only four stops, we decided to get off and head back, but when we looked around we found ourselves back in Paddington train station and we knew where we were. So we decided to explore the station, and after a while, we found the biggest set of escalators that we had ever seen and we went up and down them for about two hours, but then we became bored with them. So we thought it would be fun to slide down the metal panels that went down the middle of the escalators, from the top all the way down to the bottom.

I was so excited that I couldn't wait to slide down them and we both scrambled and pushed at each other as we climbed on to the top of the escalator casings. And when we reached the top, we both laughed and we shouted at everyone to get out of the way, as we began sliding down the stainless steel panels. Simon went first and I grabbed hold of his jumper, and as we slid down I began to spin out of control, and it was great, I had never felt anything like it before.

Then we began to go faster and faster and we realised that we couldn't stop. I screamed with excitement as I loved every second of it; but as we hit the last panel, I flew up into the air and two workers just managed to catch me by my legs as I flew through the air, and they just managed to break my fall before I hit the floor. Then as they put me down, they asked me if I was ok, and I just laughed at them as I walked off. I could see Simon, he was lying on the floor and he was laughing to himself, and then he asked me if I wanted to do it again and I said yes. So we just turned around and ran up to the top of the escalator and we did it all over again; we spent the next few hours using the escalator panels as a slide, and by the time we left the underground station we were as black as coal from the dirt in the station.

We headed back towards mum's, but I said that I was not going in; and as I walked away, I told Simon that I would be back for him in the morning, and then I went off looking for a doctor again and I soon found one. I went inside and, after talking to the receptionist, I managed to get an appointment for the next morning to see the doctor, so I left the doctor's and I walked off towards Tracy's house. As I walked up towards the front door, I could see that someone was peaking through the living room curtains at me. I knocked on the door and, within a second, Fred opened the door and said 'Hi'. I looked up at him, but I couldn't smile at him and I didn't even want to look him in the face, but I had to and I asked him if my sister was in and he said yes. I walked in past him, I went through into the kitchen, and she was standing next to the sink washing some vegetables. I didn't want to tell her about what had happened earlier at mum's house, so I just said hi, and we spent the rest of the day talking and cleaning around the house.

But all I could really do was think about what had happened to me earlier at mum's house and I knew I did not want to go back to mum's ever again. When evening came, I made a couple of excuses so I could hang around and I kept making excuses until it got too late for me to head back to mum's. And then Tracy asked me if I would like to stay for the night and I said yes, thanks, and we spent the rest of the evening watching TV; then Tracy said that I could sleep on the couch and then Fred and her went off to bed.

But I couldn't sleep and I felt uncomfortable on the couch, so I walked up the stairs and went to the toilet; but as I came out of the toilet, Fred was standing in the hall waiting for me. And within a second, he thrust both of his arms out and grabbed me by my breasts; and within an instant, I thought to myself, 'Oh my God, I've got nowhere to go, to get away from him,' and then I thought to myself that everyone around me was a pervert. I had left my mother's house because of one pervert and now I am here with another one standing in front of me.

I pushed him away as hard as I could and then I ran down the stairs and out of the house and I headed back towards mum's house, hoping that everyone would be asleep by the time I got back; and they were, so I went straight up to my bedroom and I locked my door. Then I checked the window, making sure that it opened just in case I had to use it to escape from Jim; then I put a chair up against the bedroom door, so I would hear Jim as he pushed the door against the chair as he tried to get in. But nothing happened that night and the next morning, as I walked downstairs and into the kitchen, my mum said that some social workers were coming around to visit us, and they were going to give her some money for three new beds and a TV for us kids.

I looked at her and I said that we have beds and a TV, but she said that we were going to take the old ones out of the house and hide them in the garden. That way, when the people arrive, they would see that we had none and then they would have to give her the money for new ones. Then she and Jim went about hiding everything out of sight and I just stood and watched them while they ran around. I shook my head from side to side in disbelief at what was going on and all they could do was laugh and talk about what they were going to do with the money when they would get it.

Then as soon as they had finished hiding the beds and the TV, the social workers arrived and after walking around the house, they agreed that mum needed beds and they gave her £500 cash; and with that, she thanked them and she almost pushed them out of the door. Then once they had gone, she gave Jim £200 to keep him happy and he went out the door and off down to the pub to spend the money on drinks, and then mum spent the rest of the money on Christmas presents for the two children that she had with Jim, my step brothers.

And the only reason she got the money in the first place was because of her lie that she needed to buy beds for us children who had just come over from Ireland. I could not take any more of it, she made me sick; so I went outside, looked around and found Simon sitting on the wall outside the house. After a couple of minutes, we both went off for a walk along the street and then I went off to my appointment at the doctor's. As soon as I walked into the doctor's office, I told the doctor that I had just come over from Ireland and that I needed some tablets for my head as I couldn't cope with all the pressures around me, and to my amazement he said ok and he gave me a prescription for some pills. And that was it, it was that easy to get medication.

And once I had taken some of the pills, my mind seemed to relax, things felt better and I felt more relaxed. Then I knew that I had to have the pills forever, or I wouldn't be able to cope with my family and all their problems. I hated it at mum's house and I couldn't take living there any longer, as I could no longer take Jim's constant pestering and sexual advances towards me. It had now become so bad that whenever he walked past me he would push me up against a wall and whisper into my ear that he would leave me alone and stop bothering me if I had sex with him, just once. Just the look of his dirty old face was enough to make me feel sick; and each time he approached me, I would tell him to fuck off and then I would get out of his way before he tried to touch me.

So I decided to try Tracy's house again. But it wasn't any better there either. I stayed at Tracy's for a few nights, but every time Tracy wasn't looking, Fred would try to grab or poke at me, trying his very best to touch me up. He would pull at my clothes or walk in on me while I was in the toilet. I just couldn't get any peace from him. So I decided to go and live with one of my other sisters, Karen; she was only eighteen years old, but already she had a two-week-old baby girl, and she lived on the 12th floor of a tower block, not far from my mum's house. And it was handy for me to stay close to my brother Simon and my sister Daisy.

At first, everything was fine and Karen gave me the freedom of her flat; and for a while, I was happy. During the day, I used to give Karen a hand looking after her baby and it kept me occupied, but whenever anyone else came around to the flat, we would all end up arguing about who was going to look after the new baby. And it would always end up with Daisy, Simon and me, all sitting in a row and taking turns at looking after her. But then Jim began to come around to Karen's flat looking for me, he would pound on the front door of her flat, demanding that I went back home with him. But Karen never let him in and I always hid from him until he gave up knocking and went away; and because he could not get at me, he began to turn his attention onto my brother Simon. But Simon was not having any of it. So, he also left mum's house and he went to live with one of our older brothers, Kevin. Simon was only twelve and he needed a home, and Kevin was able to give him that home.

After a while, things began to get a bit difficult for me at Karen's, as she now had too many people coming and going every day; and because she had very little money to live on, looking after me was beginning to cause arguments between her and her partner. So I had no choice, I moved out and I went back to mum's; but I hated being at mum's, I never went to school and she never fed me. And I hated her for allowing Jim to touch me all the time. Even after me telling mum about him, she did nothing to stop him, and he never gave up; and almost every morning, when mum took my stepbrothers to school, Jim would come into my bedroom and try to touch me.

Sometimes I would be awake and waiting for him to come up the stairs, and as he entered my bedroom, I would get up and call him a dirty pervert as I ran past him and out of the house. But on other days, I would still be asleep when he entered my room and I would be woken by him putting his dirty hands down the front of my knickers and from him shaking my bed because of him wanking beside it. I would sit up in my bed, I would call him all sorts of things and then I would get up and leave the house for a few hours until he went to work; then I would go back to the house, go back to bed and try to get some sleep.

By now, I was sick of everything and I had had enough of Jim again. And I could not go to Tracy's house because of Fred constantly touching me, so I decided to make myself a home in some bicycle sheds that were at the bottom of the building that Karen lived in. Karen had one of the sheds to keep some old junk in and she hardly ever used it, so she gave the keys to me and she said, 'Do what you like with it', and I did. The shed had a huge open space at the top of it that ran along the whole length of all the sheds and the space joined them all together. The space was for ventilation and it had chicken wire running across the front of it; and when I got up inside it, I was able to see through the wire and watch as people walked by the sheds. It looked a bit like a huge rabbit hutch that was ten feet above the ground and it was all mine.

But I had nothing to put into my new home, so Karen and I went and stole a few scaffold boards from a builder's yard and we laid the boards across the top of the shed's walls, and I was able to cover the whole area with the boards and make a floor for myself. I even put some old carpet down on top of the boards, to stop stuff falling through the gaps between them and so that my knees wouldn't hurt so much from crawling around on them.

At first, it felt like fun, a bit like making a camp; but after a couple of weeks, the cold evenings began to creep in and Karen went back upstairs to her warm flat and she left me all alone. I began to feel nervous and I wanted to go with her. But I knew I had to stick it out, as nobody wanted me around; so in the evenings, I would climb up onto the carpet, curl up into a ball and try to sleep. But it was the middle of winter now and it was freezing cold, and I started to shake as I was freezing; so I got up and I swallowed a few pills that the doctor had given me. Hoping they would help me to sleep, as my only other option was to sleep in with the rubbish bins in the shoot room. And after a while, the pills did nothing for me, so I tried sleeping in the bin room; but rats were running around the floor, the room smelt, and every time someone threw rubbish down the shoot from the floors above, I could hear the rubbish get louder as it came flying toward me and it was horrible. Then when the rubbish crashed into the bins, it would send dust up into the air and I would have to hold my breath for a while, until all the dirt settled again.

It was dirty, and I just couldn't cope with it, so I left the bin room and I spent the rest of the night sleeping in the corner of one of the lifts, as it went up and down the building all night. In the morning, the lift got busy as people went to work, so I got out on Karen's floor and I went and had some breakfast with her; then we both went out for the day and, as we walked around the streets, we hunted around for things to put into my shed-home. We found a mattress in a skip, and an old chest of drawers that someone had put outside the rubbish room; and later that day, Karen gave me some blankets and that was it. I had everything that I needed, and I was happy again.

As I sat looking at all the things I had, Simon came around and we spent the rest of the day playing chase in the lifts. Simon would be in one lift and I would be in the other, and we spent the whole time going up and down the building, trying to catch each other as we stopped the lifts on different floors. We had never seen lifts until we came to London and they fascinated us; at first, we couldn't understand how each time the lifts stopped and the doors opened we were on a different floor. And the people who lived in the building could not help but find us amusing, but we got used to all the people looking at us and we just carried on as if it was a fairground ride.

I spent the next twelve months living above the sheds on my own; and during that time, I was my own boss, I did my very best to stay away from my mother's house, so that Jim couldn't touch me, and I also stayed away from Tracy's, so that Fred couldn't put his dirty hands on me too. However, I began to get a bit out of control and I started smoking cigarettes and then came the drugs. At first, I smoked weed, but then some older people got me to take cocaine. I tried to keep a distance from most of the drugs and I stopped using cocaine soon after I first took some. But after a while, I found myself addicted to sniffing glue and I was always getting as high as I could, by swallowing handfuls of painkillers that my doctor had prescribed for me. They were very strong painkillers that he had given me, and my addictions got so bad that most days I would openly walk around the streets out of my head.

I also got addicted to the glue sniffing that I did and, during the day, I would walk around with a bag of glue literally stuck to my face; and most days, I would end up at Saint Mary's hospital, Paddington, choking and unable to breathe because of the glue. At the time, I thought it was funny and I used to walk into the hospital with all my clothes stuck together and my face covered in glue, and I would tell the doctors that I was suffering from an asthma attack. But I would still have the tube of glue I used, stuck to my pocket and I would be laughing as they took care of me and used chemicals to un-stick my clothes.

I was only fifteen and I was out of control, but eventually the hospital staff got so fed up with me doing the same thing day after day that they eventually called the police to me. And after a bit of help from all of them, I was able to stop what I was doing and I eventually sorted myself out. After the hospital got the police involved, the police realised that I had no one to look after me, and they found out about me living all on my own above the sheds under my sister's block. But instead of them moving me on and pushing me onto the streets, or forcing me to go back home to my mum's to be abused again, they decided that the best thing for me was for them to allow me to keep sleeping above the sheds, and to keep an eye on me. And every evening, the police would walk past the sheds to make sure I was ok and, as they walked past, they would just smile up at me as I looked down at them through the chicken wire; and then they would walk away, leaving me alone again.

After a few months, Simon said that he wanted to stay above the sheds with me; he said that he no longer wanted to stay with our older brother Kevin at his house, as it was no fun anymore. I could tell that something was up with him, as lately he had become a little withdrawn and he was beginning to look unhappy. He was only thirteen years old and he was my baby brother and I loved him, so I said yes and we both went off to Kevin's, to get his clothes. When we got there, Kevin wasn't in and, within a couple of minutes, Simon ran in, grabbed his stuff and we left the house and headed back to my place.

When we got back, we settled down for the night; but after a couple of hours, Kevin turned up and he was looking for Simon. Kevin looked up at us and he told Simon that he had to go back with him and that he wasn't allowed to stay above the sheds with me. I looked at Simon and I told him that he didn't have to go back with him, so he said, 'No, I'm not going.' Kevin went mad, he began shouting at both of us, calling us ungrateful little bastards, and then he walked away. Now I knew that something was definitely up with the both of them, but I left it at that and we both fell asleep.

The next morning, Simon became very aggressive towards me and I knew that something had changed him. For the first few months, since we came to London, he had been happy; he thought it was great having bigger brothers to hang around with, he liked to play fight with them, and being around everyone made him feel wanted. But now something had changed him again and he had become his old unhappy self again; he was acting just as he did after he was abused back in Ireland. I said nothing, but I watched him as he became angry towards everyone again, and I noticed that Kevin was always trying to hang around with him. He would play with him, acting like a child, and every day he would give him handfuls of sweets and lots of attention; but as time went on, Simon only got worse.

Then one day, as Simon, Kevin and I were playing in the rain, Simon slipped and I slipped too and we both fell to the ground; then as Simon got up, he stood over me and he hit me as hard as he could into my back. I was shocked at what he had just done to me and I looked up at him, then Kevin grabbed Simon around this neck, threw him to the ground and then he began to beat Simon. I looked at them both, but I could not understand what was going on; then they broke into a huge fight, so I got up and rushed over towards them, and I screamed at them both to stop. Kevin was beating up his own little brother and Simon was begging him to stop; he was shouting, 'Please, Kevin. Please don't hit me', and I could see the fear on Simon's face. I could see that Simon was very afraid of Kevin and, at that moment, I knew something very bad was wrong between the two of them.

Then they stopped and I said, 'Come on, Simon' and we both walked away, leaving Kevin still standing in the street with a look of murder on his face. We walked up the road, we went up to Karen's flat and I told Simon to take his top off, so that Karen and I could see if he had any cuts on his body. However, as he lifted up his top, we could both see that he had hand and finger marks all over his arms and neck that had come out in bruising all over him and it looked very bad. We told Simon that he looked ok and Karen told him that she wanted to take photos of his back so that he could see the marks that Kevin had caused him. He said ok, she took photos of the marks and we left it at that until Simon left, and then Karen took the film down to the chemist and she had it developed within an hour.

When we got the photos back, Karen and I studied them and we could see that Simon had grab marks all over him that did not come from the fight he had earlier. That evening, when Simon came back to the shed, I asked him about all the marks over his body and he said that he had got them while play-fighting with the boys. Then he said that he had to go back and stay at Kevin's house as Kevin said that if he did not come back, then he would have nowhere else to live when I give up the shed. I said that I was never going to give the shed up, but Simon still left and he went back to Kevin.

A few days later, Kevin came to the shed without Simon. He said that he had been drinking heavily since the day of the fight, and that he needed to tell me something, as he was feeling suicidal and he wanted to kill himself by jumping into the Grand Union Canal. I looked down at him, then he climbed up into the sheds and he confessed to me that he had been abusing Simon and having sex with him since the day he came over to London. He said that he had been getting Simon drunk, and he had been dropping sleeping pills into his drinks, then molesting him and having sex with him while he was unconscious.

I was shocked and I felt sick and weak looking at him. He even tried to put the blame on to Simon, saying that he wanted it to happen. But I knew it was not true and I knew that he had taken advantage of his baby brother. Simon was only thirteen years old and Kevin was almost thirty. I do not know how a grown man could do such a thing to a child, let alone his own brother, but he did and now he was feeling guilty about what he had done to Simon and he was asking me for my forgiveness.

I was so disgusted with Kevin that I got up and I walked away from him; I didn't give a shit about his feelings and I wasn't interested in his excuses. As far as I was concerned, he should have committed suicide right there and then in front of me, and I would have been happy to help him do it. I felt so angry that I wanted to go back and kill him myself; but now that I knew what was wrong with Simon, I knew that I had to do something to help him. But what could I do, as I had nothing. I didn't want Simon to know that I knew about what Kevin had done to him, so the best I could do for Simon was to be there if and when he needed me, and I spent all of my time following him around the streets and trying to keep him safe and out of Kevin's hands. But Simon couldn't cope with all the pressures he had and he began to drink alcohol and he took all kinds of drugs to help him forget about everything, and after a while he began to look a mess. I did what I could for him and somehow he just managed to keep himself together.

Then a couple of months after Kevin told me about the abuse, Simon's best friend, Tim, came over from Ireland. And it just so happened that Tim and I used to have a soft spot for each other back in Ireland, so I was also happy to see him. He was the same age as me, fifteen, and he had no place to stay, so I said that he could stay with me above the sheds if he wanted to and he said yes. I was so happy and we spent the next few months all hanging around together; and for a while, it seemed to make Simon happy having his best friend with him again. But every night, Simon still had to go back home to Kevin's house and he hated it.

After a couple of months, Tim and I began to spend most of the day with each other and, after a while, we began to have feelings for each other. Not long after my sixteenth birthday, I became pregnant by Tim and I was so happy and so was Tim. We still slept above the sheds and I even stuck a few family photos of my brother and Tim on the walls, to make the place look more like home. But it was freezing in the sheds and I knew we couldn't stay there forever; plus, for some reason, Tim began taking little digs at me and after a while the digs became thumps into my arms and legs and I didn't like it.

So, after a few more months above the sheds, I decided that it was best for me to go back to mum's house. Not for myself, but for my baby's sake, as I thought that Tim might not hit me if some adults were around. And after talking to mum, she agreed to let Tim stay with me at her house. So we went back to the shed and we packed what little belongings we had up and we moved in with mum. At first, mum seemed to be happy for us and she gave us our own room with a double bed in it; and for a while, things looked good for the both of us.

Then one day, Jim said that he had a job for Tim if he wanted it; he said that it was working as a labourer building roads; and straightaway Tim took the job. At first, Tim found the work hard. But when he got his first pay cheque, we were both very happy and it felt great having some money to spend on baby clothes. And now the bump in my belly was getting bigger and already I loved my baby, but Tim seemed to be more interested in going out after work and drinking with the boys rather than coming back home to me.

And each time Tim went out with Jim and the boys, he would come back even drunker than the time before and I began to hate him for what he was doing. I would sit up all night, waiting for him to come home and to give me some attention, but all he could do when he finally came home was stagger into the living room and collapse on the sofa. Every night, Tim was so drunk that he had no idea what he was doing, and Jim seemed to love it because he had Tim all to himself, and Tim was now his best friend and his new drinking partner.

Soon Tim and I began to have huge arguments about why he was staying out all night and drinking with Jim. I also asked him about what he was getting up to in the evenings with Jim, instead of being with me, but all he said was that everything was fine and for me to stop complaining. Soon after the conversation, Tim began to hit me again, but he would only hit me on parts of my body that people could not see.

Then one evening, while I was in bed waiting for him to come in, I heard them both as they came through the front door, and they were laughing and swearing at each other as they walked through the house. Then everything went quiet and I heard a door close. I stayed lying in my bed for a moment, expecting Tim to come in to see if I was ok, but he didn't; so after a couple of minutes, I decided to get up and to go see what he was doing. I opened my bedroom door and it was still very quiet in the house, so I went downstairs and I walked into the living room, but he was not there; so I walked back up the stairs to my room as I thought they must have gone back out of the house.

It was still very quiet when I walked back into my room and, as I closed the bedroom door, I heard a faint squeaking noise coming from the direction of the spare bedroom, so I went back into the hallway and I walked over to the spare room and I listened for a moment. And as I opened the bedroom door, I could see Tim lying face down on the bed naked, and Jim was also naked and he was just about to lie on top of Tim. I looked at them both and then I ran to my mother's bedroom and I told her what both of them were doing and she just said, 'Leave them both alone and let them get on with it.' I looked at her in disbelief at what she had just said to me and then I ran back to the spare room and I shouted at Jim to get the fuck off him and to get out of the room.

He got up and, as he left the room, I woke Tim up and then we had a massive argument, and Tim told me that Jim had been having sex with him for the whole of the time that we had been staying at mum's house. And to my shock, it didn't seem to bother him and he thought nothing of what they had been doing. We spent the rest of the night shouting at each other about our future, and when morning came Tim said that he couldn't take any more of my family and he said that he wanted to go back to Ireland, and I said ok. I even helped Tim pack his bags, and within an hour we were both on the underground train heading towards Paddington train station; and when we arrived at Paddington, Tim said goodbye to me and he got on a train and, within a couple of seconds, he was gone.

And in that split second, my whole life had changed and I was on my own again, but this time I was six months pregnant. I turned around and I went back to mum's; and when I got back, I went into the kitchen and I swallowed a couple of painkillers, but they never helped, so I took another four and I lay down on my bed, wishing I was dead. Now I hated Jim even more than I did before, because he had made my only company and the father of my child leave me. Now that I was pregnant and my belly was big, Jim had no option but to keep his dirty hands off me; and for a while, he left me alone, and I spent most of my time wandering from one sister's house to another.

Then one weekend, mum went out for the day to visit her sister and she took my stepbrothers with her, leaving my young niece and myself alone in the house. At first, everything was fine and we just sat and played games together, but then Jim came in from the pub and he accused me of eating all the food in the house; and he picked on me because I was pregnant and because he couldn't molest me anymore. He said that I had eaten a pot of bacon cabbage and potatoes all on my own, but I was feeling sick and I hadn't eaten a single thing all day and he knew it.

But he also knew that I had money hidden in my bedroom that I was saving to buy a pushchair for my baby. And the problem was that he wanted me to give him the money so that he could go back to the pub and buy more drinks for himself with it. He was so desperate for the money that he began to shout at me that he knew I had it and that I had to give it to him as rent for the room; then he said that I was a dirty little bitch and a slag, and nothing but a dirty bastard's child. And that I was no good to anyone, then he said, 'No wonder your boyfriend left you.' And with that I stood up and I shouted at him that my boyfriend left me because he could not take his dirty hands off him and because I had caught them having sex together. Jim went mad and he said that if I didn't get out of his house, he was going to kill me and my baby by kicking me into my belly. Then he ran towards me and, as he came face to face with me, he said, 'Don't you eat any of my food again.'

I thought he was going to kill me, so I grabbed my niece by the hand, and we both ran out of the house; and on the way out the front door, I called him a pig. I shouted that I was going to get him all the food that he wanted and I was going to get him a load of pig because he was a pig. Then I ran back into the house and up the stairs to my room and I got my money, then I ran back out of the house and we both walked up the high street to the local supermarket to buy some food. Once there, I got a shopping trolley and I spent all the money I had saved for a pushchair, buying him all the food he wanted. I got him ten heads of cabbage, ten pieces of boiling bacon, and ten turnips; and just the thought of what we were doing was enough to make us both laugh aloud. Once we left the shop, we struggled with the shopping trolley all the way back to the house. And on the way back, a few people asked us if we needed a hand, but all we could do was laugh and say that we were going to feed the old drunken pig all the bacon that he can eat.

When we got back to the house, Jim was fast asleep, lying drunk on the sofa, snoring his head off. So I crept into the kitchen and filled the fridge up with as much food as I could and then I lined the rest of the food up on the side next to the front door. And then I told my niece to open the front door and to get ready to run. I shouted at Jim, 'Wake up you pig' and I began to throw the rest of the food at him. At first, he didn't know what was hitting him; but as he got up and he look over at me, he realised what I was doing, and at that moment I hit him right in the face with a piece of bacon. I shouted at him that pigs are dirty just like you and you deserve to eat your own kind, and I chucked the rest of the turnips and bacon at him, and then I ran out of the house.

He jumped up to chase me, but he was only wearing his underpants, so I managed to get a head start on him and I was able to get a good way down the road before he managed to get his trousers on and out of the front door after me. He ran down the road, shouting at us and calling us little beggars and tramps. 'You cunt's', he shouted. Then he threw a turnip that he was still holding at us, but it missed and I couldn't stop laughing as it rolled past me, and I was trying to hold my belly at the same time to stop it from bouncing up and down as I ran.

Then I got a stitch in my side and I had to slow down, but I continued up the road and I ran towards my sister Tracy's house. As I got closer, I could see her standing outside the house and she was washing the windows. I shouted at her as loud as I could to open the front door, and she turned around just in time to see Jim chasing me down the road. Then she ran to the front door and she waited for us to reach the house and, as we ran inside, I slammed the door shut, hitting Jim in the face with it; and then I shouted at him through the letterbox to fuck off. Then Tracy shouted at him from the window and she told him that she saw everything that he was doing to us, and that she was going to tell mum everything; then he turned around and walked away. Tracy then turned to us and said, 'What the fuck have you two been up to?' I just laughed at her and after I had finished telling her what had happened, she said well done and she laughed too.

Later that evening, mum came up to the house to see us, and

she said that when she got home the fridge was full of cabbage, turnips and bacon; and she had asked Jim where it all came from, but he wouldn't answer her. We all looked at each other and then we all fell about laughing, while mum just stood in front of us looking puzzled. Then I told her what I had done to Jim with the food, and I told her that I could not go back to her house anymore, and she said ok and then she left.

I spent the next few weeks staying with Tracy at her house and my condition was far from perfect, but Fred could see the condition I was in and he left me alone for most of the time. Every day, mum would come to Tracy's house for a cup of tea and to see if I was ok; and every day, I would ask her if she could ring the council for me, to ask them if they could find a home for me, as I needed my own place for me and my baby; but she never did. She always said that she would ring them when she got home, but she never did; she just couldn't be bothered with it, as she was not going to get anything out of it.

Every day, I would have nothing to do but just wait around all day, and walk from one sister's home to another just to pass the time, and I was angry with everyone. I just couldn't sit still for a moment, and I continued to wander the streets and my belly just kept getting bigger and it felt like it was going to burst. I felt sorry for myself, as I was only sixteen and I felt very alone and a long way from home and I wished I had been back in Ireland.

Then one evening, while I was visiting Karen at her flat, I walked into the living room, and as I entered the room one of her husband's friends was sitting on the sofa; and as I walked in, he looked over at me and he said, 'Hi.' I turned towards him and, in that split second, the expression on my face wiped the smile clean off his; and after that, he never said another word to me. I had given him a look that had shown him how disgusted I was with men and then I walked into the kitchen to put a couple of painkillers into my mouth, drank some water and then I left the flat without saying goodbye to anyone. I hated all men and especially the ones who tried to talk to me. Little did I know then, but in about seven months' time I was going to meet him again; and next time, it would be the beginning of the both of us spending the rest of our lives together.

Even though Tim had left me and gone back to Ireland, I still kept in touch with him all the time and I rang him almost every day; but each time I spoke to him, he said that if he had to live with my family, then he would rather stay in Ireland. I told him that I was trying to get my own place for my baby and me, and he said that if I did manage to get my own place, then he would come back to me.

I was now almost nine months pregnant and my baby could have come at any moment, but Tim still refused to come back to London, so Tracy said that she had an idea. She said that she had already arranged to go back to Ireland to see daddy, so she suggested that I should go back with her. That way I could show Tim my big belly and then persuade him to return to London with me. I only had a couple of days to go before the baby was due, but I still said yes as I didn't want to have the baby on my own, and the very next day we left for Ireland.

I found the travelling very difficult and my belly hurt, but I had to go and I was so close to my due date that everyone on the train and ferry couldn't help themselves and they just had to stare at me. I was only sixteen years old, barely five foot three tall, and my belly was almost as round as I was tall. When we arrived in Ireland, we still had a long way to travel to get to our dad's house and the only transport that we could afford was the coach. And every time it went over a bump in the road, I thought I was going to have the baby, but I wrapped my arms around my belly and I never let go until we arrived at daddy's house.

As we left the coach, we walked towards the house and I still recognised it and daddy was standing by the old wooden gate, waiting for us; and by the look on his face, I knew that he was happy to see us. But it was now very late in the evening and I was feeling sick and tired from all the travelling, so I went straight upstairs to bed and I fell straight to sleep.

When I woke up the next morning, I got up and, without any breakfast, I went straight out to look for Tim. The village was small, so it wasn't long before the word got around that I was looking for him and soon Tim came and found me. I told him that I was only staying in Ireland for two days, then I had to go back to London to have my baby, and I told him that I wanted him to come back with me. He looked at me and then he looked at my belly, and once he realised the condition I was in, he agreed and he said that he would come back to London with me and we both walked off towards my dad's house.

However, when we got back to the house, Tracy was in a raging temper and she said that all dad wanted from her was money for drink; and he said that if we did not have any money for him, then we should leave him alone and go back to London. I was not the slightest bit interested in what was going on and I just stayed out of everyone's way for the rest of the day.

The next morning, I left the house and I paid for an extra ferry ticket, so that Tim could travel back with me, and off we went back to London, leaving our dad to his daily routine of drinking himself stupid all the time. Tracy couldn't wait to get back to London as she was missing Fred a lot; and all the way back, she kept begging me not to have the baby on the ferry, and then she did the same on the train and I said ok. However, I was in pain and I was suffering. I was having very bad pains in my belly and I really thought I was going to have the baby before I got back to London. But for everyone's sake, I just kept smiling and eventually we made it all the way back without any major problems; and once home, I settled down and I felt much better.

The next morning, Tracy rang our mother and she told her to get on the phone to the council and to get me a place to live, as I was about to have a baby; and within half an hour, mum rang back. She said that she told the council about me and they gave her an address of a hotel that I could go and stay in for now. She could have done that for me weeks ago, but she just could not be bothered.

I was so happy and Tim and I went off with the address to look for the hotel; and within an hour, I was in my own room. For the first time in my life, I had my own real place to live in. The council had sent me to a hotel in Kilburn that was an old Victorian house and it had a sign outside the house that said, 'Hotel, cheap rooms to rent'; but inside it was rotten and infested with cockroaches. And my room was right at the top of the house in the attic, but I loved it; they even gave me breakfast for nothing, if I got up early enough that is. Tim was feeling much happier now because he didn't have to sleep at my mum's house; but after a few days of being together in the hotel, he began to hit me again. And even though I was ready to give birth, it did not seem to make any difference to him, and that made me feel very sad.

A week later, I had my baby and I had a long and difficult labour, and after twelve hours of screaming, I was ready to give up. I was so exhausted from being left to do all the work of giving birth by myself, that I couldn't give birth on my own and I ended up with a room full of doctors and nurses all rushing around and panicking. They had left it almost too late and now both the baby's life and my life were in danger, and they had to use forceps to get the baby out of me as fast as possible. And the doctors had to cut part of my body open with scissors to get the baby out of me before it was too late.

I was exhausted, I had given up and I was not able to push anymore. I had only just turned seventeen three weeks earlier and now I felt like the doctors had destroyed me. Once the doctors got the baby out of me, they began to relax, and I was so happy when they handed me my baby. I looked at my baby and I could see that it was a boy; and for the first time in my life, I felt completely happy with myself. I now had Tim with me and my own baby boy, and a place to live. What more could I want? I now knew that nobody could come near me and ever touch me again, and I knew that I could stay away from my family if I had to, as I now had my own family to look after me.

And a week later, I was strong enough to leave hospital and I went home. At first, everything was fine, my baby was beautiful and healthy, Tim was taking care of me and he got a job on a building site; but then, one night, my brother Simon came to the hotel. He told me that he didn't want to stay with Kevin anymore, and he asked me if he could stay with Tim and me in my hotel room, and I said yes. He was my baby brother and I would have done anything for him; and a few hours later, he moved in with Tim and me.

But then, a couple of weeks later, Tim's younger brother turned up at the hotel. He had come over to London from Ireland and he had no place to stay, so he had come to us. But Tim told him to go away and to go find somewhere else to stay, but I shouted at Tim that he was wrong to send his own brother away and I told his brother to come in, and that he could stay with us for as long as he wanted. So now there were four of us, all aged between fifteen and seventeen, plus a baby, all living in the one hotel room and I loved it because there was always something going on.

However, after a week, Tim gave up his job and he began to spend all of his time with the two boys; they would all go out in the morning and they wouldn't come back until the very early hours of the next morning and, for most of the time, they left me on my own with the baby. I tried to talk to Tim about what he was doing and I asked him why he was leaving me alone all of the time. I told him that me and the baby should come first before the boys; but instead of him saying, 'Yes, you're right', he told me to shut up and to leave him alone So I had no choice but to put up with him, but then he started to come home drunk, and when we were alone he began to hit me again. I asked him to stop hitting me, but he said that it was entirely my fault that he was back in London, and he said that he didn't want to be stuck with me and the baby any longer and he hated everything about me.

And for the next couple of months, we argued constantly, and things just got worse between us; he began to hit me even more, it was as if he was taking his anger out on me. Then one night when he came home drunk, he dragged me around the room by my hair and then he punched me into my chest. And as I fell back, he hit me again, then I felt one of my ribs snap from the punch, and I felt the rib move up into a vertical position under my skin. I fell to the ground and Tim stopped hitting me and stood over me. I looked up at him and then got up and we both looked at the rib poking up in my chest. I shouted at him, 'Look what you've done' and we both just looked at each other in shock; but I had to do something, so I began to move the rib back into place and Tim helped me.

The pain was terrible, but I pushed and eased the rib back into a position that looked normal and then Tim helped me into bed. He gave me some painkillers and he looked after the baby for me while I tried to sleep. The next morning, the pain was just as bad, but I never went to the hospital for fear that they would take my baby away from me. So I just kept taking the painkillers and Tim helped me to bandage my chest up to stop the rib from moving; and after a couple of months, the pain felt a little better, so I removed the bandage. But the rib would still make a cracking noise if I bent over or took a deep breath, and I couldn't do a thing about it, so I just left it at that and I tried to forget that it ever happened. And eventually, the rib stopped making a noise and the pain went away.

CHAPTER 11

New Friends

By now I was sick of Tim going out and leaving me all alone with the baby, so I decided to do what he was doing; and one night, I picked my baby up and I went off out. And I went around to my sisters' houses and, to my disbelief, I found out that Tim had been hanging around with my own family every day, while I was sitting in my hotel room on my own, and he was even spending time with one of my own sisters and nobody said a thing to me. I was gutted, but I wasn't going to let it stop me from enjoying myself; after I had found out what he was up to, I never confronted Tim again about where he went or what he was doing, as I knew it would only make things worse for me.

But I was not going to sit around and do nothing, so every day I would get up and go out with my baby. At first, I just spent most of the day walking the streets, pushing my baby around with me from one sister's house to another. Then, after a while, I found myself staying out longer; and after a couple of months, I was in a routine of walking home at one or two in the morning all on my own. And all the time Tim would be hanging around with my brothers and sisters and none of them, including Tim, were bothered if I was around or not. And some nights, Tim would get back to the hotel just after me and I would ask him why he never came home with me, but all he could say to me was 'Sorry, I was busy.' I knew what busy meant; it meant he was hanging around with the rest of my family and not me. But if I tried to confront him about what he was doing or I tried to talk to him about what he had done all evening, he would begin to hit me again. So most of the time I said nothing to him, as I didn't want to get hurt again.

I didn't know what to do and I didn't want to lose Tim and be left all on my own with a baby. So I thought that the best thing I could do was to continue going out to my sister's and to leave him alone; and after a while, it worked and he stopped hitting me. But I soon became fed up being left on my own again and I began to follow my sisters out to pub; and everywhere they went, I followed, pushing my baby with me. I always fed my baby and I kept him well dressed and wrapped up warm and I never once neglected him; he was a part of me and it didn't matter if it was day or night, we went everywhere together.

My baby was now six months old and because of him, I was able to make a few new friends with some of the local young girls and nobody ever took any notice of me bringing my baby into the local pubs with me. Most people were happy to see me with my baby and they would all treat me very nice; and the girls would play with my baby, picking him up and feeding him for me. They would change his nappy for me as if he was one of their own, and it made me feel very happy.

Then, after a couple of weeks of me getting to know my new friends, they invited me out for a drink with them to a local pub for a girls' night out, so I went and I took my baby with me. It wasn't much, just the same few girls, but it felt great being invited out by them and I felt happy. The girls made me feel like I was one of them, and as the evening went on a few of the girls got a bit drunk and they began to act a bit silly; and then one of them said that she wanted a photo of us all together with the baby, but none of us had a camera. However, one of the girls said that her brother had a camera back at her mum's flat and she lived right next door to the pub; and because I was the only one not drinking, she said that it would be better if I went to her mum's and got the camera from the flat. They said that they would all look after my baby for me while I got the camera and she told me the flat number and her brother's name and off I went to get the camera.

It was only 7 pm, but it was already getting dark and a bit cold outside, so I wrapped myself up and I went off to her mum's. Thinking nothing of it, I knocked on the door and her dad answered. 'Is Tony in? I need to get a camera from him', I said. And he said, 'Yes, but he is in bed.' 'That's ok. Can I go and get the camera from him, because his sister told me to get it.' 'Ok', he said. Then he told me to come in and go up the stairs to his room.

I walked up the stairs and, as I knocked on his bedroom door, I walked straight in; the room was pitch black and I couldn't see a thing, so I put my hand against the wall, I felt for the light switch and within a second I found it and switched the light on. He was lying on the bed fully dressed and he was almost asleep; I stood in the doorway looking at him and then he lifted his head and looked over at me. And before he could say a word to me, I said, 'Do you have a camera? Your sister said you have one.'

Then I recognised him, he was the same man who had tried to talk to me back at my sister's house six or seven months earlier, when I was pregnant and miserable. And I remembered the look that I had given him back then and, within an instant, I felt my face turning red with embarrassment. He looked puzzled, and then he said yes, but he didn't know where it was; so I said, 'Not to worry. But if you find it, can you bring it down to the pub, as I am having a drink in there with your sister?' He said, 'Yes, ok' and then I said ok and I walked out of the room, closing the door behind me. As I left the flat, I smiled to myself and then I walked back down to the pub, hoping that he would bring the camera down to us.

And within twenty minutes, he was standing at the entrance of the pub looking in. I stood up and waved to him to come in and as he walked towards me I smiled at him; he smiled and sat down next to me. 'I found the camera', he said, and we all just laughed. I said thanks, he handed me the camera, and then he said that he had to leave as he had some things to do and then he had to go training; then he got up and left the pub. He seemed nice and now that I had become friends with his sister, I hoped that we would be seeing each other again, and I had an idea that we would. And because I was spending more time hanging around the area, it wasn't long before we bumped into each other again.

I was walking along the street with my baby in my pushchair when someone on a huge motorcycle beeped their horn as they went past me; and as I looked over, I realised that it was Tony on the bike. I smiled and then I waved at him, and he did a u-turn in the road and stopped his bike next to me; then we said hi to each other. He asked me how I was and, for a moment, I felt like I wanted to tell him everything about my life, but I just said that I was fine and before he left I asked him if he wanted to come to the pub later that evening; and he said yes, then he said goodbye and rode off.

Later that evening, I went to the pub with the girls and I sat there waiting for hours and I thought he wasn't going to turn up, but I never told the girls that he was coming just in case he let me down. Then a couple of hours before closing time, he walked in and we all spent the rest of the evening talking and having fun together; and once the pub closed, we all said our goodbyes and I walked off home, pushing my baby all the way home on my own. I didn't mind walking by myself because I was happy, but it was a long way home, about three miles and the evening was cold and dark; but I always walked home on my own, so it didn't bother me.

The next day, I spent a couple of hours hanging around with Tony's sister and she told me a few things about him; she said that he spent most of his time working and travelling around Europe on his motorcycle. And when he was home in London, all he ever did was go to the gym and train with weights. Then she said that she would get him to come down to the pub again that evening, and I spent the rest of the day just waiting around for the evening to come.; and this time, he arrived a little earlier and I felt happy that I had someone to talk to.

We spent most of the evening talking to each other about all sorts of things and I completely forgot all about everyone else sitting around me. And as we all left the pub at closing time, Tony asked me why I was always walking home on my own. Then he said that he didn't think it was very safe for someone as young as me to be walking home on my own, with a baby in a pushchair. I said I was fine and that I had been walking home on my own for a very long time and nothing bad had happened to me yet.

Then Tony asked me about my boyfriend and why he wasn't walking me home, and I said that my boyfriend was off doing his own thing. Then I said bye and I began to walk home. 'Would you like me to walk you home?' I turned around and Tony asked me again, 'Would you like me to walk you home?' 'No thanks', I said. 'I will be fine.' But before I could get any further along the street, Tony said, 'Come on, I will get you a cab. You can't be expected to walk all the way on your own and your baby needs to get home.' I said, 'No, I will be fine', but he had already stuck his hand out and he was stopping a black cab. 'Come on, I will help you with the pushchair.' And he opened the door of the cab and helped me push the pushchair into the back of the cab, then we both got in the back and we chatted all the way back to my hotel.

On the way back, I asked him more about himself and then I asked him his age; he said that he was twenty-six years old and that he worked for a film studio, working on generators and film equipment, and it sounded like he was good with his hands. But he didn't seem to want to tell me too much about himself, and he seemed to be the type of person who kept his affairs private.

When we arrived at the hotel, he helped me out of the cab with the pushchair and within a second he was back in the cab. I said thanks and he said, 'No problem, you're very welcome', then he closed the door, the cab drove off and he was gone. I walked into the hotel and up to my room, and when I opened the door, Tim was sitting on the bed waiting for me. I looked at him and he asked me where I had been all night and I told him that I was at the pub with the girls. He looked at me and then he spent the rest of the evening playing with our baby and I went to bed.

The next day was the same as all the rest, with Tim going out early and me being left alone with my baby; so as usual, I went around to the girls. But I didn't see Tony, he must have been at work or something. I spent the next few days doing the same things as usual and I wandered from one sister's house to another; and in the evenings, I went to the pub to see my friends.

Then one evening, as I was about to walk home, Tony came walking along the road. I smiled at him and, as he got closer to me, he smiled back at me and he stopped and asked me how I was. And after a couple of minutes talking, he asked me if he could walk me home and I said yes. The walk back to the hotel took about 45 minutes and, for most of the time, he asked me things about my baby and myself; and he said that he could not understand why I was still walking home on my own, so late at night. Then, as we got to the door of the hotel, he said goodbye and then he was gone again. And I thought to myself, 'That's life' and I went up to my room feeling very sorry for myself. I liked Tony and even though he had just left I felt like we were a thousand miles apart.

The next day, I went back around to my sister's, but I didn't see Tony anywhere. For the next couple of weeks, I continued going to my sister's flats day after day, hoping to bump into him, but he just didn't seem to be around the area; so I decided to go and see Tony's sister at her mum's flat. I wasn't missing him, but I was wondering what he was up to, but he wasn't there either; so after a couple of hours, I asked her about him, and she said that he was off somewhere in Europe, riding around on his motorcycle. 'Ah that's nice', I said and at the end of the evening I went home.

When I opened the door to my room, I walked in and I was all alone again. I sat on the end of the bed and I looked over at my baby, then I picked him up out of his pushchair, I put him on the bed next to me, and we both fell to sleep. When I woke up, it was three in the morning and Tim still hadn't come home, so I got into bed and I closed my eyes, wishing that my life was different; but it wasn't. This was it, this was my life and I had to make the best of it.

For the next few weeks, I hardly saw Tim as he spent most of his time hanging around with my family, and his behaviour towards me made me feel fed up all the time. Then one afternoon, as I was walking along Kilburn high road, I saw Tony ride past me on his bike; it was easy for me to spot him because he had the biggest motorcycle I had ever seen. It was a Honda Goldwing and he had music playing on it, and he must have seen me too because he stopped in the middle of the street, did a u-turn and pulled up next to me and we both looked at each other. Him on his bike and me with my pushchair and I had butterflies in my belly. We both spoke at the same time and then we both laughed as he asked me how I was. And after a quick conversation, we arranged to meet up later at the pub, and then he said that he had to go and he rode off and I walked home happy.

That evening, I went to the pub and after an hour Tony walked through the door and he sat next to me; and from that moment on, he would meet me every evening and escort me and my baby home. Then, after a couple of weeks, he began to buy me things that I needed for the baby, like nappies and food and I liked it. At first, I said no to him and I told him to stop buying me things, but I was beginning to like him even more than I thought I would and I was happy that he was helping me. But I still wasn't sure how he felt about me and every time he left me outside the hotel I felt sad and lonely and I missed him.

He never once tried to do anything inappropriate and he never once said a word out of place; he would just make sure that my baby and I had everything that we needed and that we got home safely, then he would say goodnight and leave us standing outside the hotel. So I decided that I had to do something to see if he liked me the way I liked him and I decided to meet him in the pub on my own. And the next day, I asked one of my sisters if she would look after my baby for me while I went out and she said yes.

So off I went to the pub and I waited; then just before closing time and just as I expected he came through the door to walk me home. I jumped up and, before he could say a word, I told him that my sister was looking after the baby for the night, so we can walk home together. He smiled at me and he said ok, but instead of him walking me in our usual direction, he stopped at the end of the street and he asked me if I would like to go home on the back of his bike and I said yes. He said that his bikes were parked in his garage just across the road, so we walked over to his garage and I stood back as he opened the garage door; then he walked into the darkness and for a moment everything was silent. I stood still and I wondered what he was doing, and with a loud screech of the bike engine, the garage lit up from the bright lights of the bike, and then he backed the bike out of the garage.

It was the first time that I had seen his bike at night and almost every part of it had a light on it. He smiled at me and then he asked me to walk around the bike and into the garage with him, and in the corner of the garage was a custom chopper motorcycle. I stood and looked at the bike, as he smiled and told me a few things about it and I could tell that I had competition; then he put a crash helmet on my head and he told me to climb on the back of the Goldwing motorcycle.

He closed the garage door, then he got on the bike and as we set off the whole bike seemed to come alive with lights, and music seemed to be coming from every part of it. God, I felt like I was so special. He shouted back at me to see if I was ok and I leaned forward, hitting him in the back of his head with my crash helmet, and I said yes. Then I told him that I didn't need to go straight home as no one was there and I told him that my sister was looking after the baby all night. We set off and, within a couple of seconds, he pulled up at the junction to the main road and he moved his left hand towards some controls on the bike and then we rode off up the road. And as we rode along, the radio on the bike came on and I sat back to the sound of Dire Straits, 'Brothers in Arms' coming through a sound system that seemed to fill the whole street with music. I couldn't help but smile to myself and after a couple of seconds Tony said, 'What do you want to do?' 'Anything', I said. 'But I don't want to go home.' It didn't matter to me what we did as long as we didn't go back to the hotel, as I was sick of being there on my own.

Then I sat back again, I looked around and everywhere we went people stopped and looked at us, you just couldn't miss us. The bike shone with a deep red wine colour and the bike was covered in lights of all colours and the sound coming from the four speakers was so loud and crisp that you could probably have heard us coming from a mile away. I smiled to myself again and I couldn't stop smiling because I felt so happy; then I asked Tony, 'Where are we going?' and he said, 'Just sit back and relax', so I did.

It was now almost midnight and the sky was clear, I was a bit cold, but I loved being on the back of the Goldwing and I soon forgot all about everything; and after a while, I noticed that we had ridden onto a motorway. I looked at the signs, but they never meant a thing to me, so I just sat back and listened to the music and the feeling that went through my body was fantastic and I wanted the moment to last forever.

Then, after about half an hour, we turned off the motorway, we headed down some country roads and then we rode along some back streets; and as we got to the end of one street, he stopped. I looked up and in front of me was a castle and it was all lit up with bright lights and it was massive. God, I thought to myself, this is fantastic. 'Where are we?' I asked. 'It's Windsor castle.' I looked around, then he stopped the bike and we got off. It was very quiet and no one was around; so we spent a while walking along the narrow cobblestone streets that surrounded the castle, looking in the shop windows and then we walked back towards the bike.

Tony started the engine, I climbed on the back and he drove us to another part of the castle and we spent the next couple of hours lying on the grass bank of the castle, talking and getting to know each other better. And then he took me home. The ride back was just as impressive as the ride out and it was about three in the morning when we finally pulled up outside the hotel. He turned the engine off and I got off the bike; and as he parked the bike up, I asked him if he wanted to come in and he said yes. And within that split second, I knew that I had him.

He still hadn't made any advances towards me, but now I knew that he liked me and I knew that it was the age difference between us that was stopping him from making a move towards me; but I wanted him and I wasn't going to let that stop me. He finished parking the bike up and then he followed me into the hotel and we walked up to my room. I knew Tim wouldn't be home, as he spent most of his time at my sister's, so I asked Tony into my room and he sat on a chair and I sat on the end of my bed.

We spoke for a while and then I decided to make a move, and I told him that I was cold because of the bike ride and that I needed to get into the bed to warm up, but he still never made a move towards me. I looked over at him and I could tell that he was being a gentleman; and I thought to myself, 'Is he stupid or what?' So I asked him to get up and to turn the light off, and he did and then I said, 'Get into the bed with me'; and then he touched me for the first time. And as he put his lips against mine, he kissed me and then we made love, and I hoped that this was the turning point in my life.

After Tony left, I went to sleep and the next morning I went to my sister's house to pick up my baby; and then I went looking for Tony, but no one had seen him, so I went home hoping that he would ring me. But he didn't. And for the next week, I walked around feeling sorry for myself and I felt like I had been used. Then one evening, as I was walking home, Tony pulled up next to me and I stopped. 'Why didn't you come around to see me', I said. He looked at me and said, 'Sorry, but I am confused. You have a baby and a boyfriend, and I don't know what to do.' I looked at him and he looked sad; we both talked for a while and then he told me how he felt about me and that he had liked me for a long time. I told him that I had feelings for him too and, from that moment on, we made the decision to be with each other.

At first, we managed to keep our affair hidden from everyone, but everyone knew that Tony was walking me home every night and that he was helping me out with things that I needed for my baby. They also knew that his behaviour towards me was part of his good nature, as he had also helped them in the past, by buying them things when they had little money to live on. Plus Tim knew that another man was giving me some attention and taking the time to help me, but it didn't seem to bother him because it gave him even more freedom and a chance to stay away from me and my baby even longer.

Tim didn't know it, but his actions towards me were helping me get over him; and as time went on, my feelings for Tony got even stronger. No one had ever treated me with the kindness that Tony was showing me, and he even accepted the fact that my baby came first and without my baby, there would be no me. After a few months, Tony and I had become almost inseparable and we were spending as much time as possible with each other, while Tim did his own thing, spending most of his time drinking and hanging around with everyone else in my family apart from me; and when he was around me, all he did was hit me.

Then everything came to a head when I couldn't take the beatings from Tim anymore and Tony and I told everyone what had been going on between us. Most of my family seemed to be happy for me, and I think they had an idea about what we were up to anyway, but Tony's family were not so happy and neither was Tim. We could cope with Tony's family and I knew that Tim was cheating on me anyway, and I think he had an idea of what was going on between Tony and me from the very beginning; so Tony and I just got on with what we were doing and we did our best to make the situation work for everyone.

In the beginning, there was a lot of arguing between Tim and me about whose fault it was, with a lot of 'if only we had done this and if only you had done that' going on between us and with each of us blaming the other for the situation we were in. But at the end of the day, I had made my mind up; I was sick of Tim hitting me and I did not want to stay in the relationship anymore. So I told Tim that it was all over between us and within six months I moved into a council flat; and a couple of months later, Tony moved in with me and he treated my baby as his own.

At first, things were not great between us and it took a very long time for us to get used to living with each other. But he was good to my baby and me, so I did my best to behave myself; but I was still just seventeen, and he was twenty-six, so it was difficult for us to have a serious conversation on the same level as each other. I felt like I needed to go out and have some fun and he thought that our family should come first; he had a good steady job, he went to work every day, and he had an idea of what a home should be like. But I didn't have a clue and I think that most of the time he must have felt as if he was a one-parent family looking after two kids, rather than having a partner and a child.

But he stuck with us and, after a few restless years, I did my best and I tried to settle down into a family life. Then at the age of twenty-two, I became pregnant again and I had my second child; and a year later, I had my third child and they were all boys. Tony kept working, but as our family grew money became an issue; so Tony had to sell the love of his life, his bikes, to make ends meet, and we eventually settled down into a family life. I brought my children up to be good and, over the years, things slowly got better for all of us. We even got to a point where we could afford to go on holiday each year; and as the kids grew up, the quality of all our lives improved.

I still had a problem coping with everyday life and, ever since coming to London from Ireland, I had been living on medication for the pains in my head that never went away. And every now and then, I would lose the plot and, for no reason at all, I would cause a lot of trouble between Tony and myself. I would scream at him and call him all kinds of names and I would even take my anger out on him and hit him whenever I felt angry; but I still don't know why I did it, I just felt like I needed to.

Then one day, while arguing with him, I felt like I wanted to kill him for talking back to me, so I decided to shut him up for good and I made him a drinking chocolate laced with a few sleeping pills. I gave him the mug of hot chocolate and I sat down and watched him as he drank it all down. But after a while, I began to panic and, in the end, I decided to tell him what I had done, as I had gone too far. He looked at me and he just smiled, then he began to gently laugh; and he got up and walked away from me and he walked out of the flat and he never said a word about what I had done.

Later that evening, he came back and I asked him if he was ok and he said, 'Yes, I am fine' and then I told him that it served him right for nagging me and for talking back to me. He smiled and said that he walked around for hours to stay awake and then when he felt better he came back. I tried to say sorry, but I just couldn't, we left it at that and we went to bed. And after that, I never did it to him again! I knew that he was only trying to help me, so I tried to help myself too; but every day my mind felt like it was going to explode and I felt like I was living in my own private hell. My family was never far away and they would constantly remind me of my past, and sometimes they would be a bad influence on me, by offering me drink and drugs, and it would cause problems between Tony and me.

I tried to stay away from my family as much as I could, but Simon, my youngest brother, still needed me, as he had never forgotten about what Kevin had done to him when he first came to London. And my family always seemed to be involved in everyone's business all of the time; and over the last few years, all the pressures of Simon's life seemed to catch up with him. Simon had a girlfriend and they had a baby together, but eventually they split up because he could not cope with all the pressures and the responsibility of being a parent; and soon after they split up, he became mentally ill. And he had no idea about what he wanted or if he even wanted to live; the abuse that he had suffered as a child back in Ireland and then the abuse he suffered at the hands of his own brother had almost driven him mad. He was now taking drugs and he was in a mixed-up relationship with a male partner, who was much older than he was, and his partner was no good for him.

Simon tried to find comfort in painting and he would spend days alone, locked in his flat, mixing colours and creating paintings that expressed his feelings; but locking himself away only suppressed how he felt for a while and whenever he came out of his flat he would emotionally fall apart. I tried to comfort him and I went to see him at his flat all the time, but he did not always let me in to see him and I would have to stand outside for hours, just to catch a glimpse of him as he looked out of the window.

Then one morning, I received a phone call from the police. They said that they had found Simon wandering around the streets late at night on his own, and he had no idea of what he was doing or where he was going. So, they brought him to the hospital and they had to section him under the Mental Health Act, just in case he went off and hurt himself or someone else. I said thanks to the police for helping him, then I went straight around to the hospital and the doctors allowed me to go in and talk to him. His clothes were all dirty and he had grown a long beard. At first, I hardly recognised him and it wasn't nice seeing him in the condition he was in, so I went home and I brought back some clean clothes for him to put on and the hospital allowed me to help him get cleaned up. I walked him into a shower room, I helped him to get undressed and then I gave him a wash. He was only twenty-six years old, but he looked like an old man of fifty. Once he was clean, I helped him change into clean clothes and then I put him to bed and, after a couple of hours, I went home. I loved my brother and I felt like he was my baby.

The next day, I went back to the hospital and he was still asleep, so I sat next to his bed for a while and I watched him as he slept like a baby. Before I went home, I gave him a kiss on his forehead. Later that evening, I returned to the hospital and a member of the staff said that they had contacted my mother, but she had told them not to let him out as he was a danger to her and her family and she said that he kept going around to her house and causing her trouble.

I was so disappointed with my mother. She had discarded us like rubbish when we were children and now she had turned her back on her son when he needed her again. I hated her for what she had done to him. I wanted to help Simon, but I couldn't tell the hospital about his past as it would have caused a lot of trouble for my mother and my older brother Kevin. The hospital said they felt that he needed their help, so they were going to keep him in the hospital for a while.

I spent the next six months visiting him every day, but nobody else from our family ever went to see him; they just couldn't be bothered with him. He never did get much better; but after six months, the doctors said that he was ok and they wanted him to leave the hospital and go home. I asked them if they could do anything more for him, but they said, 'Sorry, but no.' And the next day, they let him leave the hospital. I took him back to his flat, I made sure that he had food, and then I left him alone so that he could get back into a normal routine.

But he slowly got worse and, after a while, he would not allow me back into his flat; so all I could do was to wait for him to come to me. Then one day, while I was sitting by my kitchen window, Simon walked along the car park and he looked up at me; I recognised him, but he looked like a stranger. I knew it was Simon, but he had changed again and he looked terrible. He looked up at me and I could see he was holding a few paintbrushes in one of his hands, and then he turned around and walked away. I sat at the window for the rest of the day wishing that he would come back, but he never did; and by the end of the day, I felt very sad for him and I thought about everything that he had been through all of his life.

The next day, I was sitting by the kitchen window again when I heard a knock on the door. So I got up and, as I opened the door, Simon was standing there. He said, 'Hi' and then he walked in. 'I just wanted to tell you that I love you and the kids', he said in a soft voice, and then he turned around and walked out of the flat. In my heart, I knew that was going to be the last time I would ever see him alive again. I followed him out into the hall and, before he could get into the lift, I gave him a big hug and I told him that I loved him; and as I let go, he walked into the lift and then he was gone. I rushed into the kitchen and I looked out of the window, hoping to catch a glimpse of him as he walked away; and as I looked out of the window, I watched him as he walked away for the very last time and then he was gone.

The next morning, I took the kids to school and then I returned home and sat by the kitchen window and I had a fag and then the phone rang. I slowly put the fag out and I looked out of the window, hoping to see Simon looking up at me, but he wasn't there; so I got up, I walked into the living room, I picked up the phone and I just listened. There was silence for a moment as neither one of us said a word, then a voice said Simon's dead, he took an overdose and they couldn't help him. I felt cold and sad, then I asked, 'Where is he?' and I realised I was talking to one of my sisters. 'He's in Saint Mary's hospital, Paddington.' 'Ok', I said and then I rang Tony and I went to the hospital.

When I arrived at the hospital, most of my family was already there and for some strange reason I felt happy for Simon. I think it was because no one could ever harm him again and he was now at peace, and far away from all the people who ever did him harm. I looked at everyone, then I walked towards Simon and I told him that I loved him and he looked like he was sleeping; and then I left the hospital and went home.

A few days later, the hospital said they could not release his body for at least three weeks, as they had to have an inquest into his death. I thought it was a bit strange, but I never really knew much about inquests and things like that, so I said ok. And when they finally let Simon's body go, we had the best funeral you could imagine for him. His life had been full of unhappiness and disappointments, but it wasn't his fault, as he had no control over the things that people did to him. For the whole of his young life, he suffered at the hands of paedophiles and disgusting people, who psychologically prospered from his suffering, and one day they will pay for what they did to him.

At his funeral, we had a horse-drawn carriage and hundreds of people from all around the area came to walk with us. And when we reached the cemetery, we stopped the carriage and all of our brothers carried Simon's coffin the final steps to his resting place and we made the final moments of his existence a happy one. A couple of weeks after the funeral, the police contacted us again, as they wanted to know everything we knew about the people Simon had hung around with, but we never told them everything.

And a couple of days later, they rang us again and they told us that we were allowed to go into his flat to recover anything we wanted from his belongings. So, the next day, we collected his flat keys from the police station and we all went around to the flat; my sisters and brothers all began looking for things of value, but all I wanted was his painting jug with his paintbrushes in it. As soon as I found the brushes, I picked them up and I left the flat.

Then, when everyone else had finished taking what they wanted, I got the keys from my mother, I went back to the flat and I collected all of his paintings. But while I was there, I noticed a couple of odd looking books sitting on the side next to his phone. I knew he wasn't much of a reader, so I picked one up and on the front cover in big print were the words 'euthanasia' and 'how to kill yourself'. I was shocked. I knew Simon would never read something like that and someone must have given it to him, because he couldn't read very well and he wouldn't of wasted his time trying. I looked around, but there was nothing else strange in the flat, so I left and went home.

The next day, while I was looking through Simon's paintings, the phone rang and it was the police again; and this time, they told me that they were still investigating his death, as something was still bothering them, but they could not tell me what it was. They said that they would contact me as soon as they had more information for me, then I put the phone down and I continued looking at his paintings and I began to cry. We had been through so much together; now he was gone and I felt like a big piece of me was missing and I had a pain in my chest that wouldn't go away.

Then, about a month later, the coroner's office contacted the whole family and they asked us if we would object to them recording Simon's death as suicide. We said that we didn't have a problem with that, but we did not understand why they had to ask us for the permission; and then they told us that someone had taken out a large life insurance policy on Simon about a year ago. They said that for now they could not prove that it was in any way connected to his death. But they had a good idea that it was and if they could record Simon's death as a suicide, then the insurance company would not have to pay the person the money.

They also told us that Simon had taken a certain type of tablet and just the right amount to kill him; and once the tablets were in his system, there was no going back. But he did manage to call 999 for help, but by the time the ambulance crew got to him, he only had a short time to live and he begged them to help him, as he didn't want to die; and he said that he was forced to do it. They also said that they did not think he had done it all on his own, but they had no proof to use against any other person.

We were all shocked, but then again there were rumours going around that the man Simon had lived with had been living with another young boy in Europe, many years ago, who had also killed himself. We told the coroner what we knew and they said that if this man's name were ever linked to another death in the future, they would look into it. There was nothing we could do, as no one wanted to get involved, so we agreed and recorded his death as suicide; and we hoped that someday the police would get back to us with better news. For anything more to be done, we would need to be open with the police about Simon's past and whom he was involved with; but for that to happen, we would have to tell them what we knew about the man that he had been living with. But we knew very little about the man, apart from rumours.

We would also have to tell them about our older brother Kevin abusing him, and if we did that, it would have caused a lot of trouble within the family. And our mother would have said that we were all lying and then she would have done her very best to support Kevin and make everyone believe that Kevin had done nothing bad to his baby brother. So, we said nothing, as it was only going to hurt everyone and probably destroy what little we had left of our family.

We never did hear anymore from the police.

CHAPTER 12

Memories of Ireland

For the next few years, I got on with my life and I tried to concentrate on bringing up my three children, but I could never get Ireland out of my mind and I continued to take huge amounts of painkillers to relieve the pains in my head.

Then, about fifteen years after, I came to London and I got a phone call from the Irish police. They said that the institution I had lived in back in Ireland was under investigation for child abuse and they were following up on a lead about a man who had tried to kidnap me and several other children back in Ireland, in the late 1970s. They also said that the staff and the nuns at St XXXXX were under investigation, along with a number of priests from the same area, for abusing children who had been in their care, and they wanted to know if I had any information that could help them. I said, 'No, sorry, I don't have any information about the man. But I can tell you a thing or two about the nuns and some of the other people who abused me at the time.'

The police officer was a bit surprised, but not shocked, then he asked me if he could come over to England to interview me and I said yes; but it took him over two years to get the permission to come to England and, the day he arrived, he had another police officer with him. The other officer was there to make sure everything went as it should and that the interview was conducted in the correct manner.

The police officer asked me many questions about the years I spent back in Ireland, and I spent hours talking to him about the nuns and some of the other people that had abused me while I was in Ireland; and in the end, I also told him about the man in the car who tried to kidnap me. The other officer wrote everything I told them down, and once they had finished they told me that it was going to take them a very long time to investigate all the allegations, as there were so many people involved and because it all happened such a long time ago, but he would do his best. He said that he believed everything that I had told him, but it was not up to him how the government would deal with the investigation; and then he thanked me and they went back to Ireland.

It was almost another two years before I heard from him again. And when he rang me, he said that the investigation had gone well and if I wanted to prosecute anyone, then I would have a very good case against the nuns and the convent staff. However, if I wanted to take it any further, then I would have to go and see a solicitor first and then I would need to spend time back in Ireland, going over everything again. He said that the nuns had conveniently misplaced almost all of the documents relating to the nine years that I stayed with them in the convent and they had lost most of the names of the people they sent me to stay with during the school holidays. But worst of all, because my accusations related to things that had happened to me such a long time ago, the people they did manage to contact wouldn't admit to anything.

He also told me that the nuns said that the church would never have allowed things like that to happen to the children in their care. Furthermore, most of the people the police did manage to interview had very vague memories of my stay with them, and some of them said that they did not remember me at all, and they would not admit to any wrong doings towards me or any other children in their care.

I told the police officer thanks for trying and that I hoped the information I had given him had helped him in his investigation, but I had decided to leave it at that for now, as it was all too much for me at the moment. I felt that it was too difficult to push on with and I did not want my young children to know anything about my past. Plus what chance would I really have, all on my own, in court fighting against the church?

I never spoke to the police again after that, as I just wanted to forget my past and get on with the rest of my life. I tried to forget all about the time I had spent in the institution, but there was always something or someone that brought the bad memories back to me. I even tried to block the memories out by taking handfuls of sleeping pills and nerve tablets, but nothing helped. In the end, I took any kind of painkillers that I could get my hands on, just to top my other tablets up, but nothing worked. I even swapped tablets with my sisters to see whose tablets worked the best, but the effects of the tablets did nothing to help me.

I spent hours at the doctor's begging him for stronger tablets, but he would only allow me to continue with the ones that he had prescribed me. His only other option was to have me sectioned under the Mental Health Act, and he did not want to do that to me as he had known my family and my history from the day I had come back to London. He also knew what I had gone through back in Ireland and that it was not my fault, as I had told him all about my past, so he did his best to help me with what little he had to offer.

The only other help I had was from Tony; he never once thought less of me because of my past and, for most of the time, he was able to cope with me and guide me in the right direction. However, we still had a few problems, because I could not stop thinking about all the things that had happened to me in the past and my memories were driving me mad. My relationship with Tony had suffered because of my problems and, in his words, 'I had become a cold hard person'; well, almost his words! And our physical relationship was almost nonexistent and sometimes he even wondered how we had ever managed to have children.

Then one day, I went to the doctor's for a check-up and he gave me a birth control injection. I didn't ask for it, he was just giving them out as if he was giving out flu jabs. I went home and, within an hour, I had gone nuts; the hormone imbalance in my brain had caused me to see no sense at all and, after just one day, I had thrown Tony out of the house for no reason at all. But he didn't wander far and the next day I told him to get back before I did something to him or myself.

I spent the next six months screaming at him and making our life together hell; and at one point, he almost left me. I was keeping him awake all night, arguing with him until the early hours of the morning, just for spite, and he would beg me to stop, but I wouldn't and he used to go to work in the morning exhausted. And it got to the point where he could not take much more of the verbal abuse that I was giving him and he pleaded with me to stop, as he hung on to what was left of our relationship; but I kept it up and he stayed with me for the kids' sake. Eventually, the effect of the injection began to wear off, and I eventually calmed down and things got better for us as I came back to my reality.

Later that year, we went away on a family holiday and it was fantastic; it was Tony, the three kids and me, and God knows we all needed it. We spent two weeks at a villa in Portugal, and we had never had as much fun together as a family before; and when we came back to London, everyone apart from me felt like new people. However, my happiness was short lived, as a couple of days later the phone rang and one of my sisters told me that our brother Kevin had killed himself. She said that he was in Saint Mary's hospital and the doctors were only keeping him on a life support machine until we could all get over to see him; and then they were going to turn the machine off, as he was brain dead.

I put the phone down and, for some strange reason, I didn't feel like going to the hospital; I just couldn't be bothered, I felt like he deserved to die and I was happy he was dead. I sat in the living room and lit a fag; but after a short while, I heard a car horn

216

beeping outside my kitchen window and I knew it was one of my sisters, she had come to take me to the hospital with her. I didn't want to go, but I knew I would never hear the end of it if I didn't, so I walked downstairs and I got in the car.

When we arrived at the hospital, the doctors held us back for a moment and they explained that they were very sorry but he was not a pretty sight; the doctor said that some people had found him floating face down in the Grand Union Canal and we should be prepared for a bit of a shock. We said ok; and as we walked into the room, it stunk and he stunk, and his head was twice the size it should have been. I looked at him and I felt nothing, no emotions at all; then I thought to myself that he should have died years ago for what he had done to my baby brother Simon. Then I walked away and went home as the doctors turned off the life support machine.

Later that evening, the police came to see all of us and they said that some people had found him floating next to a canal boat earlier that day. They then said that Kevin had told a friend of his that he was going to kill himself because he could not take it any longer, and then the police officer asked us if we could tell him what the statement meant. We all knew what that meant; it meant that he could not live with himself anymore because of what he had done to our baby brother Simon, all those years ago. I didn't cry for Kevin, I had no tears for him; he did not deserve anything, not even my tears.

We never told the police officer about Kevin and what had gone on between him and Simon; and a few days later, we arranged for Kevin's body to be flown back to Ireland, as we wanted him as far away from Simon as possible. And a week later, most of us flew back to Ireland for the funeral. Once the funeral was over, we all flew back to London and that was the end of it and I got on with my life.

A couple of years passed and, during that time, I began to see my GP even more than usual, as I never felt happy and I only felt normal if I swallowed handfuls of nerve and sleeping tablets every day. I tried to stay away from my family and especially Tracy because of her husband Fred. He was still a creep and he was still trying to be my friend, but for all the wrong reasons, and Tracy still brushed everything he did to one side; always finding some sort of excuse for his behaviour and then laughing it off as if it was nothing.

As time went on, my children grew up, and I tried to keep my past and my family's past a secret from them, as I did not want them to find out about all the abuse I had been through. I knew I had to keep my children away from my family for as long as possible, as they would have told my children terrible stories about me and my past before they were old enough to understand; and I did a pretty good job of it. I even found the time to go back to Ireland for a few days to see my dad and I took one of my kids with me; we had a wonderful time and no one said a thing about my past while I was there.

Then, about a year later, when everything was going just right again, the phone rang and one of my sisters said that daddy was dead. She said that the police in Ireland had rung her and they told her they had found him on the beach dead and it looked like he had died from a head injury. I said ok, put the phone down and headed over to my sister's to be with the rest of my family. The next day, we arranged to travel back to Ireland and within a couple of hours we all boarded a plane and headed off.

But the moment we arrived at the airport in Ireland, our mother walked off and she went straight to our father's solicitors, she told them that she was his wife and that she was entitled to everything that had belonged to him. She then went off and stayed with some friend of hers, leaving the rest of us to arrange everything. The next day, we began the arrangements for our dad's funeral; and at lunchtime, the solicitor contacted us and he told us that our father had left everything to us, his children. Then he said that our mother was not entitled to a single thing, as her name was not in the will; but he said that she was contesting the will and it was up to us whether she would get anything.

I hated her. I hated her for giving me up when I was little and I hated her for this now, and she was an evil bitch and she always will be. She had left our father over thirty years ago and now that he was dead and he had left us some money she wanted to be his wife again; and because they had never divorced each other, the solicitor said that she was legally still his wife and probably entitled to everything he had. The solicitor also said that we had a choice of either giving her half of everything or she was going to take the lot of us to court and then she would take everything and leave us with nothing. We thought for a while and then we decided that she could have half of everything he left us.

However, before she got her hands on the money, the solicitor said that we could spend as much money as we liked on his funeral and she could not stop us as it was in the will. So we did and we spent thousands of pounds on flowers and thousands on the best coffin we could get; and we could see that it was making our mother sick, she was fuming and she even came up to us and asked us why we were spending so much money on a dead man. We told her that he was our daddy and we loved him and we always will. She looked disgusted with us and she walked away grinding her teeth together, as we carried on spending the money on the best of everything for him.

Then when it was all over, we all went to the solicitor's and in front of us he gave our mother a cheque for over twenty thousand pounds, and the rest of us got almost two thousand pounds each. Her mouth dropped open with shock and she looked disappointed at the amount printed on the cheque; then without saying a word to any of us, she marched out of the solicitor's office, got back on a plane and went back to London, leaving us to deal with his relatives and his friends. She had taken half of the money our father had left us and she never once thought a thing of it or of us or our feelings; she was only interested in how much money she could get out of the solicitor's, to spend on our stepbrothers and Jim.

Before we left, the police told us that we would have to come back to Ireland for the coroner's report, but they said they had a good idea of what had happened and how he died. They said that he had been walking along the sandy beach in the early hours of the morning, when he wandered off into the sandy mud and he became stuck in what must have felt like quicksand to him; and because he was old, he was unable to get himself free. Then the tide came in and he drowned, and he hit his head on the rocks lying around the beach, and it had been all over in around 10 minutes.

However, we knew that daddy had been walking the same beach day after day all of his life and it was no accident. We said thanks and then we went back to London; and a few weeks later, we all returned to Ireland for the report, and we were told the same story at his inquest. We left Ireland and I never went back to visit daddy again. My mother never even went to the inquest.

CHAPTER 13

Living Through It All Again

A few more years passed and the only problem I had was that I was still taking far too many tablets to keep my mind relaxed and to stop me from thinking back to when I was a child. The tablets were becoming less effective on me, and every year I had to take stronger and stronger tablets for them to have the same effect on my mind; and I was drinking a lot of alcohol to help me forget everything.

Then, one day, one of my sisters said that she had seen an article in a local newspaper relating to Irish children who grew up in the institutions back in Ireland. The article mentioned that a panel of people, were being put together to deal with child abuse claims against the church and its followers, who ran the institutions on behalf of the church; and anyone wanting to file a claim against them was invited to do so.

It sounded interesting, so later that day I spoke to Tony about the article and I asked him what he thought I should do. He said that if I felt like I could cope with talking to strangers about what went on back in Ireland, then I should give it a shot. But if talking about my past became too stressful for me to cope with, then I should not continue with it. Ok, I made up my mind and I contacted the panel of people at the address printed in the paper; and a few days later, they sent me a questionnaire form that I had to fill in and send back to them, so that my claim could be scrutinised by them. Then if they felt that I had a case against the church, they would contact me again and then advise me on what steps I should take next.

And a few weeks after I had sent the form off, they contacted me again. First, they said that I had to get a solicitor to represent me and they said that I had to go and see a specialist in the field of child abuse and psychology, so they could assess me and compile reports on my behaviour and mentality. I agreed and I did everything they asked me to do; and six months later, they sent me an appointment to attend a meeting at the Priory hospital in London.

But before I attended the meeting, my solicitor asked me to make a statement for her, explaining everything I could remember about my nine-year stay at the institution run by the nuns. I said ok; and by the time I had finished telling my story to my solicitor, she was in tears. She said that she had never heard anything like it before and she asked me if I could go home and put it all down on paper for her in my own words. So that she could present it to the panel of people who were going to judge me, and when the time came for them to cross-examine me she would be familiar with my story, and she could tell them that I was not lying about everything I told them. I said ok, and I went home and began putting my memories of Ireland onto paper.

I had to go back to the solicitor's many more times before the enquiry ended and because the process took such a long time. My solicitor and the panel of people, who were representing the government and church back in Ireland, suggested that I have counselling for the duration of the enquiry; they said that it was to help me cope with the trauma of having to go through all my bad memories again, and they told me whom I should go and see.

However, after about six months of going to see the counsellor, I began to feel worse and I had to stop going to see her. The counselling sessions had a negative effect on me and I hated going to it; plus the only person really getting anything out of it was the counsellor, as she was getting £140 an hour just for letting me sit in a chair in her office, while she just looked at me from behind her huge wooden desk. She would hardly speak to me and I spent most of the time just looking at the clock on the wall behind her, wishing for the time to go fast; and when the session was over, she would just say thanks and I would leave the room and go home.

However, within a couple of weeks of me stopping the sessions, I began to feel better and I never went back to see her again. Anyway, not only was she representing me and my solicitor, she was also working with the panel of people back in Ireland; and somewhere down the line, I think they were all connected to the compensation money set aside by the church and they were all making a fortune out of it. Soon afterwards, I received a phone call from my solicitor and she told me that my claim had been accepted. Then my solicitor and I waited and it took another two and a half years before the panel of people said that they were ready to look at my case.

And a couple of months later, my solicitor told me that the panel of people had made a decision and they did not want to see or speak to me at all, they only wanted the solicitor to attend the hearing without me. The solicitor said that my case against the church was so strong that the panel of people probably thought they had a better case against me and they could offer me less money if I did not attend the hearing. My solicitor also said that it was their right to refuse my request to attend the hearing, as they were the ones that had written some of the rulebook relating to the compensation scheme and they did not have to report to anyone but themselves. Even the police had no say in what was going on, as they were set up and run by the government and church; and they held all the financial strings of the church's purse and everything they did was behind closed doors.

The day eventually came for my solicitor to represent me in Ireland; and when the hearing was all over, they gave me a short time period to either accept their offer of compensation or to refuse it. And if I refused the offer, then the same panel of people who gave me the first offer would look over my claim again and then if they thought the amount of compensation was not correct, they could either reduce the amount offered to me or offer me a higher amount. The problem was that the same panel of people, were also representing the church and making the decisions about the amount of compensation awarded to the victims.

And for that reason, my solicitor advised me to take the first offer, as the second would probably be of a lower amount than the first; and if I refused the second offer, then they would not give me a single penny and my case would be closed. She said that she was sorry, but she had felt very intimidated by the people at the hearing, and really we did not stand a chance against them and we were at their mercy. So I said ok and I signed on the dotted line.

And a few weeks later, I was sent a cheque in euros that was probably only an eighth of the amount that I would have gotten if I had taken the church to court. I even lost a lot of money changing the cheque from euros into pounds and I think they did that on purpose just so they could have the last say in the whole matter. However, if I had taken the church to court, then I would probably have got nothing at all from them, as they are answerable to no one but themselves.

Moreover, the panel of people knew they were for most people their only hope of ever getting a penny out of the church, for all the abuse they had suffered. Plus they knew that most of the people claiming compensation would be easily tempted by the small amounts of compensation offered to them, as to them the amount offered was more than they had and would ever see in their entire lifetime. It was easy for the panel of people to take advantage of the situation and they used it to their advantage.

Once I got the money, I only spent a very small amount to pay off a few bills and I kept the rest in the bank for a year, while I decided what to do with it. If everything had been left to me, then I would probably have spent all the money in the first year. But Tony was better with money than I was and he said that it was better for me to leave the money in the bank for a while and for me to forget all about it, while he worked out the best options for me.

Then, after eleven months, we made the decision to buy a house with the money; and for the next few months, Tony searched the whole country for me, using the internet, and he found that the only place that I could afford a house was in Wales. He said that he had found a few houses for me to look at, but I felt a bit confused about the whole thing so I left it all to him. I had never been to Wales, the only time that I had seen the place was when I travelled through it on the train from Ireland to London and back again, and I knew nothing about the place. I said ok and I left him to get on with it.

But he had no transport to go looking at the houses, so he went to a motorcycle showroom and, on his 44th birthday, he bought himself a new Harley Davidson; and he never used a single penny of the compensation to pay for it. Instead, he signed an agreement to pay the amount off each month for the next five years and the money came out of his wages. And once he got the bike, off he went to look at houses for me and he spent months riding up and down the M4 motorway, looking at crap. I had been given such a small amount of compensation that it was beginning to look like I would never be able to find a house for the small amount of money I had; and for a while, we gave up looking.

After several months, Tony decided to try again, so he went back onto the internet and he tried again; and this time, he got some details about a few houses that were up for auction, so he got back on his motorcycle and he headed up the M4 motorway again. This time, it began to rain and it never stopped, it was going to be a 500-mile round trip to where the houses were and back again, and it was going to take the whole day.

About half an hour into the journey, the rain became a full-blown storm, but he continued on; however, it never stopped raining. He eventually crossed the Bristol Channel and he continued riding into Wales; but after 200 miles, he had to stop. It was still raining and he was freezing cold, so he pulled off the motorway and he headed into a small town. He had no idea what he was looking for, but he needed a rest, so he pulled up in what looked like the high street and he got off his bike and looked around. Nothing but rain, no people, just freezing rain. So he decided to get back on his bike; but as he turned around, he noticed an estate agent's on the corner of the street. The windows were all steamed up with condensation, but the lights inside were on, so he walked across the road and he pushed the door open and walked inside; and there were four estate agents, all sitting at their desks doing nothing.

He took off his crash helmet and he asked them if they had any houses for sale in his price range and one of them said yes, just one, and the person walked into the back of the office. And within seconds, he came out of the back office with a tatty sheet of paper that had a photo and some details about a house on it, and he handed it to Tony. Tony said thanks, but his hands were soaking wet and the ink on the sheet of paper began to run, so he stuck the sheet of paper into his pocket and he left the shop; then he got back on his bike, he headed back to the M4 motorway and he continued on his journey.

The weather got worse and fog began to cover the entire motorway, so he decided to stop again; he had been sitting on the bike for over four hours and the weather conditions had become unbearable, so he decided to give up and he left the motorway at the next exit. But there was nowhere for him to turn around and the fog got so bad that after a while he got lost, so he decided to pull over and have a rest by the side of the road.

He pulled up at the first junction he came to and looked for a place to stop; but as he pulled up by the side of the road, he seemed to recognise the road sign in front of him. But he had never been there before, so he pulled his gloves off and he took the piece of paper out of his pocket. The paper was soaking wet and it was falling to bits, but he could still make out the name of one of the roads on the piece of paper and the name was the same as the road he had stopped at. That's strange, he thought to himself, so he decided to go and look for the house on the paper, but the ink on the paper had run even more and almost all of the address had vanished and all that was left was the picture of the house and nothing more. He knew that he was on the right road, so how hard could it be to find the house, he thought.

And off he went, but the road went on for miles and miles and he went past village after village, but none of them looked or felt right. He soon found himself riding along a valley road and, as he rode up into the hills, it began to get misty and foggy and he had to slow down to almost a walking pace. It was still raining and he could only see a few feet in front of the bike and the conditions got so bad that he had to ride the bike onto a grass verge to let some cars go past him, as he was holding them up; and then he decided to stop, as the visibility continued to get worse.

He was now exhausted, so he decided to give up and head back to London; he switched the engine off and he got off the bike and looked around and all he could see was mist and fog; he knew he was in the middle of a valley, but he could see nothing. Then, as he walked back towards the bike and as he turned the key, the mist began to clear and he found himself standing at the corner of the street that the house stood on. He had now travelled eight miles along a valley road, not knowing where he was heading, and he had stopped because he had to and not because he wanted to and he was exactly where he wanted to be.

He got back on the bike, but it was still foggy and he could hardly see a thing as he rode along looking up at all the houses; and as he caught glimpses of them through the fog, they all looked the same and something just didn't feel right. Then he found himself a split in the road, so he decided to ride up a steep hill; and as he turned the corner at the top of the hill, he was facing the front door of the house. He pulled the front brake and his whole body tingled as he stopped outside the house; he looked around and it was as if fate had brought him straight to the front door. And the house was just what I had been dreaming about for most of my life. A house surrounded by trees, fields and countryside, in every direction you looked.

He got straight on his mobile phone and told me about the house, then he rode back to the estate agents and told them that we were interested in buying the house. And straightaway, they drove Tony back up to the house so that he could look inside, and after a short conversation over the phone, we made an offer on the house that same day. Then Tony got back on the bike and rode back to London and it never stopped raining until he got off the bike.

After a few days, the offer on the house was accepted, but it took nine months to complete and then the house was all mine. And Tony and I spent the next three years restoring the house; but by the time we had finished the restoration, we could not afford to live in the house as we had spent all of my compensation on buying the house and most of Tony's wages over the three years on the restoration of the house. We were now broke and the only time we could use the house was on weekends and school holidays, but we didn't mind as it was perfect for me to get away from everything when I needed to.

For the next couple of years, we continued using the house as often as we could; and each time I had to leave the house and go back to London, it became harder and harder for me, as I had become attached to all the peace and quiet of the countryside. I was still taking my medication to help me cope with everyday life and Tony still did his best to help me through each day, but now he was exhausted from everything and he began to feel ill. He had spent the last twenty plus years looking after me and putting up with all the problems that came with me and now it was his turn to be sick, but he never said a thing to anyone and I had no idea that something was wrong with him.

Then one day, while he was at work, he began to get pains in his chest and he knew it was time to go to the hospital; and as soon as he arrived at the hospital, the doctors took him in and then they rang me. They said that he had arrived at the hospital on his motorcycle and that he was still using it while he had chest pains and they were concerned that he could have had an accident if the pains had become unbearable. Then they said that they wanted to keep him in for observation because they thought he might have had a heart attack. I said ok and then I went straight to the hospital.

When I arrived, Tony was lying on a bed, with wires and tubes stuck all over him and he had a drip in his arm, but he was awake and he said hi. Then one of the nurses took me to one side and she shook her head from side to side and she said that he had to stay in the hospital so they could do tests on him. Then she asked Tony what he did for a living and he couldn't remember, so she asked him his name and he laughed as he said that he knew that, but the nurse didn't laugh, instead she asked him again and after a couple of seconds he told her. Then she gave him some tablets and she told him that they wanted him to stay in the hospital; he was not happy about staying, but he knew something was wrong and he said ok. I spent the night sitting next to him while he rested and they did more tests.

And in the morning, a doctor came to see us and he said that it was good news; he said that Tony hadn't had a heart attack. However, they still wanted to keep him in the hospital while they did more tests, as his heart was beating at twice the speed it should, and it would not slow down on its own. They were also having a lot of trouble slowing it down with drugs and his blood pressure was at a dangerously high level. But the worse thing was that nobody was allowed to make Tony laugh, as even laughing seemed to make his heart race out of control and his blood pressure go up to a dangerously high level; and the nurses would have a lot of trouble trying to bring everything under control again.

And he had to spend a week in the hospital, trying to relax, while the doctors tried different drugs to gain control of his heart rate and blood pressure. After the doctors got his heart and the blood pressure under control, they said that he still had an abnormality on his cardiographs, but they didn't know the cause of it, and they asked Tony if he had any explanation; but he had no idea what the problem was. So the doctors decided to send him for a stress test and they sent him off to run on a treadmill. Once there, they covered him in wires and sensors, then they connected him up to a machine and they told him to start running; and he kept running until his heart rate got to over two hundred beats a minute. Then they told him to stop and he went back to the ward and, after a couple of hours, they decided that he was well enough to go home. However, he would have to take tablets every day for the rest of his life, to control his heart rate and blood pressure. (I think he just needed a rest.)

Anyway, once he got home, I could see that the tablets were working and after a week he went back to work and everything was back to normal, apart from my brain. I felt so tormented by everything around me and I felt that I couldn't cope any longer and I felt like I wanted to kill myself. I seemed to be spending most of my days lying in bed and I didn't even want to get up to make dinner or to do anything else for that matter. And Tony said that my behaviour was beginning to affect him, as doing everything on his own was just too much for him now.

I knew something was wrong with me, so I went to see my doctor and he said that he wanted to change my medication for another type and I said ok. He gave me a new prescription and, after collecting the tablets, I put my old medication into a box and I began to take the new ones. At first, they seemed to make little difference; but after a week, my old tablets must have worn off and I went nuts. For no reason at all, I began shouting at everyone and no one could speak to me, as they could not make any sense of anything I was saying.

Then one weekend, while we were all at the house in Wales, I felt like I could not cope with myself anymore, so I went upstairs to my bedroom and I slashed at my arms with a metal nail file and my arms began to bleed. I sat on the bed and I thought to myself,

'What have I done?' I got up, opened my bedroom door and then I called out to Tony. He walked up the stairs and as he walked towards our bedroom, I opened the door and I stood in front of him. "Please don't be mad with me", then I held out my arms and I showed him what I had done. He said, 'Please, no more, I just can't cope with anything more. Please, no, not that.' I looked at him and he looked pale, then I said sorry and he sat on the bed next to me and I told him how I felt; and I begged him to ring the doctor's and get him to change my medication back to my old tablets for me and he said, 'Ok, I will.'

The next morning, Tony rang my doctor, he explained to him what I had done to my arms and he told the doctor how I was feeling. But my doctor said that he would not change my tablets back unless I went to see a mental health adviser, but I said no, I just could not go to see anyone and I certainly didn't want to see another counsellor. So, Tony spoke to the doctor again and this time my doctor agreed to change my medication back, so long as I would go and see him as soon as we got back to London and I said ok.

When we got back, I went to the doctor's, but I took Tony with me for support. Tony told my doctor what had been going on with me and, after he had finished speaking to him, my doctor said that I would have to go and see the mental health adviser or he would have me sectioned under the Mental Health Act. I said ok and we left the doctor's with a new prescription for my old medication again; and after a couple of weeks, I felt normal again or as normal as I would ever feel.

Then the appointment to see the mental health adviser arrived in the post and I felt like the abuse was starting all over again, so I sat by the kitchen window, I lit up a fag and I wished I had been dead. A couple of days later, I went to the appointment and I told the doctor almost everything about myself; and when the appointment was all over, he was shocked, but I felt no different. A week later, I went back to see him again and this time I told him everything about me and my baby brother Simon and how I missed him; and when I finished, he said that I should write a book about my life, so I did.

How Do I Feel Now?

I feel sad for myself, I feel angry at everything, I hate everyone and I feel sorry for my children. Almost everything about my life has been bad, I am not happy and I never will be. If I live a thousand years, I will still feel the same as I do today. What everyone did to me when I was young was wrong, this is my life now and I have to live with it. I deal with each day as it comes, but my past still haunts me to this day and it always will.

The problem is that when you experience life as a child, it should be with your mum, dad, brothers and sisters and other children, playing and exploring the world around you. Going to bed happy, smiling, and waking up with excitement and anticipation as to what you will learn and discover throughout the day. When you are a child, your mind is free to absorb its surroundings and absorb the feelings your body experiences, both physically and emotionally. This is how you learn good from bad and right from wrong.

Still as a child, you learn to read and write and to make friends. I never had any of that and now I am beyond the reach of any counselling or education and I have been so from when I was four years old. From the first day that I was abused, my life changed forever; and when I walked through the institution's doors in Ireland, my life was set on a path that has destroyed my soul. I never had a childhood and I never will; for me, my childhood was over before it began and my life with the nuns was hell. My emotional pain today is as strong as it was the day it began. From a very early age, I suffered at the hands of the very people who said they would take good care of me and at the hands of many other people around them who they called their friends.

For me, my pain will never leave me alone. When I go to sleep, it is in my head; and when I wake up, I can see it in the mirror. It is a part of me that I grew up with and is now and always will be embedded within me. You cannot change me or the way I am with counselling, education or money and you cannot split me into two like my personality.

No matter how much counselling the doctors give me, it will not help me. Counselling does not work and it never will; I have been through many counselling programs and they do not work. I did try. I took up the offer of counselling, hoping it might help in some way, but it did not. Money will not change me or the way I feel; it will not make me happy, it cannot buy me love, friendship or a childhood and if I had one wish, I'd wish I had never been born.

However, I do have three children who I love very much. They have suffered because of my upbringing and my personality; and if anyone deserves something, then they do. And they deserve more than what I can give them. This is where I would get the satisfaction and the benefit of money. I am not and I never will be a greedy person and perhaps that is why I have very little. The damage to me was done a long time ago and it will stay with me and haunt me until the day I die.

Who knows what I might have become if I had the chance to be myself in the beginning? A doctor, a cleaner, a mother. The time that I spent in the institution has made me into a very complicated, difficult and unhappy person and my emotions are cold. I am only waiting to die and I feel like it is taking too long. My family began the path to my destruction, they used me and they abused me, but they never ever loved or wanted me, or my baby brother Simon. If I have a soul, then it is lost somewhere between hell and Ireland, and I do not think I will ever find it; but time will tell.

Little Children

The first step through the institution's doors began a struggle that many children lost by paying the ultimate price with their lives. Some gave up the struggle while still in the institution and others, like my brother Simon, gave up at a young age, when they could not cope with the pressures of real life any longer and the abandonment they felt when no one wanted them.

Many of my friends from the institution are now dead; taking their own lives was their way out and a means to peace. I am still alive, but only because I found someone who truly loves me for whom I am; and without his help, I would be dead. I am not going to kill myself, because I have put too much into living this long and it would be a waste to give up now, but I am not happy having to live the rest of my life without my beautiful baby brother Simon by my side.

I dedicate this book to my baby brother Simon.
God bless you all if it means anything.

The End